The Tragic Fate of the
U.S.S. Indianapolis

The Tragic Fate of the
U.S.S. Indianapolis

The U.S. Navy's Worst Disaster at Sea

Raymond B. Lech

Cooper Square Press

All the names in this book are real, with one exception.

First Cooper Square Press edition 2001

This Cooper Square Press paperback edition of *The Tragic Fate of the* U.S.S. Indianapolis is an unabridged republication of the edition first published under the title *All the Drowned Sailors* in New York in 1982.

Copyright © 1982 by Raymond B. Lech

Designed by Louis A. Ditizio

Published by Cooper Square Press
An Imprint of the Rowman & Littlefield Publishing Group
150 Fifth Avenue, Suite 911
New York, New York 10011

Distributed by National Book Network

Library of Congress Cataloging-in-Publication Data

Lech, Raymond B., 1940-
   The tragic fate of the U.S.S. Indianapolis : the U.S. Navy's worst
disaster at sea / Raymond B. Lech.-- 1st Cooper Square Press ed.
      p. cm.
   Originally published: All the drowned sailors. New York : Stein and
Day, 1982.
   Includes bibliographical references and index.
   ISBN 0-8154-1120-0 (pbk. : alk. paper)
   1. Indianapolis (Cruiser) 2. World War, 1939-1945--Naval operations,
American. I. Title.
   D774.I5 L43 2000
   940.54'5973--dc21
                              00-064490

⊖™ The paper used in this publication meets the minimum requirements of
American National Standard for Information Sciences— Permanence of
Paper for Printed Library Materials, ANSI/NISO Z39.48-1992.
Manufactured in the United States of America.

To my Captain: Bernadette
To my Crew: Barbara and Christopher
          and
To the surviving survivors of the
U.S.S. *Indianapolis*

Contents

List of Illustrations

Illustrations following page 100

1. The U.S.S. *Indianapolis* has been lost in the Philippine Sea as the result of enemy action.
2. The next of kin of casualties have been notified.

NAVY DEPARTMENT COMMUNIQUE
NO. 622, AUGUST 14, 1945

Responsibility extends from the Commander in Chief, Pacific, to the Lieutenant Operations Officer, Tacloban, and into the Bureaus of the Navy Department.

MEMO FROM NAVAL INSPECTOR
GENERAL TO THE CHIEF OF
NAVAL OPERATIONS.
JANUARY 7, 1946

The Tragic Fate of the
U.S.S. Indianapolis

1.

Mission

DURING the summer of 1945, the Pacific island of Tinian was the largest air base in the world. Isolated from the normal hustle of the field sat a silver B-29, poised for one fateful mission. The carefully trained crew of *Enola Gay* was eager to make the drop that, it was hoped, would end the four-year war with Japan. But first, the weapon had to be delivered from the middle of an American desert.

A quarter of a world away, the heavily armed convoy rolled from Los Alamos to an Albuquerque airfield where a trio of lumbering DC-3s anxiously awaited their precious cargo. Loaded down with technicians, security people, and "The Bomb," the planes fought their way into the southwestern sky and eventually arrived at Hamilton Field.

Now that the key components of the weapon were in the heart of California, the obvious question was, "How do we get them to the island?" By air or by sea?

The air route was the most desirable since it would eliminate the time problem, but the scientists who had painstakingly developed this awesome weapon weren't sure what it would take to set it off. They knew theoretically it should work, but the arming and detonation of this atomic power had not yet been tested (and wouldn't be for another few weeks). If, by chance, the plane crashed during takeoff, it was soberly terrifying (and conceivable) to the people at Los Alamos that the city of San Francisco just might be blown off the map of the United States.

Fourteen miles to the east of Hamilton Field and just twenty-five miles northeast of the famous San Francisco Opera House was the Mare Island Naval Shipyard. Sitting there for over two months was a war-weary heavy cruiser, repairs just completed from a devastating kamikaze attack off Okinawa. It was decided by Major General Leslie Groves (Manhattan Project) and Rear Admiral William Purnell that this sixteen-year-old ship would be their transport and that she would sail westward to rendezvous with *Enola Gay*.

The captain was hurriedly called into the office of Admiral Purnell in San Francisco. Also present was Navy captain William Parsons, who was to assemble the bomb on *Enola Gay* while she was flying toward Hiroshima. The skipper of the heavy cruiser listened intently to his very simple orders, which were to deliver a particular cargo, as fast as possible, to Tinian. He was also told that this freight was to be guarded with his life and the life of his ship, and that if they were sunk en route and there was only one lifeboat left, the cargo was to be put on that boat. Furthermore, neither he nor his crew had a "need to know" what the cargo was. Bewildered, the officer left.

The death warrant of his ship, of 880 men, and, finally, himself, had been signed.

On July 15, 1945, the U.S.S. *Indianapolis*, former flagship of the Pacific Fifth Fleet, dropped her heavy anchor in San Francisco Bay off Hunters Point Naval Shipyard. Around noon on this Sunday, "The Bomb" was brought aboard. (Actually, it was only the internal components of the weapon that were being shipped and not the outside casing, which was already on Tinian.) A metal cylinder or "lead bucket," weighing about two-hundred pounds and containing the deadly uranium, was carried aboard, securely strapped to the deck up in Captain's Country, and guarded by Army officers from Los Alamos. At the same time, a fifteen-foot heavy wooden crate holding the detonating mechanism, or "cannon," was lashed to the deck in one of the ship's hangars and protected by members of the Marine detachment. Except for the vigilant sentinels, no one dared go near the "bucket" or the "cannon."

At 5:30 A.M. the next morning (Monday, July 16, 1945), an enormous blast, coupled with a blinding flash, rolled its way across the New Mexico desert, while a poisonous mushroom reached into the early morning sky. As if set off by a nuclear starter's pistol, at 8:00 A.M., the *Indianapolis* hoisted anchor and a half hour later, all 9,950 tons of her slipped between the narrow confines of the bay and passed beneath the Golden Gate. Of the entire crew aboard her at that moment, 73 percent would be dead in two weeks. Fate had destined that this vessel would go down in the record books as the greatest disaster of a ship at sea in the history of the United States Navy.

On this very same day, while the *Indianapolis* was breaking out into open water, Lieutenant Commander Mochitsura Hashimoto ordered the lines cast off and, with the music of a band echoing in the background, the Imperial Japanese submarine I-58 gently slipped away from her pier at Kure. In exactly fourteen days, this 2,600 ton underwater weapon and her 105-man crew would annihilate the heavy cruiser *Indianapolis*.

Captain Charles Butler McVay, III, son of the former Commander in Chief of the United States Asiatic Fleet, was slated for the top of the Navy ladder. Appointed to Annapolis by President Wilson, he graduated in 1919 and in the ensuing years ran the normal gauntlet of posts required of up-and-coming officers. He served on various types of vessels from tankers to battleships, did his stint at the Navy Department in Washington and as Naval aide in the Philippines. Prior to taking command of the *Indianapolis* in November 1944, he was executive officer aboard the cruiser U.S.S. *Cleveland* where, on the night of March 5, 1943, off the Solomon Islands, he won the Silver Star for conspicuous gallantry against enemy Japanese forces.

The 46-year-old McVay ran a tight ship and, because his orders from Admiral Purnell were to get to Tinian as fast as possible, he pushed everyone, but most especially his engine room.

On her first day at sea, the unescorted cruiser hit some rough weather and could make only 28 knots, but on Tuesday and Wednesday her sharp bow cut more deeply into the blue Pacific and a speed of 29 knots was being continually registered. The morning of the fourth day, ship and secret cargo reached Hawaii, and Captain McVay discovered when arriving at Pearl that they had set a world speed record from Farallon Light (outside San Francisco) to Diamond Head. The old record of 75.4 hours, established in 1932 by the *Omaha*, now held second place to the 74.5 hours recorded by the *Indianapolis*.

Six hours after reaching Pearl Harbor, the *Indianapolis* was gone again, with a full supply of fuel and stores. The westward march continued at 24 knots for another 3,300 miles. One week later, on July 26, 1945, she reached Tinian and, just over a half mile offshore, dropped anchor.

Brass from every branch of the armed services swarmed over her decks, and both the "lead bucket" and "cannon" were gently hoisted over the quarterdeck rail into a waiting barge tied along her side. While this was going on, the Advance Headquarters of the Commander in Chief, Pacific

Fleet (Fleet Admiral Chester Nimitz), gave Captain McVay his new orders.

The *Indianapolis* had taken on board a group of passengers in San Francisco. Some had debarked at Pearl and others at this Marianas airfield, but there were still a few remaining (primarily members of Admiral Spruance's Fifth Fleet staff) who were slated for Guam, an island just south of Tinian. The first part of his instructions, therefore, stated that after unloading, the ship would make the overnight trip to Guam and put ashore any remaining itinerants, which was welcome news for both crew and captain. Since they had left the West Coast, these passengers kept getting in the way, and it had reached a point where the crew could not even conduct a decent drill. A few months later, McVay complained, "Passengers always interfere with drills, because although you try to confine them to a certain rendezvous, they are wandering around the ship, and you proceed to jump down their throats and want to know where their battle station is—and they say they are just passengers. It makes it quite difficult, in my opinion, to really hold top-notch drills when the ship has extraneous personnel on it."

Once the *Indianapolis* arrived in Guam, Captain McVay was instructed to report to the port director of the Guam Naval Base, who would route him westward, across the Philippine Sea, to the island of Leyte. Upon entering Leyte Gulf, he was to transmit a message immediately to the commander of Task Force 95 (CTF-95), Vice Admiral Jesse B. Oldendorf, who was steaming off the coast of Japan, informing him of the *Indianapolis*'s arrival in the gulf and reporting to him for duty. However, before the cruiser sailed northward to become part of Admiral Oldendorf's armada, it was to spend ten days in the Leyte Gulf area undergoing refresher training, since over 25 percent of her crew came aboard at Mare Island and were inexperienced.

Once anchored in the gulf, McVay was to report physically to Admiral Oldendorf's direct subordinate in the area (and at that point his immediate superior), Rear Admiral Lynde D. McCormick, Commander of Task Group 95.7 (CTG-95.7). Admiral McCormick was at that time anchored in Leyte and was flying his two-star flag on the battleship *Idaho*.

By a copy of this order, McCormick would know that the *Indianapolis* was coming, arrange a program, and put the ship through the ten-day training cycle. (See Appendix A for the actual orders.)

Copies of these instructions were sent to seven diverse commands: the Tinian port director; the port director on Guam; Vice Admiral George Murray, Commander of the Marianas (within whose area of responsibility she would be sailing from); Fleet Admiral Nimitz; Admiral Spruance; Vice Admiral Oldendorf; and, finally, Rear Admiral McCormick. It was obviously no secret to anyone where the *Indianapolis* was coming from, where she was going, or what she was doing.

The message was received and understood by everybody— everybody, that is, except one.

After she completed unloading, the *Indianapolis* left Tinian and set sail south for the overnight trip to Guam. That evening, a coded message directed to CTG-95.7 in Leyte Gulf was received in the cramped radio room of the battleship *Idaho*. This was a copy of the *Indianapolis*'s orders. McCormick's communications staff began to decipher the dispatch but as soon as they started—quit, and they never bothered to decode the body. Some unknown member of McCormick's communications group carelessly decoded the addressee as 75.8 instead of Task Group 95.7 and it was, therefore, automatically assumed that the message did not belong to them. Consequently, the staff did not feel it was worth the time or effort to decipher the contents. A repeat still should have been asked for, however, since the message was directed toward a task group commander and not some isolated ship at sea.

The primary reason that the admiral's staff opted to disregard the message, however, was because it was classified as "Restricted." If the security classification of the dispatch had been higher, such as "Secret" or even "Top Secret," a repeat would have been demanded. In protecting (or excusing) this blunder, Admiral McCormick later remarked (and agreed) that the message, because of its security classification, "did not have sufficient significance" for them to either decode the body or ask for a repeat. In a few days, this stupid mistake would have tragic repercussions for the men of *Indianapolis*. The unit the cruiser was to report to never knew she was coming.

2.

Route

LIEUTENANT Commander Hashimoto's ten-month-old boat was better equipped, larger, and faster than comparable submarines anywhere in the world. Her twin diesels drove her along the surface at almost eighteen knots and her deadly oxygen-powered torpedoes were the envy of navies everywhere. Quite simply, the Japanese I-Class submarine was a weapon not to be ignored.

Hashimoto's fourth war patrol consisted of a flotilla of six submarines, known as the "Tamon Group,"* leaving on staggered dates. Three of the submarines were already at sea, and I-58 was the fourth to leave. After departing from Kure, Japan's massive naval base situated in the southwest corner of Honshu, they made a fifty-mile journey southward to the Kaiten base of Hirao, where six of the huge torpedoes were securely strapped to the submarine's back.

The Kaiten was an oxygen-powered torpedo, forty-eight feet long and weighing eight tons. It had an underwater

---

*The name of one of the four Buddhist gods responsible for protecting Japan against her enemies.

speed of 30 knots and carried 3,200 pounds of explosives in its warhead. The unique thing about a Kaiten, however, was not its size, speed, or explosive power but that it carried a man. Essentially, this torpedo was the underwater equivalent of the suicidal kamikaze. Upon spotting a target, the pilot climbed through a hatch into the torpedo, the straps holding it to the sub's deck were released, and off he went. It was strictly a one-way trip.

For a week, I-58 roamed the Philippine Sea, searching for a target without luck. On Friday, July 27, 1945, the day *Indianapolis* sailed into Apra Harbor, Commander Hashimoto moved his boat to the east/west shipping lane between Guam and Leyte. He decided to sit there patiently and wait.

Three days before the *Indianapolis* steamed into Guam, the U.S.S. *Underhill* had been escorting a southern convoy of fifteen small ships from Okinawa to Leyte. At 9:00 A.M., the lookouts aboard the destroyer escort noticed a Japanese plane following them, and *Underhill's* skipper instantly sounded Battle Stations to his crew and the ships in his charge. The trailing aircraft, with its red ball blatantly embossed on its side, constantly radioed back to its base the position of the ships. In turn, this information was being fed to I-53 (having left Japan on July 14 as part of the Tamon Group), which was speeding toward an intercept.

The *Underhill* remained on the alert and, six hours later (3:07 P.M.), having made a sonar contact, began a depth-charge run. Four minutes after the attack began, her anxious lookouts spotted a periscope about 100 yards off the star-board bow. The captain ordered hard a-starboard, full speed ahead, and directed the helm to ram. Within seconds she made contact. There were two slight jars, three rapid explosions, and suddenly there were two *Underhills*.

The ship split in half; the bow silently floated off in one

direction, the stern sailed in the other. The death toll came to 119 men, and, while the ships from the convoy were rescuing the remaining 109 crew members, two more periscopes were seen. Unknowingly, *Underhill* had rammed a Kaiten released by I-53.

Shortly after the incident, Naval Intelligence at Pearl Harbor broadcast an emergency message to all commands in the Pacific: *Don't ram.*

During World War II, the submarine fleet of the Japanese Empire had two basic missions: (a) reconnaissance, and (b) supplying their distant island garrisons. The Tamon Group was unique, however, in that they had orders to perform only one task, to sink ships. The war was drawing to a close, and the Japanese were desperate. Anything that could fly (or float) and kill the invaders was ordered to do so.

United States Naval Intelligence knew this. In Washington, Captain William R. Smedberg, III, held the very high post of assistant combat intelligence officer for Fleet Admiral Ernest King, Chief of Naval Operations. He and his combat intelligence division were charged with estimating the enemy's capabilities, intentions, dispositions, and strengths.

Captain Smedberg knew that during the war, Japanese submarines had many opportunities to attack U.S. shipping and had not done so. For example, in the Marianas campaign, there were hundreds of American ships sitting in exposed anchorages for over three months, and there were no successful attacks against any of these vessels during that campaign. However, during the month of July 1945, submarine activity intensified and Captain Smedberg and his staff knew of the four Japanese submarines of the Tamon Group. Furthermore, he was cognizant of the fact that these subs were assigned strictly offensive missions and that they were operating in the general area of the east/west Guam to Leyte route and north and south of it.

The key to this intelligence coup, however, was not just knowing that there were submarines assigned offensive missions but knowing, to a fairly high degree, where they were—and Smedberg knew that also. In fact, in early July, he prepared a chart of the Pacific Ocean covering the general area between Japan, the Marianas, the Palau Group, and the Philippines. On that chart, he had pinned fairly exactly the four submarines of the Tamon Group. I-53 was shown at the spot where *Underhill* was sunk; two more were further north, and the last one was in close proximity to the Guam/Leyte shipping route. This submarine was Commander Hashimoto's I-58. After the war was over, Captain Smedberg was asked if he considered this information "hot," and his simple reply was, "Oh, yes."

Combat intelligence in Washington did not hoard their data but immediately sent it to Pearl Harbor for dissemination. Meanwhile, Fleet Admiral Nimitz, Commander in Chief, Pacific (CinCPac) had his own overworked intelligence section and it generally had the same information Captain Smedberg did, and sometimes even obtained it before Washington.

In charge of the combat intelligence section for Fleet Admiral Chester Nimitz was Captain E. T. Layton. This highly respected officer had the same information Captain Smedberg in Washington did and kept his plot of the Tamon Group operations constantly updated. He knew where those four subs were at all times and was keenly aware that enemy submarine activity was classified as greater than normal. As was his responsibility, combat intelligence of CinCPac passed this "Ultra Secret" data down the chain of command

and, more specifically, to senior officers in the Pacific and their staffs.

The overnight voyage was uneventful, and after the usual antiaircraft practice on the way in, at 10:00 A.M., July 27, 1945, the *Indianapolis* dropped anchor in Apra Harbor, Guam. While the ship was discharging her passengers and taking on food, fuel, and ammunition, the captain left the vessel and headed for the Advance Headquarters of the Commander in Chief, Pacific Fleet, on the island of Guam. In charge of this forward post was Nimitz's assistant chief of staff and operations officer, Commodore James B. Carter.

McVay asked for the commodore and was ushered into his office. The captain's primary concern was the desperately needed refresher training, and he immediately brought the topic up, asking whether the ship could have her program conducted in the waters off Guam rather than sending him across the Philippine Sea.

As far as CinCPac was concerned, the top priority of the ship was to have her ten-day training cycle completed; everyone was anxious to get Admiral Spruance and his staff back aboard and once again have the *Indianapolis* as the prestigious flagship of the Fifth Fleet.

But Carter told McVay that the *Indianapolis* would have to go to Leyte for refresher training. "We no longer give such training here in Guam," he said.

Captain McVay did not like the idea of sailing across the Philippine Sea with his green crew and would have obviously preferred staying right where he was. He complained to the commodore that at the rate things were going, his refresher training would probably be conducted in Tokyo Bay.

McVay asked Carter how soon the cruiser would have to leave and was told that the only big rush was to get the training completed. Therefore, the *Indianapolis* could finish taking on fuel and sail the next morning.

Captain McVay pointed out to Carter that he hadn't been in the area for about three months and consequently wasn't at all familiar with conditions "out there." Who, he wanted to know, would provide him with up-to-date intelligence? Being in charge of Nimitz's Advance Headquarters, the commodore naturally knew of the Tamon Group mission and was apprised by Naval Intelligence of the relative position of each of the four patrolling subs. Furthermore, he was aware that one of these submarines had sunk the *Underhill*, just three days prior to this conversation with McVay. Instead of taking a few scant seconds to say to McVay, "We know of four subs recently sent out on offensive missions," or, even more simply, "We know of one sub operating in the vicinity of the Guam to Leyte route," Commodore Carter told him nothing.

"I don't remember that we discussed any intelligence information," Carter said later. Why not? Because, "It wasn't normal for captains to request that of me. He was only in my office a very short time; and that intelligence was provided by the port director at the time the ship was routed, as a normal procedure."

When the short meeting was over, Carter sent McVay to the Guam port director's office for sailing instructions. Upon walking out of the Advance Headquarters of the Commander in Chief of the Pacific Fleet, the senior officer of the *Indianapolis* had as much information as he walked in with— zero. As a matter of fact, McVay felt the situation "out there" was quite normal. "I got no impression up there [Carter's office] at that time of any unusual conditions in the area—I will say that."

After leaving Commodore Carter, McVay stopped off and

had lunch with Admiral Spruance, who happened to be on the island at the time. After the meal, the captain headed for the office of the port director, Guam.

The director of the port, Lieutenant Commander W. Brooks, wasn't in when McVay got there but nearby was a Quonset hut housing the port director's convoy and routing office, and at about 4:00 P.M. McVay entered. Inside these cramped quarters was Lieutenant Joseph Waldron, a former newspaper executive and now convoy and routing officer of the Guam Naval Base. Approximately 90 percent of all vessels leaving the Marianas were routed by Waldron. He figured his office had sailed over 5,000 ships during the past ten months. Being proud of the routing office, he was pleased to point out that they had a reputation for having their information up-to-date and for giving the most complete instructions of any port in the Pacific.

The purpose of the captain of the ship meeting with the routing officer was to make preliminary arrangements for the vessel's sailing. After he left, the orders would be typed up and made ready for delivery. Waldron delegated to two members of his staff the task of making these arrangements with McVay, and Lieutenant R. C. Northover and Ensign William Renoe got to work.

They first asked the captain what speed he wanted to make and when he wanted to leave. McVay was a little shocked by these questions, since he remembered that the last time he was in the area, in order to conserve precious fuel, ships were not permitted to exceed 16 knots, except under special circumstances. McVay reminded the two officers that when figuring out how fast he should go, they should take into consideration that the cruiser had just completed a high-speed run from San Francisco. McVay preferred that this next run be at medium speed in order to rest his engines. Furthermore, he wanted to arrive off Leyte Gulf at dawn, since the early morning light would allow him to practice some antiaircraft fire on the way in.

After some quick math, it was concluded that he could arrive Monday morning if the ship did between 24 and 25 knots. This was totally unacceptable to McVay, so they worked out what speed was required to arrive on Tuesday morning and decided that leaving at 9:00 A.M. the next day (Saturday, July 28, 1945) and steaming at an average speed of 15.7 knots would do it. The captain agreed.

The next question was the route, about which there was really no question to be raised because there was only one available. This was a direct east/west straight line from Guam to Leyte, known as "Convoy Route Peddie." Neither the routing officer nor McVay had the authority to change the route since the port director's sailing Bible was Wartime Pacific Routing Instructions, which clearly stated that "under normal procedure, combatant fleet components proceeding to or returning from combat operating areas *shall be* sailed on standard routes whenever such routes are available." "Peddie" was the *only* standard route from Guam to Leyte.

At the very moment these instructions were being drawn up for the voyage of the U.S.S. *Indianapolis*, sitting smack in the center of "Peddie," and just waiting for a target, was Commander Hashimoto in I-58.

Although a routing officer or a captain of a ship cannot, on his own authority, change a sailing lane, the system was not so rigid that senior commanders could not modify these ocean highways. In fact, at that very time serious consideration was being given to altering the Guam/Leyte route, and it had almost been accomplished, needing only a signature.

Captain Samuel Clay Anderson was the Pacific Fleet operations officer for Fleet Admiral Ernest King, Chief of Naval Operations. Because of his position, he was privy to all the information obtained by Naval Intelligence and therefore knew of the Tamon Group and their mission. This knowledge caused him to be concerned about the safety of shipping in the area where the submarines were operating.

Captain Anderson was forced to take direct action on the day *Underhill* was sunk, since this proved to him that the routing of combat ships in the Western Pacific was erroneous. Consequently, he immediately drafted a dispatch to Admiral Nimitz at Pearl Harbor, calling CinCPac's attention to the fact that he believed it was a mistake to route combat vessels over their present lanes (and by implication asking they be changed, including Route "Peddie").

The prepared dispatch was sent up the ladder until it reached the Vice Chief of Naval Operations, Admiral Edwards, who told Captain Anderson that the matter would be taken up at a higher level. Further investigation shows that this higher level was Admiral King, who, for reasons known only to himself, would not give his authorization to send this message to Pearl Harbor. The final outcome was that the route of the *Indianapolis* was not changed, and McVay, Northover, and Renoe went on to the next subject.

Now that the ETD, speed, ETA, and route had been settled, the next topic was an escort. The cruiser had absolutely no underwater detection equipment, and if a sub were lurking beneath the waves anywhere along the route she simply wouldn't know about it without sonar. However, the routing officers did not think an escort would be available, and Captain McVay didn't give it another thought as he had traveled many times without escort. As a matter of routine, Lieutenant Waldron went to the phone and called the headquarters of the Commander of the Marianas and was put through to his surface operations officer, Captain Oliver Naquin. Naquin wasn't in, but his assistant, a Lieutenant Johnson, answered the phone. Waldron later recalled that "the surface operations, ComMarianas, was contacted by me personally, and I was informed no escort was needed. This was in agreement with the general policy that ships below a certain degree of latitude could proceed unescorted in that area. It was merely a routine check in case surface operations knew of an escort that was going out there with which we could combine the ship."

Although Captain McVay was accustomed to sailing without escort, this rejection of one from surface operations prompted him to say later on, "I don't believe a ship should proceed in any waters considered submarine waters without an escort, where it is possible to provide one, unless that ship has underwater sound gear."*

The last topic was intelligence, and Waldron and McVay didn't go into it deeply since all up-to-date information on enemy activity would be contained in an intelligence brief attached to his routing instructions. Before leaving, McVay mentioned that his navigator would stop by for the formal routing orders and intelligence addendum in a few hours.

---

*After the sinking of the *Indianapolis*, an enormous fuss was made over sending the ship out without escort. Hundreds of pages of testimony and documentation were devoted to this subject, but the author feels that this was—and is—a minor point vis-à-vis others that had disastrous consequences. Standing orders at the time stated categorically (and rightly so) that ships capable "of taking care of themselves" should sail on their own; there were just so many escort vessels to go around and they had to be allocated sparely—specifically, to ships carrying troops and smaller vessels in convoy. Furthermore, the Okinawa campaign had recently ended, with the invasion of Japan contemplated, and this type ship was badly needed in the war zone, rather than escorting combat ships in "rear areas," which Guam and Leyte were considered to be. Even allowing for the fact that if two ships are sailing together and one is sunk the other can pick up survivors, or, if both ships go down, the chances of getting off an SOS are far greater, the author believes that the Navy chose to focus the public's attention on the escort problem rather than reveal some of the more serious flaws in the system that led to the disaster.

Heading back toward his ship, Captain McVay mentally reviewed what had just transpired and felt secure: "There was no mention made of any untoward incidents in the area through which I was to pass. I definitely got the idea from CinCPac Headquarters and Port Director, Guam, that it was a routine voyage."

At 7:00 P.M. that evening, the cruiser's navigator, Commander John Janney, entered the Quonset hut and met with Lieutenants Waldron and Northover. He was handed two sheets of paper; the first being the routing instructions and the other was entitled "Intelligence Brief for Guam to Philippines."

The instructions were quite simple, indicating that the ship would leave at 9:00 A.M. the next morning (Saturday), cover the 1,171 miles to Leyte at an average speed of 15.7 knots, and reach the Gulf at 11:00 A.M. on Tuesday, the thirty-first. The orders stated further that "commanding officers are at all times responsible for the safe navigation of their ships" and that the cruiser would "zigzag at discretion of the commanding officer." These instructions were basically boiler plate and, as Waldron stated, "It was acceptable form and general policy to indicate zigzag at the discretion of the commanding officer—no routing officer attempts to tell the captain of a combatant ship what he should do while at sea."

After briefly reviewing the intelligence addendum, Janney returned to the *Indianapolis* with the orders and immediately met with McVay and Commander Joseph Flynn, the ship's executive officer. The three men went over the instructions thoroughly and found nothing unusual.

One of them made the comment that once again they were traveling unescorted.

Next they spent some time on the intelligence brief. Three possible submarine sightings were listed, which was about average for any given week. The report noted that one submarine was spotted on the surface just after midnight on July 22, but by this time that information was obviously stale. Two other sightings were indicated for July 25, and everyone recognized them to be extremely doubtful (which they were). One of the two had the comment, "Unknown ship reports sighting a possible periscope," and the other was interpreted as, "indications at that time pointed to a doubtful submarine." As a matter of fact, the three submarines on the brief were already known to Commander Janney from other sources and were plotted on the chart of the *Indianapolis* days before they received this brief.*

It is more important to note what was not in the brief rather than what was in it. The sinking of the *Underhill* was not mentioned nor were the positions of the four submarines of the Tamon Group. Most importantly, it was not mentioned anywhere, or to anyone, that I-58 was hanging around Route "Peddie."

In secret documents, the United States Navy admitted that "Captain McVay was informed that there was nothing out of the ordinary in the area which he was about to traverse" and he "was given no information from any source with regard to unusual submarine activities in the area, to the westward of Guam or in the Philippine Sea." Furthermore, the Navy secretly admitted that "Captain McVay was not informed of the presence of four enemy submarines operating in the Western Pacific with offensive orders, nor was he informed of

---

*Fleet headquarters at Pearl Harbor, on a daily basis, sent out "Blue Summaries" to all commands and ships in the Pacific, which gave an overall picture of the war situation for that day. These summaries always indicated where antisubmarine operations were taking place. If a ship did not receive a summary, however, it would still get the information, since its radio watch would intercept and plot all activities in the area it was in or going to.

the sinking of U.S.S. *Underhill* by an enemy submarine to the westward of Guam on July 24."

Vice Admiral George Murray, Commander of the Marianas, insisted that "the information contained in the routing instructions was the best information we could provide," but, as we have seen, the intelligence brief wasn't worth the paper it was printed on.

Actually, it is quite simple to explain what happened: when the flow of this "Ultra Secret" information on the Tamon Group reached a certain point in the chain of command, it stopped as if it had hit a brick wall. The reason that it stopped was its security classification—"Ultra Secret"—which was the highest and most secure of categories. Essentially, it was so secret that people were afraid to talk about it.

Captain E. T. Layton, in charge of combat intelligence at Pearl Harbor, knew that intelligence, no matter how secret its classification, was wasted if it was not passed down to combat officers who needed it to make proper decisions. Captain Layton's only rule was that "Ultra Secret" information could not be passed down the chain of command in the form the senior commanders receive it, nor were these commanders to betray to their subordinates the source of the data. Otherwise, this senior intelligence officer expected all secret evidence to be disseminated. As a matter of fact, Captain Layton's personal concept was that "Ultra" information should go into the intelligence report attached to routing instructions, with the proviso that it be worded in a general manner. For example, "Hunter-killer groups are commencing antisubmarine measures in certain areas," or "Danger of enemy submarines exists on the Guam/Leyte route," or any wording of that nature. This would give the person reading the report sufficient notice that there was some unusual and perhaps potentially dangerous activity taking place along his assigned route. Unfortunately, Captain Layton had too much confidence in the chain of command.

Commodore Carter received his information on the submarines from Layton and, although he did not convey it to McVay, he verbally passed it to (and discussed it with) Captain Oliver Naquin, surface operations officer for Commander, Marianas, the same officer Waldron called requesting an escort for the *Indianapolis*. At this point in the command structure, the information went no further. Captain Naquin did absolutely nothing with it.

The intelligence department of Guam Naval Base was the next step in the chain of command to which Naquin should have funneled this knowledge (especially the critical information about Hashimoto sitting in the middle of Route "Peddie"). After all, it was at Guam that the intelligence reports were attached to routing instructions.

According to Commander J. R. Lawrence, operations officer for the Guam Naval Base, his intelligence department depended *entirely* upon Commander, Marianas, and, more specifically, on Captain Naquin, for information on enemy activity in their area. But, on the day the *Indianapolis* sailed, Commander Lawrence and his intelligence crew knew nothing of the sinking of *Underhill*, of the dangerous Tamon Group, or of I-58 just a few days off their western beaches.

Meanwhile, back at the routing office, Lieutenant Joseph Waldron and his crew were busy routing ships and attaching to their instructions intelligence reports that were essentially worthless.

The following morning (Saturday, July 28), the U.S.S. *Indianapolis* made preparations for getting underway. Admiral Spruance had a conference to attend in Manila and was thinking of asking Captain McVay for a ride but at the last minute changed his mind. At 9:00 A.M., the skipper gave the order to stop topping off fuel, hoist anchor, and "we cleared the harbor about 0910, July 28, minus ten time."*

An hour and a half after the *Indianapolis* cleared Apra Harbor, Lieutenant Waldron's routing office composed a message for transmission to all interested parties describing the anticipated movements of the cruiser. It pointed out that the vessel left at 9:00 A.M. on the twenty-eighth, would do an average speed of 15.7 knots along Route "Peddie," be outside Leyte Gulf at 8:00 A.M. on Tuesday, the thirty-first, and finally anchor in the gulf at 11:00 A.M. The dispatch also noted that since the ship was sailing from one command area (Marianas) to another (Philippine Sea Frontier), she would cross over, or "chop," the imaginary 130° East line of longitude separating the two commands sometime on Monday,

---

*Throughout the history of this disaster, there has been general confusion about times, including (but certainly not limited to) the time, and even the date, the ship was sunk. It is not unusual to read in many sources (and documents) that the ship was sunk on Sunday, July 29, rather than on Monday, July 30. The reason for the various discrepancies is neglect in converting time zones to ship's time.

Z (Zulu) time is Greenwich time. Guam operated in a minus 10 (hour) time zone so add 10 to Zulu for Guam time; e.g., 2300 Z (11:00 P.M.) of July 27 converts to 9:00 A.M. on the twenty-eighth.

Leyte operated in a minus 9 zone; i.e., a one-hour difference from Guam.

To make matters more confusing, halfway between Guam and Leyte is a "minus 9½" zone, in which area the ship was sunk and to which her clocks were adjusted. However, I-58, although operating in a 9½ zone, *did not* make the one-half hour adjustment and her clocks remained at minus 9 from Greenwich. Therefore, there was always a one-half hour difference between when the sub said something happened and when it actually happened aboard ship. The best example of this is when I-58 noted her torpedoes fired at about 11:35 P.M. on July 29 and the ship sinking prior to midnight while in reality they didn't hit until after midnight or technically, the next day, July 30.

Whenever possible, all times in this book have been converted to ship's time.

July 30. The *Indianapolis* was never to cross that imaginary line.

The message was immediately sent to the operations office of the Marianas; the port director at Leyte; Rear Admiral McCormick (CTG-95.7) aboard the *Idaho*; Admiral Spruance; the commander of the Philippine Sea Frontier; Commodore Carter; Fleet Admiral Nimitz; Vice Admiral George Murray (Commander, Marianas); commander of the Western Carolines sub(ordinate) area under Commander, Marianas; and finally, Vice Admiral Jesse Oldendorf (CTF-95) off Japan. Everyone involved received the message and they all posted the *Indianapolis* on their respective plotting boards—everyone, that is, except one.

This time around, McCormick (CTG-95.7) had the dispatch decoded, but his superior, Vice Admiral Oldendorf (CTF-95), didn't.

Upon reading the message, Rear Admiral McCormick became very confused. He thought that either in San Francisco or Guam the *Indianapolis* had been put through her refresher program and therefore he wondered what her purpose was in reporting to Leyte. Naturally, if his staff had decoded the previous message, he would have known the reason for the stopover. Even after receipt of this dispatch, however, he wasn't convinced that she would ever enter the gulf since two heavy cruisers had recently been detached from the Okinawa task force, and McCormick assumed that along the route the *Indianapolis* would be diverted northward as a replacement for one of them. If, however, by some slim chance she did enter the gulf on Tuesday, he knew that the cruiser would report to him and he ordered his staff on the *Idaho* to grease her on the plotting board for a scheduled ETA of 11:00 A.M. on the thirty-first.

Vice Admiral Jesse Oldendorf was totally in the dark as to the movements of *Indianapolis*, due to his nonreceipt of Wal-

dron's message. The system dictated that the routing office
not send the dispatch directly to the task force but to the joint
communications center at Okinawa, where it mysteriously
disappeared. Oldendorf bitterly complained that the center
was notoriously inefficient in forwarding messages to those
to whom they were addressed. Therefore, although he knew
that at some time the *Indianapolis* would be in Leyte he
didn't know when, since he had no idea as to her departure
date from Guam.

While the *Indianapolis* was leisurely sailing across the
shark-infested Philippine Sea, the two commands it was
necessary for her to report to each had only one piece of a
two-piece puzzle. McCormick knew she was coming and
when she was due but couldn't figure out why; Oldendorf
knew why, but not when.

3.
Sailing

SEVEN hours after *Indianapolis* embarked on her final voyage, the merchant ship S.S. *Wild Hunter* quickly keyed an emergency message across the Pacific:

> URGENT PLAIN
> SSS SSS DE WQ3VB
> BT 10R 25 NORTH 131R 45 EAST
> PERISCOPE SIGHTED
> BT 280720Z AR

Twenty-eight minutes later, again:

> URGENT PLAIN
> NPN DE WQ3VB BT
> SIGHTED PERISCOPE AGAIN
> FIRED ON SAME BT 280748Z

In tandem with several planes, the destroyer escort *Albert T. Harris* was sent to investigate and this hunter-killer group scoured the area. By Sunday evening, however, they lost contact, broke off, and went home.

In all probability, there was no submarine (at least none

known to Naval Intelligence), but the interesting aspect of this sterile action is that it was taking place within the jurisdiction of Commander, Marianas (just east of the "chop" line), and about 170 miles ahead and 60 miles off the track that the *Indianapolis* was on. Copies of the Action Dispatches between *Wild Hunter,* the planes, and *Harris,* were constantly flowing into Vice Admiral Murray's headquarters but at no time did he or any member of his staff consider diverting the cruiser from her planned route.

Secretly, the Navy admitted that "shortly after her departure [from Guam] there were actually 'hunter-killer' operations in progress along the route over which the *Indianapolis* was sent, which presumably were known to CinCPac Advanced [sic] Headquarters (Carter) and/or Commander, Marianas (Murray), and which would have appeared to have been sufficient reason to have diverted the *Indianapolis* from her routing, but no action was taken."

Saturday was a normal work day for the crew and by the next day all abandon ship equipment and provisions had been thoroughly inspected and pronounced to be in A-1 shape.

On Sunday, the *Indianapolis* overtook an LST also heading for Leyte, and Captain McVay recalled that "we used him for a surface problem. We were constantly tracking planes, using them for AA drill during the twelve to four [watch] that afternoon."

Lieutenant Commander Lewis Leavitt Haynes was a doctor, born and raised in Manistee, Michigan. He received his medical degree from Northwestern University. Doctor Haynes had been in the Navy for eight years and, prior to joining the cruiser, was with a destroyer division in the Atlantic. He had also spent eighteen months aboard the battleship *New Mexico*. Of all the ships he had served on, he liked the *Indianapolis* the best. The discipline was good, the spirit was fine, and there was the utmost cooperation between all departments. He enjoyed being on that ship.

For most of Sunday, Doctor Haynes cloistered himself in Number 2 mess hall, subjecting many unhappy members of the crew to cholera shots. After a full day of jabbing sharp needles into muscular arms, he left for dinner, where he sat at the same table with Commander Janney, the navigator.

Conversation was light, and after a while Janney passed the remark that sometime during the night they would be passing an area where antisubmarine operations were taking place. They kidded about it for a few minutes, and, as Haynes recalled, "He said they were listening to the TBS* conversation and that we would pass sometime around midnight in that area, sometime during the night, he didn't say midnight, where they were having a 'hunter-killer' mission. And we joked back and forth at the table about it, a sort of good-humored joking back and forth."

As was his custom after dinner, Doctor Haynes went for a walk on the forecastle deck and savored the warm Pacific breeze. His stroll completed, he stopped down at sick bay for a final check of his patients and at 10:45 P.M. was back in his room and asleep.

The officer of the deck for the six to eight watch that Sunday evening was Lieutenant (jg) Charles Brite McKissick, of McKinney, Texas. When he took over, it was still light, the ship was zigzagging on a course of 262°, and the sea could be described as between choppy and rough. Overhead it was partly cloudy, but upon looking over the sharp bow toward the distant horizon McKissick noticed that they

---

*Talk between ships. In this case, *Wild Hunter, Harris,* and the planes.

would soon be running into some heavy low-lying clouds. It certainly wasn't the most pleasant Sunday evening he could have had for taking over a watch.

Prior to formally relieving his counterpart, Lieutenant McKissick went over to the communications board and removed a silver metal folder that held various "All Ships" dispatches, messages to "All Commands Interested in Combat Reports," and general intercepts made by the cruiser's radio room. One of the dispatches told of the *Wild Hunter* periscope sighting and the subsequent killer operation headed by *Harris*.

The report McKissick saw wasn't very detailed, simply saying "ASW operations in progress 10-26N, 131E . . .," but he recalled, "I had seen a routine dispatch while I was on watch to the effect that there was in the area—not in the area we were in but 200 to 250 miles south of our course [sic]—there was a report that a DE—now, I can't remember whether it was a CVE, but it was some sort of antisubmarine patrol that had reported a contact." Therefore, before formal relief of the watch was completed, the outgoing and oncoming officers of the deck prepared a problem whose hypothesis was that the supposed sub was after the *Indianapolis*. If the ship remained on course at the same speed, could the sub reach and sink it? And the answer was no: it was too far away.*

During the last half hour of McKissick's watch (sometime between 7:30 and 8:00 P.M.), McVay gave the order to stop zigzagging and resume their base course. Lieutenant McKissick said, "I remember the captain giving me the order at the

---

*It has been documented that Captain McVay did not know of the *Harris* operation but it is a moot point since, even if he did, in all likelihood he would not have changed course or followed anything different from standard procedure. It must be remembered that responsibility for safeguarding the passage of the ship through his area belonged to Commander, Marianas, and he was therefore the diverting authority. He was aware of *Wild Hunter*, and *Albert T. Harris* was his ship.

end of evening twilight, that is, good dark, that we were to cease zigzagging. As I recall it, to the best of my recollection, we had ceased zigzagging during my watch. When I turned the deck over to my relief we were steady on course."

Under the circumstances that existed on that Sunday evening, the captain of the *Indianapolis* felt secure in giving the order. It was a bad night, with heavy clouds and a choppy sea, but the most important reason for this decision was the cruiser's faulty intelligence report, according to which there were no prowling submarines along his route that evening. McVay, therefore, used his discretionary power to cease zigzagging and later stated over and over again: "The knowledge which I possessed indicated to me that there was little possibility of surface, air, or subsurface attack, in fact no possibility."

Most submarine officers do not feel zigzagging to be an extremely effective torpedo deterrent anyway, and a ship that is not zigzagging can sometimes create more problems for the submarine than one that is. Captain Glynn Donaho, who sank 200,000 tons of Japanese shipping as skipper of the *Flying Fish* and *Barracuda*, felt that with his modern fire-control equipment, high-speed torpedoes, and a well-trained crew, the zigzagging of his target never affected the results. In fact, Donaho admitted that "I have personally found that a target not zigzagging would have confused me." The only time the zigzag maneuver can be effective is when the target changes course (either zigs or zags) *after* the torpedoes are fired. But if luck isn't with the ship, she may find she has changed course into the path of the underwater missiles. By zigzagging, what the master of a target has accomplished at best is to extend the life of his ship for another few minutes. In the meantime, the submarine commander would be reloading his tubes, getting the timing of the target's zigzag pattern down, and setting up for another salvo and, hopefully, the final kill.

At 8:00 P.M., Lieutenant McKissick was relieved as O.D. It was a very dark night, with no moon and very poor visibility. He immediately hurried to the wardroom where a movie was starting in five minutes. After the show, McKissick went straight to his room and was sound asleep by 10:00 P.M.

When Lieutenant (jg) K. MacFarland took over the four-hour shift as O.D. at 8:00 P.M., the *Indianapolis* was steering a straight course, both her air and surface search radars were operating, a low, true wind was blowing, and the sea was choppy, with long swells moving in from the northeast.

Joining MacFarland for this last four-hour watch in the life of the *Indianapolis* was the gunnery officer, Commander Stanley W. Lipski (supervisor of the watch);* the chief engineering officer, Lieutenant Richard B. Redmayne (training to be supervisor); and Quartermaster 3rd Class Vincent Allard. It was so dark Allard could not recognize people on the bridge and the only way he knew who was who was either by their voices or by standing right in front of their faces.

As soon as the watch settled down, Commander Janney came to the bridge and dropped the night orders off; the captain would come up later to sign them. In passing, the navigator mentioned to MacFarland and the others that around 8:00 A.M. the next morning the ship would be passing through an area where a destroyer escort (*Harris*) was searching for a sub.

The officers reviewed the orders and found them to be fairly routine. They stated the course, speed, ports of departure and destination, said that all submarines were to be

---

*Captain McVay: "The supervisor of the watch was normally a head of department, who was put on the bridge because he was an older officer with more experience, who could advise the officer of the deck and oversee what was going on. He was not involved in the conning of the ship, but kept the general situation in mind, was free to go to the combat information center on the deck below if necessary, was to keep general supervision over the officer of the deck, lookouts, helmsmen, course, speed, and, in general, be a supervisor of all activities controlled from the bridge."

considered enemy, and that if there were any changes in sea conditions or weather, or if there were any radar contacts, the captain was to be notified.

Just prior to 8:00 P.M., the cruiser picked up her speed to 17 knots. This increased pace would make certain the *Indianapolis* maintained her average overall tempo of 15.7 knots, and McVay thought it was adequate since he felt the chance of submarine attack was negligible. Furthermore, the skipper believed that sailing straight ahead at 17 knots was better protection for the ship than slowing his speed of advance by zigzagging, especially during alternating conditions of darkness and occasional moonlight.

The captain came to the bridge at 10:30 P.M. He remembered, "It was a confused sea, with long swells, long, deep swells, light wind, and a dark night. It was apparently overcast. . . . It was very dark; the visibility was well below average." He went into the red-lit chartroom where Commander Janney was patiently waiting, and together they reviewed the orders for the evening. McVay recalled that "I always discussed the situation with the navigator. He wrote the things in the night Order Book which I discussed with him (earlier) to cover the general situation. He then submitted it to me, I read it, made any changes that I wished to make, signed it, and then gave it to the officer of the deck."

After the meeting, Captain McVay went out on the open part of the bridge to get some fresh air. He remained there for about ten minutes and at 10:45 P.M. headed down to his emergency cabin and prepared for bed.

At 11:00 P.M., Captain Charles Butler McVay, III, United States Navy, went to sleep.

At 11:00 P.M., Lieutenant Commander Mochitsura Hashimoto, Imperial Japanese Navy, woke up.

After being roused by the petty officer of the watch, Hashimoto put on his undecorated uniform and entered I-

58's shrine to pray. At 11:30 P.M., he was in the conning tower.

The officer of the deck reported nothing unusual, and Hashimoto had the speed increased to three knots. At the same time, he ordered the boat raised to sixty feet below the waves of the Philippine Sea and the night periscope broke the surface.

Glued to the rubber eyepiece, Hashimoto swept the surrounding 360° horizon three times and saw nothing, but then the visibility improved and he could almost see the horizon. With the crew at action stations, I-58 surfaced.

The yeoman of signals screwed open the conning tower hatch and climbed up the narrow ladder to the breached bridge, quickly followed by the navigator. Hashimoto remained at the night periscope. Radar was on, but nothing showed on the scope.

Suddenly, the navigator shattered the night silence: "Bearing red nine-zero degrees, a possible enemy ship." Calmly but quickly, the captain lowered the periscope and scrambled up the ladder. Binoculars to eyes, Hashimoto noticed on the horizon "an indistinct blur" and without a second thought gave the order to dive. The entire action, from surfacing to diving, took fifty seconds.

At 11:38 P.M., I-58 was making her way into hiding, while Hashimoto kept the night periscope steady on target. The ship was too far away for him to know what it was, but the order was given to prepare all torpedo tubes and Kaitens 5 and 6. The submarine's sensitive sound gear was operating, which would help in determining if the enemy changed either course or speed. By 11:39 P.M., everything was ready to fire. Hashimoto hoped that the long wait along this east/west shipping lane would now pay off.

But something had to be wrong, and Hashimoto was both confused and worried. What was coming at him? If it was a large warship, why wasn't it zigzagging? Where were the escorts? His immediate reaction was that he was in trouble; he had been spotted, and it was a destroyer rushing down on him for the kill. Furthermore, whatever it was, it was going to be almost impossible to hit; I-58 was sitting smack in the middle of Route "Peddie," and this thing was coming straight at him, head on. His first objective was to get out of the way.

The blur was just slightly off to the right, and Hashimoto gave various course alterations in order to fire a salvo into the starboard side when (and if) the ship passed. While this was taking place, he still could not estimate the range or type of ship since she was coming bows on, and the masts would not separate as they would have to do if he were to judge their height. Very shortly, however, because of his course adjustments, "the round black spot gradually became triangular in shape," and he steadied I-58 on course; the broad starboard side of the ship would pass in front of his six forward tubes.

At about 3,500 yards, the fore and main masts separated in the periscope lens, and Hashimoto calculated the mast height at ninety feet. He now knew he was onto something big and thought that she was either a battleship or large cruiser.

At this point, the youthful Kaiten pilots were becoming restless and literally begged Hashimoto to please send them off, but the captain decided against it; this was such an easy target that there was no need to waste a life. Furthermore, other submarine captains had had some bad experiences with defective Kaitens: the darkness limited their operating efficiency and getting them away was a somewhat noisy process. He would try the torpedoes first, and if they somehow missed he could always let off a Kaiten to catch and ram the ship.

The target's course was estimated at 260° with a speed of 12

knots, and the six bow tubes were loaded with the best torpedoes in the world. The firing range was set for 1,640 yards,
and a tense silence radiated throughout the submarine.

At midnight, with visibility about 3,000 yards, the watch
changed and Lieutenant (jg) MacFarland was relieved as
officer of the deck by Lieutenant John I. Orr. The new O.D.
had been aboard the *Indianapolis* only a short time but was
an experienced watch stander, having had three years of
prior sea duty. As a matter of fact, Orr had had a destroyer
sunk from under him at Ormoc Bay, and McVay felt that he
had had his baptism by fire and certainly was qualified to
stand an alert watch. The skipper thought Orr was among
his better officers. He had been under his supervision long
enough for McVay to consider him qualified for officer of the
deck.

Visibility had improved somewhat, and Lieutenant Orr
had the authority to begin zigzagging on his own initiative if
he thought it necessary, but, because of conditions, he
decided to stay on course. "I believe," McVay said later, "that
Orr, who had the deck, would have zigzagged if he thought
conditions warranted it. He had been sunk on one ship. I
would not find him at fault [for not doing so]. The onus, I
think, is on me."

At 12:05 A.M., Monday, July 30, 1945, the twelve to four
watch had settled down. At a distance of 1,648 yards off their
starboard beam, a Japanese periscope was sticking out of the
water, watching every move they made.

The six torpedoes were set for a speed of 48 knots and a
depth of 12 feet. Hashimoto could have lowered the running
speed to 42 knots, but all that would have accomplished was
an increase in the range of the missiles. A lower speed was
unnecessary since the target was very close and essentially a

sitting duck. Five of the torpedoes had magnetic warheads, and one had an inertia type. The spread between torpedoes was three degrees, except for the middle two, which were two degrees apart.

Submarine ace Glynn Donaho explained at McVay's court martial that the spread between torpedoes was important because it is not unusual for a submarine commander to estimate either the course or the speed of his target inaccurately. Therefore, if there is an error in either one of these calculations, the torpedo spread should compensate for the error enough to allow one of them to hit home.

Twenty-seven minutes after first sighting the *Indianapolis*, Captain Hashimoto gave the command to fire. The first torpedo slipped out of I-58's tubes, and another one left every three seconds until, after fifteen seconds, all six underwater missiles were loosed. During the entire deadly process, the captain remained glued to the night periscope, lowering it a few feet after each firing to compensate for the gain in underwater buoyancy.

As soon as the last torpedo was ejected, Hashimoto brought the submarine on a parallel course to the *Indianapolis*. Never taking his eyes from the periscope, he waited for the explosions that would take place in about one minute.

4.

Sinking

FIVE minutes past midnight on July 30, 1945, the first torpedo smashed into the starboard bow of the United States heavy cruiser *Indianapolis*, and an ear-shattering explosion rocked the ship. Three seconds later, the second torpedo found its mark directly under the bridge and blew up.

The vessel lifted slightly out of the water, quivered, then promptly settled back down. At the same time, from the bridge to the bow on the starboard side, water was sent soaring into the midnight sky; flame, steam, and smoke belched out of her forward stack, and an enormous ball of fire swept through the entire forward half of the ship. Within seconds, the fire died away. Once again the *Indianapolis* was level and riding high, but now with the bow gone and two huge gaping holes in her right side.

The 40-mm guns were hastily ordered to load and, without waiting for further commands, shoot at anything that moved. One of the 5-inch guns was training out over the vast darkness, seeking a target, but in the end, not a single shot was fired by the *Indianapolis* in retaliation.

From midships forward, the cruiser was a complete disaster; no light, no power, no communication, no pressure. Although the rear half of the vessel was untouched, the tons of water that gushed into the forward part of the cruiser sealed the fate of the *Indianapolis*.

The first violent explosion threw Captain McVay from his bunk onto the steel deck, and the second blast jarred him where he lay. The tiny emergency cabin filled with smoke; the vibrations and whipping of the ship reminded McVay of the time they were hit off Okinawa. "My immediate reaction was, when I was wakened and only half awake, 'My God, we have been hit by another kamikaze,' and then I commenced to get all of my faculties. I immediately believed that there was very little chance of an enemy plane in that vicinity. I had seen many mines at Okinawa; there were very few ships, to my knowledge, damaged by them. Therefore, the most probable thing in my mind was that it must be torpedoes. It was by a process of elimination that I arrived at this conclusion." Within seconds, the Captain had picked himself up off the deck and was rushing naked to the bridge.

In the charthouse and on the bridge, the captain noticed an "acrid white smoke" and this, coupled with the darkness, made it almost impossible for him to discern anything. "We could see nothing from the bridge. It was dark. You couldn't make out anybody on deck. I could not distinguish who was on the bridge, except by asking their names." From what little he could observe during his first few minutes topside, the skipper's gut reaction was that it wasn't all that bad.

Slipping around the deck in his bare feet "and nothing much else," he shouted for Lieutenant Commander K. C. Moore, his damage control officer. As soon as the torpedoes had hit, however, Moore had quit the bridge (where he was supervisor of the twelve to four watch) and rushed below to inspect damage and close the watertight doors. Next, McVay called over the O.D. and asked if he had received any information or reports. Lieutenant Orr replied that he had not. He did point out to the captain that as soon as the explosions took place he immediately gave the order to "sound general alarm."

Captain McVay noted that Orr was extremely upset and almost on the verge of panic because he couldn't stop the huge engines. The U.S.S. *Indianapolis* continued to plow ahead at 17 knots, every second sucking tons of water into the giant holes in her right side. Orr said to McVay, "I have lost all communications, I have tried to stop the engines. I don't know whether the order has ever gotten through to the engine room." It hadn't.

The electrically operated engine room telegraph, and everything else electrical, was out of commission. From the bridge, there was absolutely no communication of any type to (or from) any other part of the ship, except for a voice tube to McVay's emergency cabin and another tube from the bridge to the conning tower. A seaman on watch had been constantly trying to contact the engine room, and the frustrated officer of the deck finally sent a messenger below to order the engineers to shut the damn things down; the spinning props were only hastening the ship's demise.

As Captain McVay related, "Lieutenant Orr was greatly concerned because he could not give the word to stop all engines, and I knew that with the damage forward we would be taking in a great deal of water while going ahead. I know what he had in mind because he mentioned backing the engines." But, from the moment she was hit until she sank, the *Indianapolis* never lost headway.

Walking out onto the starboard wing, the captain vainly searched the forward part of the ship for damage but because of the smoke and darkness saw nothing. At this point, the cruiser had very little list, and McVay figured that everything could be controlled. He was not very upset. He went back inside and told Lieutenant Orr he was going to his cabin to grab some clothes and would be right back.

While McVay was out on the open wing, Edward Keyes, the boatswain's mate of the watch, tried to get the electrically operated PA system working but with no luck. He then went over to Lieutenant Orr and asked him what he should do and was told to get everyone below decks topside. Keyes hollered to him that the PA system was out and the lieutenant then ordered him to go below and pass the word personally.

At 12:10 A.M., five minutes after being struck by two torpedoes, the *Indianapolis* had a 12° starboard list, and Captain McVay was back on the bridge, hastily getting dressed. By this time, although the list was reasonably slight, he was more aware of the fact that they had been hit hard. K. C. Moore, the damage control officer, now reappeared on deck, totally out of breath. Having made a quick inspection down below, he reported to McVay that the ship was badly damaged and going down rapidly. He asked the captain if he wished to abandon ship; he had taken a check of all the compartments up forward, and they were flooding fast.

Captain McVay, however, wasn't sure the commander was right. He found the damage control officer's report hardly believable, and he could not accept the fact that they were actually sinking that fast. McVay knew the list was slight and that from the bridge aft there was no damage at all. The damage he had sustained off Okinawa had seemed just as heavy but had been controlled, and the captain felt that this could be contained also. He knew it would be wrong to order Abandon Ship too late, but it would be just as censurable to order it too early. McVay made the decision not to abandon and told Moore to go below and check again. Commander Moore left the bridge, never to return.

McVay asked Orr whether the radio room was getting off a

distress message, but the O.D. had to reply that he didn't know. At 12:12 A.M., the skipper sent the bugler of the watch into the smokey charthouse to read the inclinometer, and when he returned McVay received the disturbing news that the list was 18°, an increase of 6° in two minutes. The 10,000 ton heavy cruiser was going down.

Eight minutes after the *Indianapolis* was hit, three minutes after Commander Moore left the bridge, and one minute after the inclinometer had been checked, Commander Joseph Flynn, McVay's executive officer, reported to the captain. Crisply, he stated that they were very badly damaged and taking on water at an enormous rate, and he concluded tersely, "I think we are finished; I recommend we abandon ship." The skipper was stunned. How could an explosion be so severe as to force him to quit her in just eight minutes? McVay sadly turned to Flynn and said, "O.K., pass the word to abandon ship."

Seconds later, Lieutenant Orr received word to abandon and told the bugler to go to the rear of the bridge and pick up life preservers for them both. When the bugler returned, Orr ordered him to abandon ship. The officer of the deck did not make it clear, however, whether he meant for the bugler to sound the Abandon Ship call over his horn (which would alert the crew within hearing distance that it was time to leave) or to save himself by getting off the *Indianapolis* before it was too late. The bugler opted for the latter course, and the Abandon Ship call was never blown.

At this moment boatswain's mate Keyes returned to the bridge and told the captain that he had completed passing the word "All hands topside" to the men below decks. Keyes had reached the after sleeping compartments and the mess hall but had been unable to notify anyone from midships forward because of the smoke and fire. Below decks, everyone had been rushing past him with the sole intention of getting topside and there weren't too many people left to pass the word to. McVay believed that anyone who could get on deck was there by now, since sailors have an "instinct" that tells them when a ship is badly wounded, often before the official word to abandon is passed.

Moments after the twin explosions rocked the *Indianapolis*, the O.D. sent an officer down to the radio room with the ship's exact position, which would be sent out with the contact report. At 12:14 A.M., McVay turned to Commander Janney and asked the navigator, because of his extensive knowledge of communications, to make sure that the distress and contact message had gotten off the ship. He told him to have the message sent that the *Indianapolis* had been torpedoed, giving her latitude and longitude and stating that she was sinking rapidly and needed immediate assistance.

After Janney left, McVay went out onto the open wing and from his perch yelled down to the patient men jammed along the port rail to abandon ship. Hands cupped to mouth, Commander Flynn was shouting the same order. Many men did not wait for the order, and a number of people had jumped off the ship at first inclination, or they slid off the deck into the water. Because the cruiser never lost headway, there was a wake of bobbing heads for miles behind it. From the fantail, sailors who had jumped or been blown off could be heard screaming. All along the port rail men were lined up, three and four deep, waiting for the order to leave.

In the area of the quarterdeck, a severely wounded Commander Lipski, the gunnery officer, was in charge. At one point he met up with warrant gunner D. R. Honner and Lipski "gave me a message for his wife. . . . He was badly burned and didn't think he would get through. I wasn't burned, and he figured perhaps I would." Once he was assured all the men were wearing life jackets, Lipski, on his own initiative, gave the order to abandon ship. Seconds later,

Commander Flynn came out of the port passageway and said, "Go over the side, men."

Lieutenant Commander Joseph Reid was the senior officer on the fantail, where hundreds of scared young men were milling about. Most of them wanted to go over the side. Reid vainly tried to hold them back, but by ones and by twos, and then in groups, they leaped over the rail. In the darkness, they could not see that the increasing starboard list was bringing the two port propellers further out of the water, and many of the men jumped into these two giant grinders and were chopped up. When Flynn told the crew in the area of the quarterdeck to go over, a sailor on the stern recalls that "all of a sudden I saw these men, commencing from forward, starting to jump into the water, and as the men forward started to jump in it came like a wave back aft, and the men toward the aft part started jumping in as the men ahead of them jumped. . . ."

A few minutes after ordering Abandon Ship and telling Janney to check with the radio room, McVay decided to leave the bridge. The navigator had not reported back, and since Radio One was just a few decks below it shouldn't have taken more than a minute or so to find out if they were getting a message off and to report back. This transmission was the captain's primary concern now that Abandon Ship had been ordered; he decided to check the radio room personally. He also wanted to inspect the damage, especially around the main deck, as he had heard rumors that it was split near the forward stack. McVay could not visualize why they were going down so fast by the bow.

Leaving the bridge, he walked through the charthouse and into his emergency cabin where he found and put on his life preserver. Stepping out of his room, he met up with Captain E. M. Crouch, a passenger who had come aboard in Guam and had been sleeping in McVay's main cabin. Crouch had forgotten his life jacket and asked, "Charley, have you got a spare life preserver?" So McVay went back into his cabin, picked up a pneumatic preserver, and handed it to seaman quartermaster Harrison, who happened to be in the passageway, with the request, "Please blow this up for Captain Crouch." He then continued toward Radio One.

McVay had just placed his foot on top of the ladder that led down to the signal bridge when the *Indianapolis* suddenly took a sharp 25° tilt to the right. At 12:17 A.M., the ill-fated cruiser was listing 60°. Everyone and everything was thrown to starboard, and the noise was deafening from material breaking loose and men yelling and screaming. Captain McVay held on for dear life and was able to stay on his feet only because he was between the railing of the ladder. He finally made it down and on hands and knees, crawled up the sloping deck of the signal bridge to the port side, where there was another ladder leading further down to the communications deck.

Struggling down the ladder, he reached the deck, and there he noticed some men getting ready to jump without life jackets. He stopped long enough to call out, "There is a floater net on Number One stack; get that, don't jump over the side unless you have some form of support. The ship should stay in its position for enough time to get that floater net off." The officer of the deck, hearing his voice, yelled down from the bridge, "That is the captain talking. Now get your floater net and your life jackets." For a few precious seconds the men tried to loosen the net but couldn't, and McVay finally said, "If you can't, you might as well let it go."

Abruptly, the ship took another heavy list of 30° more. The time was 12:18 A.M. and the former flagship of the Pacific Fifth Fleet was on her side, high in the water, where she would remain for another two minutes. Holding onto a lifeline, McVay pulled himself up the vertical deck and found himself standing on the side of the ship. Water noisily rushed in through the open hatches and stacks, and the U.S.S. *Indianapolis* began to settle.

Lieutenant Charles McKissick, who had the earlier six to eight watch as O.D., was asleep in his starboard room when the first torpedo exploded forward of him and the second, aft. At that moment, as he was thrown to the deck and heard the glass shatter in his mirror, his first and only thought was to get topside as quickly as possible. Two other officers had been asleep in the room with him, and they had already left.

Stepping into the narrow corridor, he found it jammed with men. On his deck and the main deck above him, burning oil was floating on water in the passageways, making them unbearably hot. The smoke and heat were so intense that McKissick ducked back into his room.

Searching in the dark, he located the drawer under his bunk and pulled out a flashlight. He then grabbed a towel, went over to the sink, and wet it. Wrapping it around his head and with the flashlight in one hand, he stepped out into the blistering passageway again.

The fumes and smoke were horrible. He couldn't stay where he was, so, hunched over, he stumbled forward until he reached a ladder leading up to the main deck. Struggling up the steps, he had only one thing on his mind—to get fresh air as quickly as possible.

Now that he was in the starboard passageway of the main deck, he didn't know which way to go—forward or aft. Looking down the narrow corridor toward the officers' wardroom, he saw smoke, fire, and a crowd of men. Not wishing to get caught up in the jam back there and not knowing what was in store for him if he moved forward, he crossed the listing ship to the port passageway where he knew staterooms to be.

The only thing on McKissick's mind at this point was air,

and he entered a small room with the sole intention of opening a porthole and climbing out. When he reached the port, it was tightly dogged down and he couldn't find a wrench to unscrew it. He had little oxygen and was understandably nervous and frustrated. "I remember as I was at the port I could hear the air escaping out of it, as if under pressure. You could hear it whistlying [sic] around the port, although it was supposed to be airtight and watertight." Not about to get stuck in this small room, he found himself back in the scalding passageway.

He looked aft toward the wardroom, and conditions were no better than before. Just as he began moving forward (which was his last option), a heavy steel door to the powder-handling room of Turret Number One opened and a voice called out, "Anybody want to get out?" Gratefully, McKissick replied that he certainly did, and the sailor said, "Come out this way," and led him into the room. Once inside and crawling on hands and knees, "I could feel the fresh air and felt some relief." He was led up a ladder into the pointer's booth and out the door of the booth into the open air on the port side of the forecastle deck.*

By the time he reached the forecastle, he was exhausted and nauseated. He fell to his knees and was sick from the smoke and fumes. The fresh air revived him, and after he had gotten his bearings and rested for a moment he felt better. More times than not, the moon was hiding behind distant clouds, and during those times McKissick couldn't even see a man who was only two or three feet in front of him. When a cloud slipped away and exposed the moon, visibility was quite good.

---

*After leading McKissick out, Seaman First Class James Newhall went down two additional times in an attempt to lead men out. Through his efforts, one other man was brought to safety but, while doing this, Newhall was severely burning his hands. Seaman Newhall was recommended for the Bronze Star in this action.

The forecastle deck, on which Lieutenant McKissick was standing, was, after the bow itself, the most forward part of the ship. During the last fifteen minutes in the life of the *Indianapolis* however, she had no bow; about forty feet of it was gone, "completely off, just like you had taken a saw and cut it off clean."

For the moment McKissick was relatively safe, but if he went into the water he knew he had better be wearing a life preserver. McKissick was still on the port side, which was rising higher and higher every minute, and he moved aft just a short distance to where belts were being distributed. He turned on his flashlight, found a jacket for himself, and continued to hold the light for other men who needed one. Suddenly, out of the darkness from the direction of the bridge, Lieutenant Orr yelled down, "For God's sake, put out that light. There is liable to be an enemy submarine around here." Snapping out the beam, McKissick again went forward.

Lieutenant C. Jenney,* the senior officer on the forecastle deck, ordered all men in the area to help in rescue operations, and Lieutenant McKissick quickly joined in. This part of the cruiser was in a total shambles. Everything under the deck they were standing on had been destroyed, and almost everyone killed. Beneath them were three spaces where between 100 and 120 men had lived and slept, including the entire Marine detachment, the steward's mates, and some officers. When the torpedoes hit, most of the Marines, all steward's mates, and many of the officers were killed. Nevertheless, there were still people down there, alive, who had to be pulled out.

On the port side, between the Number One and Number Two 8-inch gun turrets, was a hatch leading to the hell below. Breaking out a fire hose, they shoved it down the opening

---

*Not to be confused with Commander Janney, the navigator.

and turned on the water. Not a drop came out. The explosions had ruptured the fire main, and the inferno below remained unchecked. Reluctantly, they gave up.

Directly opposite them on the starboard side was another hatch leading to the main deck beneath, and McKissick, together with six or seven other men, succeeded in pulling out a few lucky sailors. Everyone brought on deck through this hole was badly burned, either from the flash of the explosions or the 3,500 gallons of aviation gas that were stored forward. The ship's rapidly increasing list was making the rescue operation very difficult, and when the last man was hauled out they had to tie a rope around his chest and drag him up the slanting deck to the port side. When the list reached 50°, further rescue became impossible.

Standing by the Number One Turret, McKissick thought of heading aft, but the walkway going in that direction was jammed with men, all with the same idea. Not liking crowds, he decided to stay put. He believed that if the front half went under, it really wouldn't matter where he was. The entire forecastle deck, together with the Number One Turret and her three giant 8-inch rifles, was underwater. The only dry spot was the after port side of the deck where he was standing. Using his own initiative (as many other officers aboard the *Indianapolis* did during her last few minutes), Lieutenant McKissick gave the order. "At that time, I felt that it was the proper time to abandon ship, and I told the men who were within hearing distance of me that I felt that we ought to go over the side, so we held our life jackets and climbed up over the life lines, walked down the port side of the ship, and just walked into the water."

Fifteen minutes after being comfortably asleep in his room, he was now swimming as fast as he could. His only thought was to get as far away as possible. When the *India-napolis* went down, he didn't want the suction to take him

with her. For a brief moment he turned around in the night
sea and gave a last fleeting look at the steeply listing
Indianapolis.

After being relieved from the eight to twelve watch, Chief
Engineer Richard Redmayne had a quick midnight sandwich and then had just entered the officer's head when the
first blast erupted forward of him and the second directly
underneath. The cruiser shook, lights went out, and in the
blackness he could hear and smell fire beyond the head.

There was only one door out, and he figured that the sooner
he left that confined space, the better off he would be. Putting
his right hand over his face, with eyes closed, he rushed out
into the heat and flames. Running out the door, he fell and
the fingertips of his left hand went to the deck for support;
they were immediately burned. The flame was licking at his
right hand, which was covering his face, and his hair was
singeing. He headed aft down the port passageway, and it
soon became cooler so he opened his eyes. His only objective
at that time was to get to his battle station, which was the
after engine room.

About three minutes later, with the ship at a 10° list, Lieutenant Redmayne made it to his station. The officer of the
watch reported they had no communication with the bridge,
and Redmayne noticed that the engine room telegraph was
dead. Furthermore, they didn't know what was happening in
the forward engine room, which controlled the two outboard
shafts (One and Four), and vacuum had been lost on the
Number Two engine. The chief engineer, therefore, ordered
Number Two engine shut down, and, since this power plant
controlled the inside starboard shaft, that propeller immediately stopped spinning. Furthermore, since the engine that
controlled the inboard port shaft was operating all right, he
ordered it opened up, and the inside port propeller began

spinning faster. This was exactly what the bridge didn't want, but soon that enormous prop was spinning at 160 RPMs and forcing the bow deeper and deeper into the Philippine Sea.

Everything being relative, the rear engine room was in pretty good shape. In addition to all auxiliaries, the main generators functioned perfectly, and the diesel powered emergency generator started automatically. From midships aft, the entire ship had power and light and was basically undamaged.

Glancing at his inclinometer, Redmayne noticed the list between 12° and 15°. At that moment, Machinist's Mate First Class William Nightingale, who had been in charge of the forward engine room, reported to the chief engineer that he had ordered the room abandoned at 12:10 A.M. As soon as the torpedoes had hit, Numbers One and Four shafts, which spun the port and starboard outside propellers, stopped turning. The lights went out, sparks and cinders began shooting out of the ventilation ducts, steam pressure dropped, oily water poured down the engine-room hatch, and smoke immediately filled the entire room. The two main generators, which supplied power to the forward half of the cruiser, were also knocked out and the emergency generator wouldn't start. Nightingale said that it was too hot to stay down there but, with three of the four props dead in the water, he asked the lieutenant if he wanted him to go back. The reply was negative.

Right after Nightingale reported, the chief engineer became seriously worried. The list was becoming worse by the minute so he ordered that fuel oil be pumped from the starboard to port tanks, hoping for at least a small correction.

At 12:16 A.M., four minutes before she went down, Lieutenant Redmayne made the decision to go to the bridge and see what was going on. Climbing up the ladder from the innards of the ship and not knowing at this time how far down by the bow she really was, he wasn't overly concerned about her sinking.

Reaching the top of the ladder, the engineer noticed two sailors who were part of a repair party in the Number Two mess hall, which was located directly over the engine room. One of the men was on a sound-powered phone, and Redmayne asked if they had any contact with the bridge, to which they answered no.* He then asked if they knew what conditions were like up forward, and he received the same reply. Just a few minutes before, these men had met Lieutenant Commander Moore, who had been sent down by McVay to further check the damage and close all watertight doors. Moore had come into the mess hall, filthy with oil and badly burned, hands over his head and calling for help: "Somebody help me, I want somebody to come with me—please help me—why isn't anybody looking at me?" Then he left, going forward to his death. One of the two sailors made the insensitive remark, "He must be crazy." After talking with Lieutenant Redmayne, both men felt they better get out, but one of them first stopped by his locker to put in his pocket $109 cash, a ring, and a few souvenirs from his girlfriend.

The ship took a sudden 30° surge to starboard while Redmayne was on the ladder leading up from the mess hall to the main deck. He hung on for all he was worth and struggled up to the top. Debris was ripping from the port bulkheads and crashing all around him. Almost as soon as the noise started, it stopped, and when he reached the port side of the main deck, the *Indianapolis* was on her side. On the bulkhead were

---

*The sound-powered phones were not effective, because to call a station using a sound-powered phone it is necessary to attract attention by the use of an electric push button. Since no station could be communicated with, it must be assumed that the call-bell system, which requires electrical power, was completely out.

oxygen bottles, and when Redmayne reached them they were horizontal. Crawling hand over hand on the bottles, he reached a once vertically stacked pile of lumber, which was also horizontal, and stood up. He walked across the wood, out the after deck, and simply plopped into the Philippine Sea.

Looking up at the ship, the chief engineer saw men jumping off the fantail. He also noticed the ship, on its side, moving through the water. "She had some headway on her. I do not suppose it was more than five knots. She went down decidedly by the bow, because before she fully capsized you could see the screws; she completely rolled over, still having some headway on her. Of course, by that time the weight was causing her to go straight down, and as she disappeared I would say she was just about vertical with the bow down."

Lieutenant Commander Lewis Haynes lived as far forward as you could get. Dr. Haynes was a very light sleeper, and for some odd reason, just seconds before the explosions, he woke up. He started to rise in his bunk when the first torpedo hit, and through the thick glass of his porthole he saw a brilliant flash. The explosion sent him flying through the air, and his lamp, which had been bolted to the desk, went sailing with him. He landed half on his desk and half on the deck. He started to get to his feet when the second explosion stunned him.

Flames shot through the deck in his room. Quickly, he grabbed his life preserver. Stepping into the passageway he saw Lieutenant Commander K. Stout, who occupied the cabin across the way. Suddenly Stout screamed, "Look out," and Haynes lunged back into his room just as an enormous flash of flame passed down the corridor. "It was a tremendous and continuous sheet of flame that lasted for a second or two," Haynes said, and for what little protection it could afford the doctor held his life jacket in front of his face. Nevertheless, he still received first-degree burns over parts of his face, and the hair on his forehead was partially burned off.

Going back out, he headed forward toward a ladder leading topside, only a short distance away. Upon passing the only room in front of his, which held two officers, "I heard them scream, but I never saw them. I think they were unable to get out." He had taken a few more steps forward when a white flame erupted in front of him and barred his way; heading any farther forward was simply out of the question. Turning around, he began working his way aft toward the wardroom, in which there was a passageway leading up to the quarterdeck. Flames were everywhere. He noticed fire coming out of an ammunition compartment and was afraid that the shell room was going to blow.* His main concern was to get out as fast as possible since, as the doctor recalled, "The heat and smoke were very intense and the smoke had a very peculiar odor which I had never smelled before." Haynes was being quickly overcome by fumes.

Upon reaching the sanctuary of the wardroom, he noticed that although it was not actually on fire it was very hot and there was a red haze throughout. Halfway across the room he collapsed, and his hands went out to break the fall. As soon as they touched the deck they were severely burned, but the pain brought him back to his feet. In pain, he groped his way across the room toward the starboard side, hands sliding along the wall, feeling for the passageway that led up and out. "Chairs, lamps, and things seemed to be scattered about, getting in my way. I fell into an easy chair and began to feel drowsy again." Sitting in the chair in the smoke-filled wardroom, Commander Haynes relaxed and figured this was the

---

*Some newspaper reports at that time stated that the magazines blew up but that is incorrect. There were only two explosions, not multiple, and the men in the two forward gun turrets did reach safety. Furthermore, if the magazines had exploded, the ship would have been blown in two.

end; he was going to die and he really didn't care. Out of the haze, "Someone was standing over me and said, 'My God, I am fainting,' and fell on me." Haynes panicked, shoved the body off his lap, and forced himself back to his feet.

Men were yelling not to light matches, and one sailor was continually screaming, "Open a porthole—open a porthole— open a porthole." The doctor struggled to the starboard side and found a port that was open and swinging freely.* He hooked it up "and I stuck my head out and took a deep breath. It was like sticking your head into a deep-freeze cooler in comparison with the heat of the wardroom." His first inclination, after clearing his head, was to climb out the port and fall into the water. He had second thoughts about the wisdom of this move, however, since directly beneath him was the hole from the second torpedo. The sea, according to Haynes, "was littered with paper and the water seemed to be very agitated, and I said to myself, 'I can't go into the water there because I will be sucked in toward the ship again.'" While his head was sticking out the port, a rope that was attached to a floater net on the open deck above him kept hitting him in the head. He jerked it a few times and found it to be secure. With great difficulty, he forced himself out the porthole and began painfully climbing up the attached line. At one point he stopped, looked down, and saw water madly rushing into the giant hole beneath him.

Reaching the top, he crawled across the net and was on the forecastle deck. He quickly headed aft toward the port hangar (which was the emergency first-aid station) and upon nearing it heard men desperately pleading for a doctor. Shoving his way through a group of sailors, he saw his chief

---

*Commander Haynes always felt this porthole was blown open by the force of the explosions, but it was not. Ensign John Woolston and a steward's mate had undogged it and, a few minutes earlier, had climbed out and up.

pharmacist's mate, John Schmueck, administering morphine to a group of about thirty badly burned seamen. Haynes joined him, and they started laying the men out in rows. Many of them were crying, and the doctor was frustrated since there were only a few bandages and no light except for the peek-a-boo moon. He located some more morphine and began injecting those whom he thought to be in the most pain. While giving an injection, he fainted but came to in seconds when the man he fell across roughly shoved him away.

They needed more help, and Doctor Haynes sent a man down to sick bay for both morphine and corpsmen. Within a few seconds, the messenger reported back that the sick bay was no more. It was flooded and on fire, and everyone within was dead. There was no way to get near it.

After hearing this news and looking around him, Commander Haynes knew the ship was in trouble; he ordered Chief Schmueck to stop treating and get life jackets for everyone. Then Haynes climbed a ladder to the deck above. When he reached it, he found the men were all manning their guns in an orderly manner. The doctor was immediately struck by the contrast between the calm and order of the gun deck and all the agony and screaming in the first-aid station below. Several men were cutting down bags with jackets in them, and Haynes said he needed some for his patients. One of the sailors handed him an armload, and he brought them down to the hangar.

Quickly jackets were put on all the burned men. A sailor, spotted outside the hangar, was so badly burnt that the skin was hanging down from his arms. Doctor Haynes went to him with a jacket. The man pleaded not to be touched, but the preserver was forced on him anyway. Shortly afterward, the doctor noticed for the first time that the ship was listing. A man began sliding away from him, and at that moment the ship suddenly keeled, and all the patients went tumbling down towards the starboard side and into the waiting sea. Together with hundreds of other men, Haynes grabbed the port lifeline and chinned himself up the deck until he was standing on the side of the cruiser.

Looking around, he saw that the side of the ship was black with men. For some reason, he had an extra jacket, and standing next to him was a very young man who had lost his. Haynes helped the sailor on with the preserver, and then the youth jumped over but hit a bar that was sticking out of the side of the ship.

Together with a throng of other men, Doctor Haynes walked down the side of the cruiser and partially crossed the red-painted bottom. Reaching the line where sea and ship met, he held onto his jacket, and jumped.

The stern was towering straight up. Men still stood on it, and some even perched on the motionless propeller blades. After taking about ten strokes, Commander Haynes turned on his back to watch the death of his ship and silently say his final good-by.

She was at about a 65° angle, with her rear defiantly pointing into the midnight sky. Then, as a sharp knife would easily slide into a crock of butter, the *Indianapolis* slid downward into the depths of the Pacific Ocean. A large wave washed Haynes a long way from the spot. About five minutes later, from the deep, an explosion sounded. After that, there was nothing.

The detonations threw the five men in Radio I (Radio Central) to the deck and flung the port receivers off their tables. Suddenly, the room had no lights, was filled with smoke, and was essentially a wreck. The men grabbed flashlights and lanterns, and decided to abandon the radio shack. When they opened the double doors of the communications office, however, they were greeted by a wall of flame and quickly retreated back into the room. The watch officer, Lieutenant (jg) D. Driscoll, commanded them to get out by using the main entrance, but when they undogged the door, standing on the other side was the junior officer of the deck. He ordered them back into the room to send out a distress message.

Radio I was primarily a message receiving room. All dispatches, orders, or any other type of communication from the outside world, flowed into the radio receivers in this compartment. When the *Indianapolis* wanted to send a message, it had to go through the radio transmitters in Radio II (Radio Transmitter Room), which was not far from Radio I, but still in a different location on the superstructure. Therefore, during normal operations, one room (Radio I) took in all messages, and another room (Radio II) sent out. Even though Radio I did not physically have any transmitting equipment in the shack, they did have transmitting keys and, in cooperation with Radio II, did send messages. These transmissions from Radio I though had to flow through the transmitters in Radio II, and then out of the ship.

After being ordered back into the room, Lieutenant Driscoll picked up the phone and attempted to call Radio II, but couldn't get through. He then remarked that someone would have to go to Radio II and tell them to plug a transmitting line into the key in Radio I. On hearing this, Radioman 2nd Class Elwyn Sturtevant rushed to Radio II. When he reached the transmitting shack, he was told that a line had been set up for Radio I's use and that they could transmit over 4235 kilocycles.

Back at Radio I, sitting at a transmitting key, was Radioman 1st Class Joseph Moran. On a small piece of paper, Lieutenant Driscoll had written out the message that he had been given by the junior O.D. The officer held a flashlight for

Moran and the tapping began to flow out on 4235 kc, which was the frequency constantly listened to ("guarded") throughout the Pacific by all shore bases, and many ships at sea. Over his shoulder, a messenger sent up from Radio II was busy copying the message to bring back to that room. Moran transmitted, "XRAY VICTOR MIKE LOVE—WE HAVE BEEN HIT BY TWO TORPEDOES," giving the latitude and longitude of their current position. He kept repeating this signal over and over, with the follow-up plea: "NEED IMMEDIATE ASSISTANCE."

Next to the transmission key Moran was tapping, a red "pilot light" was supposed to pulsate each time the key was pressed. The light was not blinking, but the system would work with the light out. The meters in Radio II were working fine, however, and showed transmission by Radio I. Moran, having been aboard the ship a few years and knowing the equipment as well as anyone, was confident that the signal was getting out.

When the *Indianapolis* reached her starboard list of 50°, the operating positions on the port side of the shack began tearing loose and fire started creeping into the room. Lieutenant Driscoll ordered the men to clear out, and everyone abandoned Radio I safely.

Coincidentally, just a few days before, Captain McVay had decided to hold a battle problem centering on the radio rooms. The simulation had been that Radio I was knocked out of action and Radio II was depended upon to get a message out.

Radio Technician 2nd Class Fred Hart was late coming on watch and was just getting dressed when the torpedoes hit forward of Radio II. Rushing into the blackness of that shack, he heard someone yell for a light and, finding his toolbox, pulled out a flashlight and flipped it on. Then he started up the auxiliary generator, and a desk lamp and two overhead fluorescent-light fixtures switched on. Looking around, he saw that nothing was damaged except for a receiver that had come in for repair and which was now lying on the deck. Otherwise, everything that was secured remained secured. All of the transmitters were warmed up, and one was constantly kept on 500 kc, which was the frequency listened to by ships at sea.* Hart remembered that he looked at the pilot lights on the transmitters, and they were all lit, which meant that they had power for all the transmitters. As a matter of fact, Radio II had transmitting power until the ship went under, since its power source was the after engine room.

Shortly after Hart turned on the emergency generator (which provided the lights, not transmitting power), Chief Radio Electrician L. T. Woods entered the room. He was an extremely self-assured man, never uncertain about his job and hardly ever asking questions. Hart considered him the best, by far, of anyone in the shack. Woods had just come from up forward, and he knew they were going to sink. Briefly describing to everyone what he had seen, he told them to either put on or blow up their preservers and remain calm.

Woods next sat down at one of the transmitting keys and quickly went to work. While Moran, in Radio I, was busy keying out on 4235 kilocycles, four minutes after the explosions, Chief Woods began repeatedly sending out from Radio II a plain language SOS on 500 kc.

There is some doubt as to whether Moran was getting out, but Woods had power and was sending. The men in the room could see the transmitter putting out and the meter registering. As one man in the room recalled, "I knew Mr. Woods, and I knew that he knew enough about radios and transmitters

---

*Radio One transmitted on 4235 kc, which was primarily attended to by shore bases.

that he wouldn't try to send out a message if it wasn't getting out. All you have to do is observe the transmitter current meter and you can tell whether or not it is getting out."

For about five minutes, Woods kept monotonously banging out the SOS. He then left the room, checked the damage, and a few minutes later, at 12:17 A.M., returned and ordered the men to leave; the ship was going down.

No ship responded to the distress message of the *Indianapolis*, although it is possible (as we shall see) that it was received by a few ships in the area. If, by chance, nothing did get out, the only explanation offered was that the antennas had been either knocked down and/or grounded. Captain McVay had seen this happen when the ship was hit by a kamikaze off Okinawa; the insulators broke loose, thereby grounding the antennas and, although there was some evidence of a transmission, actually nothing was getting out. The only problem with the grounding explanation is that, based upon the type of equipment on board (which was the best), if the antennas had been down or grounded the current meters next to the transmitting equipment would not have shown output, and there is no doubt that these meters were registering.

Standing by himself on the side of his rapidly sinking ship, the first thought that came into McVay's mind was to die, to go down with the ship. That would have been so easy, for he wouldn't have to face what he knew was coming after this. Captain Charles McVay was actually embarrassed that he was still alive, but something within him spurred him to at least try to save himself.

He began walking aft along the ship's side and for a few seconds, he couldn't face the reality of having lost, in just fifteen minutes, a heavy cruiser of the United States Navy. Even while taking this midnight walk along the side of his overturned ship, he was not convinced that she was going completely under. Peculiar as it may seem, he played with the idea of sitting on the stern until morning light, at which time he could properly survey the situation. Suddenly, without warning, he was sucked off the side by a wave caused by the bow going down.

To McVay's complete surprise, he was in the water and swimming away. He looked up and later remembered that he "saw this hulk, just descending on me, and I swam away from the ship, thinking, 'Well, this is the end of me.'"

The plunging *Indianapolis* said her final farewell to her master by throwing hot oil over his neck. Swimming desperately now, he heard a sort of swish, looked around, and she was gone.

No one will ever know precisely how many men survived the sinking, but based upon the thousands of pages of recently declassified documents, a conservative number would be 800 (and could have been closer to 900). Therefore, approximately 400 men went down with the *Indianapolis* including Commander Flynn, E.O.; Commander Janney, navigator; Lieutenant Commander Moore, damage control officer; and Lieutenant Orr, O.D. Because the midnight watch had just changed, many men were awake at the time Hashimoto's torpedoes hit, and this permitted a majority of the crew to escape.

There was still time for the Navy to get these men out of the water.

5.

In the Water the First Day

Monday, July 30, 1945

AT 1:00 A.M., with the six forward tubes once again re-loaded with missiles, I-58 sneaked to just below the waves. Intently staring through the periscope and finding that there was nothing to be seen for 360°, Hashimoto gave the order to surface. Heading for the spot where the ship had been hit, the Japanese kept a sharp lookout for debris and flotsam that would establish proof of the sinking, but because of the darkness they couldn't see a thing. Commander Hashimoto, however, was certain the ship had gone down, since it would have been impossible for her to make off at high speed with the damage he knew she had sustained. Nervous about lurking destroyers and aircraft, he sped off toward the northeast and, about one hour later, brought the boat to the safety of the deep. During this hour on the surface (between 1:00 A.M. and 2:00 A.M.), he instructed his radio room to forward a message to Tokyo that he had sunk a "battleship of the *Idaho* class."

The United States Navy had previously broken the Japanese code (except as to ship classifications) and Naval Intelligence in Washington and Pearl Harbor were busy reading I-58's message at about the same time Tokyo was. Secret Naval documents report that "at a time which is approximately within a half hour after the recorded time of the

67

sinking of the *Indianapolis*, the Japanese submarine I-58, *which was known to be operating on an offensive mission in the general area through which the* Indianapolis *was then passing* [italics author's], sent a dispatch to his commander reporting that he had made a sinking. Our decryptors were unable to determine the nature of the sinking, as they apparently had not been able to break the grill which encodes the Japanese designation of various types of United States vessels." Nevertheless, on that early Monday morning, the Navy knew that an American ship had been sunk and were aware of the latitude and longitude of that sinking.

While the communications center in Washington was translating the message, "a check translation of this same message was received" by them from Pearl Harbor. When Washington completed their translation, they compared it with Pearl's version. They were basically identical. At this juncture, Washington took no further action on the intercept, since they knew Pearl had the same thing and all follow-up action to this intelligence coup would be handled directly by the Pacific Fleet.

The action taken by CinCPac on Hashimoto's message was—in a word—nothing. The entire matter was totally ignored, and the Navy later secretly admitted that "the delay in making the search for the survivors of the *Indianapolis* ... seems to involve deeply the headquarters of the Commander in Chief, Pacific Fleet." Furthermore, had Fleet Admiral Nimitz and his staff "taken immediate steps to have this matter investigated, it is probable that the survivors of the *Indianapolis* would have been located within twenty-four hours of the time of the sinking of the ship and many lives would have been saved."

Pearl Harbor ignored I-58's message because "it was believed it was intended to deceive." The Japanese were notorious for exaggerating their claims; they would send out a message saying that they had sunk a particular ship when in fact the vessel was 3,000 miles away. Also, intercepted Japanese combat reports contained a great deal of false intelligence, put out as "feelers." Initially, the Navy investigated all of these enemy reports, with no results. Subsequently, a policy was developed of placing a very low evaluation on all intercepted messages reporting the sinking of a ship. Therefore, when I-58's dispatch to Tokyo was picked up and translated, no one bothered to plot the submarine's position on a map or to mark that of ships in the area. If anyone had done so, it would have been readily noticeable that Hashimoto and McVay were occupying the same spot.

The potato crate gently nudged him. For five minutes after his ship disappeared, the captain was alone in the quiet darkness, clinging to a wooden box. Soon, two empty life rafts silently drifted by, and McVay heaved himself into one and lashed the other to it. A short distance away, he heard someone yell.

Quartermaster 3rd Class Vincent Allard found himself with six or seven other men, all desperately hanging onto a coiled floater net. One of them had a bared knife and was busy cutting the tangles in the net so that it would uncoil and spread out. While this was going on, Allard heard a cry for help. He quickly swam toward the sound and in a few seconds found a sailor floating on a pontoon from one of the ship's planes. He guided the man back to the group clustered around the net, but no sooner did he return when again he heard cries for help. Off he went once more and soon spotted two men holding onto a potato crate. One of the boys could swim, but the other could not and was very scared. Telling the swimmer to stick close, Allard began helping the non-swimmer to the safety of the net. On the way toward the group, he heard someone yell that he had a raft. Since it seemed that the raft was closer than the net, Allard changed course and headed for the sound. The voice called again, and Allard thought he recognized it as the skipper's. Allard called out to ask if it were the captain calling, and McVay replied that it was and to come aboard. They swam a short distance and reached the rafts.

The man who could swim climbed unassisted into the empty second raft, McVay and Allard helped the other sailor in, and then Allard joined McVay in his raft. The two men in the second raft had swallowed an enormous amount of water, and at first Captain McVay thought they were both dying. But after a while, they came around. Just before sunrise, they met up with five men on another raft that had a floater net tied to it. They lashed this raft to theirs, and, at first light Monday morning, the group consisted of three rafts, one net, and nine men. Captain McVay was the only officer. The men were Vincent Allard, Angelo Galante, Jay Glenn, Otha Havins, Ralph Klappa, George Kurlick, John Muldoon, and John Spinelli.

Some of the rafts on the *Indianapolis* were large enough to hold twenty-five men each, while many smaller ones were distributed and lashed to the various open decks of the ship. The rafts were basically rectangular in shape, with rounded corners, and were made of kapok covered by canvas. There was no floor to a raft but, instead, either heavy rope or wooden slats secured side to side and fore and aft of the bottom. Generally, to keep dry, a man did not sit in the raft but on the side, and this checkerboard effect of rope, or "grating," acted as a type of safety net; in case someone slipped, he wouldn't fall through the raft. The grating also served as a somewhat firm place to keep the feet in order to secure better seating on the side.

An inspection of the rafts turned up two canoe paddles, a

box of cigarettes, fishing gear, signaling mirrors, and a tin container that held twelve Very (star) shells and a pistol. They also found a canvas bag holding a first-aid kit and matches, but it was soaked and everything inside was useless except for some sealed tubes of ointment. During the day, a water breaker holding three gallons of water floated by. This was given to McVay to be tasted, but salt water had leaked into the archaic wooden container and the water was undrinkable. So as not to create unnecessary fear, the captain didn't pass on the bad news but told everyone it would be rationed out when he thought it was "absolutely necessary that they have a drink."

No food was found on any of the rafts, but fortunately, sometime during the day, an emergency ration can drifted by. Upon opening, they found it was dry inside, and they pulled out a number of cans of Spam and small tins of malted-milk tablets and biscuits. The skipper told the other eight men that one 12-ounce tin of Spam would be opened daily and divided equally. In addition, everyone would daily receive two biscuits and two malted-milk tablets. Under this quota, he figured they had rations to last ten days.

When the rafts crashed into the sea, their gratings had broken. Nevertheless the men made themselves as comfortable as possible and hung on while they were tossed about by the heavy swells of the unending ocean. At one moment they would be deep in a valley of waves and the next moment on top, looking down into that same valley. While on this unwanted roller-coaster ride, resting momentarily on the crest of a wave, they spotted two other rafts also on the crest of their waves. One raft was about 1,500 yards away and appeared to have one man on it who was calling for help. The other raft was much farther away and looked like it held a group of men who seemed to be in good condition. At this time though, McVay's group was too exhausted to paddle over to the near raft, and any investigation had to be held off until the next day.

During this first day, a monstrous shark decided to investigate the raft and its edible cargo. The shark kept swimming under the raft. The dorsal fin was "almost as white as a sheet of paper," while the body was a darker color. The shark could therefore always be spotted because of the visibility of its white fin in the water. The frightened men attempted to catch the pilot fish by knocking them off with canoe paddles, but this was an exercise in futility. They also tried hitting the shark with paddles, but when they occasionally did manage to do so he swam away and returned a few minutes later. In the days to follow, this unwanted nuisance was to become a real menace.

During the entire time in the water, Captain McVay's wristwatch kept excellent time. At 1:00 P.M., a high-flying twin-engine bomber flew overhead in the direction of Leyte; at 3:00 P.M. either a B-24 or B-29 passed to the south of them, also heading for the Philippines. An attempt was made to attract attention by mirror, and, in the coming days, that became a ritual—one that never worked. These attempts were a source of great frustration to all the groups. McVay felt the mirror to be completely inadequate as a signaling device.

After spotting the two distant rafts, McVay and the others assumed that they were the only survivors of the ship and, all in all, figured no more than twenty-five or thirty men, including themselves, made it off. What they didn't know at the time was that they had drifted seven to ten miles north of the main groups.

Stranded in the middle of the deep and seemingly never-ending Philippine Sea, the captain understandably became very depressed. He daydreamed about taking a bath, drinking a cocktail, and relaxing in comfort, and in the midst of such thoughts he wished to live, but soon reality broke in upon his fantasies.

He dreaded the idea of seeing again the wives of his now dead officers. While at Mare Island, he and Mrs. McVay had gotten to know these women, and now "I knew there was nothing I could say to them. . . ." His mind drifted back to Guam. He remembered the moment when he was told no escort was needed, and he cursed the people there for not having one available; if there had been an escort, it could have radioed for help and picked up survivors. His final, and unfortunately most nagging thought, was of his personal responsibility: he was the captain, like it or not.

Two hours prior to the close of their first day, a plane flew overhead, its red-and-green running lights clearly visible. McVay fired one of the star shells skyward, but it went unnoticed. The container holding the shells had sixteen fillers but only twelve shells, which was the standard issue for this type of raft. It irked McVay to see four empty slots. Why couldn't they just fill the entire thing up and be done with it?

As the day drew to an end, however, spirits were high in anticipation of the morrow's rescue. The *Indianapolis* was due in Leyte Gulf in the morning, and when the heavy cruiser didn't show up questions would be asked, a search made, and rescue would be on the way.

At some time on this Monday, the "marker" for the *Indianapolis* on the plotting board of Commander, Marianas, was removed under the assumption that the ship had "chopped" into the area of the Philippine Sea Frontier. In actuality, the cruiser never made it into Frontier waters; she went down in the territory and jurisdiction of Vice Admiral George Murray, Commander of the Marianas.

After narrowly escaping from his after engine room, Lieutenant Richard Redmayne swam from the starboard side of the *Indianapolis*. Within five minutes, he found a kapok life preserver, which he put on, and for about a half hour he rested in the water alone. Then he spotted a life raft with men on it and joined them. During the remaining dark morning hours, two more rafts and two floater nets joined the group. The three rafts and two nets were lashed together, and they continued to drift, picking up water breakers, floating food containers, and other men.

Surveying the area at first light, they found the hostile sea covered with a heavy oil slick, 5-inch powder cans, and an assortment of junk. Many of the men were terribly sick from swallowing sea water and oil, and the ones who had passed out in the water were being held up by their shipmates. A head count was attempted, and they discovered that their group consisted of approximately 150 men, including four officers and five chiefs. Lieutenant Redmayne, as the senior officer, took charge.

In addition to the three rafts and two nets, about 90 percent of the people in the water in this group were wearing life jackets; the ones who didn't have any held onto the side of the rafts or onto men who had jackets, or they hugged empty ammo cans. The rafts themselves were very overcrowded, each one averaging fifteen to twenty men, and the sailors who had been put on the rafts were the ones the officers and others in charge thought to be in the worst condition.*

---

*Of the thirty-five rafts the *Indianapolis* sailed with, only about twelve were released, which contributed to the enormous loss of life. There were essentially three reasons for this. First, "most men waited for 'Abandon Ship' to break the life rafts loose, but 'Abandon Ship' never came until the

On Monday, nothing much happened. The large group floated, drifted, survived. They spotted the same two afternoon planes McVay had seen and also fired flares at the one plane that evening, with no success.

Certain early signs of insubordination surfaced. One of the men on the floater net was Petty Officer F. Giulio. Because of his particular job aboard ship, he was well known among the crew. On this first day, he kept complaining that he should be put on a raft since the life jacket kept slipping around his legs and he had a hard time keeping afloat. Giulio was the senior ranking man on that net and therefore their natural leader.

Distributed among the rafts and nets were four water casks and about nine or ten emergency tins of food, which contained malted-milk tablets, biscuits, and Spam. During the late afternoon, Giulio and some of his followers broke into the rations and began to eat. A short distance away, Chief Petty Officer Clarence Benton spotted them and immediately ordered them to stop, since all rations were to be divided equally. For the time being, Giulio and his small group obeyed the order.

During the evening Lieutenant Redmayne allowed a small amount of food to be rationed equally to all the men in the group.

Is it possible that among all the ships at sea and the numerous shore stations monitoring 500 and 4235 kilocycles,

---

ship was over on its side [sic]." Second, the further the ship tilted to the right, the greater the strain on the straps which held the rafts in position to various parts of the ship. This pressure on the straps made it very difficult to unhook or cut them loose so that the rafts could fall free. In addition, because of the increasing list, it was almost impossible for crewmen to get over to the starboard side to attempt to free the rafts on that side of the ship. Third, lack of experience. Many men were trying to cut the thick straps with knives, but this wasn't necessary; all that had to be done "was pull a toggle pin and then the securing lashes [would come] loose." Many of the inexperienced crew did not know this.

nobody, throughout the entire Pacific, picked up the SOS of the *Indianapolis*? Many uninformed people continue to believe that the reason there was a delay in locating survivors was because the ship never sent out an SOS.

Several months after the disaster, Admiral George Murray, Commander of the Marianas, stated that he found it difficult to understand how a ship could go down without at least getting out some sort of contact report. He felt that the modern communications facilities aboard a combat ship, coupled with the urgency of the situation, would make it impossible for a vessel to sink without having time to transmit a distress signal.

The *Indianapolis*, we have seen, did have time to get out a distress signal and, in fact, was sending to the very end. A thorough study of previously secret Naval documents on this disaster reveals the possibility that some ships at sea on the night of the sinking did indeed pick up emergency signals on their radios.

About five months after the sinking, the Navy sent a memo to the Coast Guard cutter *Bibb,* which was at sea on that fateful night. It said, in part, "Rear Admiral Alexander Sharp, USN, has reported to this office that on or about July 30, 1945, the USCG *Bibb,* in which he was embarked at the time, received a fragmentary distress message which may have some concern in the matter under investigation." *Bibb* replied that this was not true, and nothing more was done about it.

The first time, however, that we know definitely that any ships or shore stations had the slightest inkling that something was amiss was Thursday, August 2, four days after the cruiser went under. Radio receivers throughout the Pacific intercepted the panicked calls from Leyte and CinCPac asking if anyone knew the whereabouts of the *Indianapolis*. (Could Admiral Sharp, a seasoned naval officer, have been off by four days when he reported *Bibb* picked something up "on or about July 30"? Four days—12:20 A.M., on Monday, July 30, to about noon on Thursday, August 2—is a fairly large time frame to be mistaken about, and Sharp did think the matter important enough to bring it to the attention of Washington.)

While in the hospital at Guam, Donald Cowen, a survivor of the *Indianapolis,* met up with a crewman of the seagoing tug U.S.S. *Pawnee.* According to Cowen's later testimony, this sailor mentioned that the *Pawnee* "picked up the tail end of an SOS the night we were sunk. Quoting him, it was, 'We are torpedoed and sinking fast. We need immediate assistance.' Identification was not received nor was location of ship. It was just the tail end of a message." These were practically the identical words transmitted by the sinking cruiser. Nevertheless, there is no record of the Navy investigating further this supposed intercept by *Pawnee.*

In November 1945, Fred Hart, radio technician 2nd class and survivor of the *Indianapolis,* was traveling cross country by train when he met Lieutenant (jg) J. F. Newman, who was senior aviator aboard the cruiser *Salt Lake City* on the night *Indianapolis* went under. Hart relates what happened next: "We were in the smoking room, just conversing, and he happened to ask me why I was going across the country, and I told him I was being called back as a witness in connection with the sinking of my ship. He asked me which ship, and I told him the *Indianapolis.* He said he was on the *Salt Lake City,* and he said it was only 300 miles from us at the time of the sinking. He said they knew about it and that they had picked up our message, but they tried to suppress it around the ship. The captain was walking around in circles (I gathered from what he said), and he gave me the impression that the officers of the ship had received our message. I asked him why, in that case, they didn't try to do something about

it, and he informed me that they were with a flotilla of destroyers and that the captain had asked him to fly over and
see if he could sight the survivors and he told them it was too
far away for the plane that he had and if he tried to go that
distance he would land in the ocean too."

A short time later, Lieutenant (jg) Newman was called into
the office of the Naval Inspector General, was interrogated,
and denied everything Fred Hart said. Newman stated that
the *Salt Lake City* was on her way to Saipan when they
heard of the sinking, but this word was not received until
after the survivors were spotted. He claimed that he did not
hear a distress message rumor but a message of sighting. He
further testified that he didn't know anything about Captain
Mitchell, the skipper, deliberating about taking the cruiser
into the area, nor did he ever discuss with the captain the idea
of sending off a plane to search the area. In addition, Newman roomed with Lieutenant L. P. Thweatt, one of the communications officers aboard the ship, and he said that
Thweatt never mentioned anything to him about receiving a
message.

Within the thousands of pages of documents relating to the
Indianapolis disaster, no further testimony was taken from
anyone aboard the *Salt Lake City*—not from Captain Mitchell, not from Lieutenant Thweatt, not from any radiomen
on watch the night of the sinking. The conflicting testimony
of Fred Hart and Lieutenant Newman was never looked into.

The day after the *Indianapolis* left Guam, U.S.S. *Hyperion*
left that island for San Francisco. In December 1945, Commander Clarke Withers, captain of the ship, received a message from Washington which stated that "rumor has been
received in this office that a distress message from the *Indianapolis* was received on board U.S.S. *Hyperion*, of which

you had command, on or about the night of 30 July, 1945."
Commander Withers wrote back and agreed that messages
were received indicating the loss of the *Indianapolis*. "I have
no records available as to the date of receipt nor have I
records as to the names of the radiomen who were on watch
during this period and do not remember definitely the date of
receipt of the message indicating the loss of the *Indianapolis*.
I do, however, remember that we intercepted a message from
the port director, either at Leyte or Samar, requesting whereabouts of the *Indianapolis* and that we had information she
was sunk prior to interception of that dispatch."

The only way *Hyperion* could have had information about
the sinking of the *Indianapolis prior to* intercepting a dispatch from Leyte asking the ship's whereabouts, was if *Hyperion* had heard the SOS. When Leyte sent their messages
out, it was strictly as a question; the port director did not
know at that time that the ship had gone down. No further
investigation was conducted by the Navy in this matter.

Shortly after abandoning ship, Doctor Haynes found himself in a group of about 400 men, the largest in the water.
Naval documents refer to this body of men as the "swimmer"
or "life preserver" group. This huge batch of survivors, which
was separated from the McVay and Redmayne groups by
miles of ocean, had not a single life raft or floater net, not a
morsel of food or drop of water. Most of the men, however, did
have life preservers.

Haynes remembered that at no time during the abandoning of the ship and in the momentary confusion following it
did he witness any acts of panic or hysteria. The men generally remained calm and quiet. During these first few hours,
someone would occasionally call out, "Has anybody two life
jackets?" and somebody would invariably answer, "Yes."

Most of the men were unrecognizable since they were black from the heavy fuel oil blanketing the water. It burned their eyes, clogged their nostrils, and choked their throats.

Lieutenant McKissick was part of this group, and he remembered the men's concern that the submarine would surface and open fire on them with machine guns. A few of the survivors claimed they saw running lights that night, but what they actually saw were life-jacket lights. Some men had these lights attached to their vests and turned them on in an attempt to attract the attention of any planes that might be flying overhead.

Soon after the ship went down, there was an underwater explosion that was heard and felt by everyone. McKissick ordered the men around him to lie prone in order to raise their bodies as far out of the water as possible and lessen the concussion if there were any further blasts.

At approximately 1:30 A.M., Quartermaster 1st Class Robert Gause spotted a fin. By estimating the distance between the dorsal and tail, he guessed the shark to be about twelve-feet long.

Quite a few sailors in his group were critically wounded. There were a large number of severe flash burns of the face, arms, and body, and some men had compound fractures of one sort or another. There were no medical supplies of any kind for the frustrated Doctor Haynes, and many of the men with fractures and burns died from shock during the first few hours. After removing their life jackets, the dead were allowed to slip away. Before the boiling sun rose over the distant horizon on Monday morning, about fifty of the original four hundred were dead.

The bravery and self-sacrifice of the men in this, the largest of the groups, was astounding. Many of the wounded, and some of the men without life jackets, had to be constantly supported. Whenever Haynes called for volunteers as reliefs, someone always came forward. Although they griped about the fact that they were stuck in the middle of the Pacific, swimming for their very lives, all the men were generally good natured and cooperative.

By daybreak, this mass of floating humanity had split into three subgroups. The largest group contained about 200 men, the second 100, and the smallest about fifty. These subgroups were separated from each other by a distance of only several hundred yards, at most. Leader of the group of 200 men was Captain Edward Parke, Commanding Officer of the Marine Detachment and holder of the Bronze Star for bravery on Guadalcanal. Strong and athletic, he was superb in his energy, leadership, and self-sacrifice. Dr. Haynes remembered him as the typical Marine, one who was very strict with the group and had the situation well in hand.

The main objective was for everyone to stay together. Captain Parke found a cork life ring with about 100 feet of attached line. To prevent drifting, he strung the line out and each man grabbed a piece of it and took up the slack. In this way, they formed a long line of men which began to curl on itself, as a wagon train would circle against attack. The wounded were brought into the middle and tied to the life ring itself by the strings on their jackets. There was no confusion, and the men stayed well grouped together. If someone did drift off the line, Parke swam over to the man and herded him back in. On several occasions, he gave his jacket to a man without one and swam unsupported until he could find another preserver.

Bravery in this enormous group of "swimmers" was everywhere. Commander Lipski, the ship's gunnery officer, who had been very badly burned, was cheerfully supported all day Monday by Airman 1st Class Anthony Maday. Lieutenant Commander Coleman, who came aboard in Guam and was a member of Spruance's staff, was the leader of a group, and he worked unceasingly to keep them together. Time after time, he swam out to bring in stragglers. Ultimately, Commander Coleman became so weak that he died from exhaustion. And there was Ensign Moynelo, who organized a large group of men. For three days, he kept the group together, rounded up drifters, and took off his own jacket many times and gave it to those without until he could fine another. Finally he, too, collapsed and died.

Fortunately, there were more than enough life jackets to go around, since two days prior to their sailing from Mare Island a supply of kapok jackets was delivered, a duplication of a previous order. Therefore, at the time of sinking, it is estimated that there were 2,500 jackets aboard. These preservers were stowed at the various battle stations on the weather decks, as well as in canvas bags in the vicinity of the Number Two stack. According to Captain McVay, the only reason anyone could have been in the water without a jacket was that he preferred to get off quickly without first going to find one.

The kapok jacket—basically a vest that the arms go through and that ties around the front—supported a man with his shoulders level with the water and his head out. These jackets were supposed to hold up for only forty-eight hours, but, amazingly, they lasted throughout the entire ordeal, though they did start to become water-logged near the end, and the wearers began sinking lower in the water.

The other type of preserver available, the rubber, pneumatic type, should be mentioned only to be condemned. This was not a jacket, per se, but a belt, worn deflated around the waist aboard ship at all times. Lieutenant Redmayne thought it was pure suicide to let people think that they could rely on these things. Because they were constantly worn folded around the waist, it was just a matter of time before holes developed, and the wearer would not know there was a leak until he used it. Certainly, wearers should have periodically tested the belts, but in most cases, they didn't. Even if a belt were in good shape, if it came in contact with anything sharp in the water the air would fizz out. It was also impossible to sleep in the rubber belt, for a wearer could flip over onto his face and drown.

Shortly after dawn on Monday, Lieutenant Commander Moss W. Flannery, commanding officer of VPB-133 based on Tinian, climbed into his Ventura bomber and headed out over the Philippine Sea on routine antisubmarine patrol. Visibility was unlimited and in order to obtain better horizon shots for navigation, instead of flying at his normal 5,000 feet, he dropped down and flew between 1,500 and 2,000 feet. At 9:20 A.M., he flew directly over Dr. Haynes and his group of 350 men. In the water, the men saw this plane coming directly at them, the sun reflecting off its front window, and they began splashing the water with their hands and feet to draw attention. Ensign Park, one of the ship's aviators, had some green marker dye in his jacket and spread it in the water. They all firmly believed that they had been seen and estimated that within five hours seaplanes from Guam would be landing in their midst.

Flannery, however, couldn't see a thing. The best way to spot something as small as a head in the ocean is not to look out at an angle but straight down, and at a height of 500 to 800 feet, not 1,500 feet. Flannery was looking out his side window, and his biggest problem was the glassy sea. The rays of the sun shot down on the surface of the water and bounced back into Flannery's face. It was as if he were in a dark room with the beam of a flashlight shooting into his eyes. Unknown to Commander Flannery, but quite appropriately, when the late afternoon sun was beating down on their exposed heads and no seaplanes were landing to relieve them of their ordeal, the discouraged men in the water were cursing blind aviators.

By 10:00 A.M., the sun was reflecting so sharply off the sea that everyone began to suffer from intense photophobia, an intolerance to light. Dr. Haynes was very concerned, since he considered this far worse than snow blindness. It caused severe pain, which was relieved only when the sun went down. Closing the eyelids did not help since the sun burnt right through. In order to somewhat ease the discomfort, the men ripped their clothing and blindfolded themselves. Fortunately, their bodies did not burn; they were all covered by fuel oil, which the searing rays of the sun could not penetrate.

For the remainder of the first day, there was constant change among the three subgroups. They would merge for a short time then break apart again. The wounded stayed in fairly good shape, and only a few men died. In order to determine death, Dr. Haynes would place his finger on the pupil of an eye and if there was no reflex it was assumed the man was dead. The jacket would be removed and the body allowed to drift away. In the background, some of the men would recite the Lord's Prayer.

By noontime, the sea became choppy again, with large swells. Practically everyone by this time had swallowed some of the oil-soaked water, and they were all throwing up. Thirst was beginning to get to the men, and Haynes, while trying unsuccessfully to find some first-aid supplies, visited all three groups and cautioned them against drinking salt water. For the moment, all the men agreed not to drink from the sea.

The survivors were beginning to see sharks in the area, but, so far, there were no major attacks. Giles McCoy, of the Marine detachment saw a shark attack a dead man. He believed that because of the dead men in the water so much food was available that the sharks were not inclined to bother with those still alive.

That, however, had been in the morning and afternoon. By the time that the merciless sun began to set, large numbers of sharks had arrived on the scene, and the men were scared. Cuts were bleeding. When a shark approached a group, everyone would kick, punch, and create a general racket. This often worked, and the predator would leave. At other times, however, the shark "would have singled out his victim and no amount of shouts or pounding of the water would turn him away. There would be a piercing scream and the water would be churned red as the shark cut his victim to ribbons."

At the Philippine Sea Frontier, Lieutenant Edward B. Henslee, Jr. (surface control officer, plotting section, operations office), read the dispatch from Guam giving the itinerary of the ship. During the day, a plot card and plotting sheet were developed for the *Indianapolis*, and the estimated position of the ship was marked on the plotting board. There was no doubt in anyone's mind at Frontier Headquarters that the heavy cruiser would be in the following morning.

At 10:00 P.M. on Monday evening, the Leyte Gulf Naval Base prepared a list of all ships expected to arrive at and depart from Leyte Gulf on the next day, Tuesday, July 31, 1945. A footnote at the bottom of the list stated, "The value of this list lies in its accuracy, completeness, and prompt dissemination." The "Leyte Gulf Expected Arrivals and Departures" list for July 31 showed thirty-six ships arriving. The largest of the thirty-six on the list was the heavy cruiser *Indianapolis*. Forty-nine copies of the list were made and distributed to all who had a need to know, from the port director to the Naval Base to senior officers of the Philippine Sea Frontier.

6.

In the Water the Second Day

Tuesday, July 31, 1945

A S the war in the Pacific intensified, communication networks throughout the theater became heavily over-burdened. To alleviate this situation, on January 26, 1945, Commodore James Carter had composed a letter, 10CL-45, which was signed by Vice Admiral Charles McMorris, Nimitz's Chief of Staff. It was forwarded to all CinCPac commands, and it contained nine devastating words: "Arrival reports shall not be made for combatant ships."

Unfortunately, the assumption drawn from this order was that if the arrival of a warship was not to be reported, neither was the nonarrival. This was not the intent of the order.

The Navy admitted that the directive (10CL-45) was poorly drafted and that if it had been composed correctly, informing the recipient of what to do if a ship *did not* arrive, at least one full day would have been saved in picking up the *Indianapolis* survivors, and many lives would have been saved.

Two months after the tragedy, Fleet Admiral King, Chief of Naval Operations, wrote a private memorandum to Secretary of the Navy James Forrestal, pointing out that 10CL-45 was faulty and was a primary reason why the *Indianapolis* was not reported missing. In closing, King told the Secretary that the responsibility for this letter and the consequent delay in reporting the missing ship, rested with Fleet Admiral Chester Nimitz, Commander in Chief of the Pacific Fleet.

When writing the order, Commodore Carter assumed that combat vessels would arrive at their destination as directed and, therefore, there was no need to report their arrival. The particular point of what to instruct the port director to do in case of nonarrival was never raised. Commodore Carter later reflected that if he had had to do it over again, he would have also included instructions as to what to do if a scheduled arrival did not show up.

Nimitz's chief of staff, Admiral McMorris, the man who signed the order, did so because the thought never occurred to him or his advisers that the phraseology might result in the omission of reports of nonarrivals.

What ultimately developed as a result of the order was a sense of complacency on the part of the officers to whom it was directed.

Lieutenant Stuart B. Gibson, operations officer for the Leyte Gulf port director, knew by sundown of this last day in July that the *Indianapolis* had not shown up, and he did nothing about it. He did not mention it to any of the other officers working with him nor to his superior, Lieutenant Commander Jules Sancho, the director of the port. Since his orders firmly stated that he was not to report arrivals, it never occurred to him that he still might be required to report nonarrivals. Gibson later claimed that it was not imposed upon him by any directives existing at the time to report nonarrivals, and he respectfully asked, "How can I be guilty of failing to perform a duty which never existed?"

Fleet Admiral King took a different view of the situation and told Forrestal that Lieutenant Gibson was indeed negligent, for since he knew the cruiser wasn't in he had a duty to report that fact. According to King, "This officer may have placed too great a confidence in the completeness of a senior's order, but he had sufficient information to have taken intelligent action when it became apparent that the *Indianapolis* was overdue in Leyte, and it is within the bounds of the action expected of responsible officers to expect that he, on his own initiative, would have appreciated the situation and taken action. The fact that there existed no specific printed instructions cannot be accepted as evidence to excuse completely Lieutenant Gibson of any connection with or responsibility in this matter."

Gibson, however, did not take this lying down at the investigation of the *Indianapolis* disaster and stated firmly, "I believe that I have been unjustly accused in this case, and that my reputation as a Naval officer has been greatly damaged. . . . This entire case proved the inadequacy of provision . . . for shipping control of combatant ships, and it is submitted that a junior officer, such as I, should not be held responsible for duties which never existed." Therefore, "I wish to . . . disclaim any fault or blame for this tragic incident."

We certainly cannot make light of the responsibilities of Lieutenant Gibson but, from what we now know, neither can the entire burden be placed upon him. He was simply a cog in the disaster wheel and on November 30, 1945, the Naval Inspector General told King that the Navy should not accept the premise that the primary failure in the naval structure with regard to this disaster was the "stupid interpretation" of an order by a port director. There were just too many other circumstances to be taken into consideration.

At 8:00 P.M. on Tuesday evening, nine hours after the *Indianapolis* was due in, the Expected Arrivals and Departures List for the Gulf was prepared for the next day. Since she hadn't come in, the ship was automatically put on the sheet again for expected arrival the next day, Wednesday, August 1.

Yesterday they had been too exhausted to paddle over to

the raft holding the one lone man, and this morning he was still calling to them. Thinking him hurt, the McVay group began the tremendous task of pulling nine men on three lashed rafts and a floater net to this isolated and scared soul. Changing the two men paddling once every half hour, it took them four and a half hours to traverse the 1,600 yards separating them and their objective. Upon finally reaching the young man, they saw that, beside being lonely, there was nothing wrong with the new member, and McVay said, "As misery loves company, he wanted somebody to talk to."

There still remained the other group farther away that had been spotted the day before, but the men were now too exhausted to try to reach them. Besides, most of the men had blisters on their hands, and these were creating saltwater ulcers. The new man told the skipper he had seen no one else in the water, and the captain was convinced that his group, plus the small pack of men in the distance, were the sole survivors, even though it seemed incredible that no one else had escaped.

In the morning there was no wind, but the sea could still be described as rough. As the day wore on, the endless water calmed down. There were very long, sweeping swells, but they didn't break and no whitecaps could be seen. Considering the circumstances, the group was comfortable and in fairly good shape.

During the day, Vincent Allard took the large canvas bag that had held the matches, first-aid kits, etc., and fashioned out of the fabric a "cornucopia" cap for everyone. The men pulled the hats over their ears, and this, together with the fuel oil that covered them, saved them from the scorching rays of the sun. To further protect their hands from sunburn, they placed them under the oil-covered water sloshing around in the grating of the rafts.

The fishing kit they found on one of the rafts was a delight to any fisherman's eye, and both McVay and Allard were excellent fishermen. But it didn't help much since there were a number of sharks in the area, and the one big monster of the first day was still performing his merry-go-round act. They did manage to catch some black fish which McVay thought to be in the parrot family; although the meat was very white, he was afraid to let the men eat it. Instead, he used this flesh as bait, hoping to catch nearby schools of bonito and mackerel. However, every time they dropped the line, the shark took what they offered, and, after a while, they gave up the idea of fishing.

During this second twenty-four hour period, two planes had been spotted; one at 1:00 A.M. and the second at 9:00 P.M. A pair of star shells were fired at both planes, but they weren't seen. The men griped about the shells, for once they reached their maximum height they burst like fireworks and then immediately died. The group wished parachutes were attached, which would float the light back and give the aviator more time to recognize the distress signal.

The plotting board at Philippine Sea Frontier showed the *Indianapolis* as having arrived in the gulf. Since this had not been confirmed, however, the pin would remain on the map, which indicated to all looking at the marker that *Indianapolis* was *presumably* in. All, that is, except Lieutenant Edward B. Henslee, the plot supervisor at Sea Frontier, who knew for a fact she wasn't.

Any ship entering the port had to pass the harbor entrance control post, which in turn notified the plot board at Frontier Headquarters. Because Henslee knew the *Indianapolis* had an ETA of 11:00 A.M. and by this afternoon the control post had not reported her passing, he knew she had not arrived. He was not in the least disturbed, however, since many ships were eight to twelve hours late in arriving. The only action, therefore, that he felt should be taken at that point was to have her inked in on the Expected Arrival Report for the next day as an overdue vessel.

The headquarters of the Philippine Sea Frontier were at Tolosa, Leyte, a few short miles from the office of the port director at Tacloban. The telephone was the principal means of communication between them and, in addition, a daily guard mail service was available. There was absolutely no reason why any information regarding the nonarrival of the *Indianapolis* at Leyte could not have been transmitted between the port director and Frontier Headquarters.

But even if Gibson at the Naval Base and Henslee at Frontier Headquarters had communicated with each other about the missing ship, it is quite possible that nothing would have been done about it anyway. The sad fact is that Frontier Headquarters and their subordinate command, the port director's office at the Leyte Gulf Naval Base, each had a qualified officer in a responsible position who knew on July 31 that the *Indianapolis* had not arrived and who passed it off as unimportant.

Just as the Philippine Sea Frontier had its board, the Marianas also plotted the ship, and on this Tuesday they removed the cruiser's marker because they assumed she had already arrived. No check was made by Commander, Marianas, with the Philippine Sea Frontier to confirm that the *Indianapolis* had indeed arrived before removing her name from their board.

Plotting boards were kept everywhere across the vast Pacific on the movements of the *Indianapolis*, and CinCPac was no exception. Commodore Carter followed the progress of the ship on an overlay of his operations board, and on this day he removed her from his plot. He assumed she had arrived and did not bother checking. In removing her, he was a victim of his own order; 10CL-45 prohibited the reporting of arrivals and, since Carter heard nothing, he assumed that the ship was in and safely anchored in Leyte Gulf.

At dawn on the second day, the isolated Redmayne group had about sixty men on rafts and another sixty to eighty in the water. Meanwhile, during the dark morning hours, some of the more seriously injured men had died.

The water breakers turned out to be a disappointment. Some of the casks were empty while the others contained either salt or cruddy black water. Lieutenant Redmayne said, "It was dirty and tasted as though the salt content was about equal to the salt content of the seawater." These casks were made of wood, and when the rafts crashed into the sea the seams on the casks split, thereby allowing fresh water to escape and salt water to seep in. The casks were large, heavy, and difficult to handle, and in the standard life raft the water would probably become salty after the first use. Once the seal was broken to pour water, it couldn't properly be resealed, thus allowing salt water to seep in. Should the cup become lost, serving fresh water from the cask resulted in great wastage.

It is a fact that on board ship constant inspection was made of the rafts' provisions, and much attention was given to fresh water. Boatswain's Mate Keyes pointed out that "we filled them every week, and if there were any empty or filled with salt water, it must have happened after we got into the water."

First-aid equipment was generally useless, since the containers were not watertight. Anything in tubes remained sealed, but there weren't enough remedies to go around for burns and eye troubles caused by salt water and fuel oil. The food stayed in good condition but, here again, there was a problem since the primary staple was Spam. Not only did this increase thirst because it was salty, but Spam draws sharks. The men discovered this when they opened a can of Spam and sharks gathered all around them.

The policy of the group was to put all men on rafts who were sick, injured, or didn't have life jackets or belts. The problem with this, however, was that men with belts or jackets began taking them off and allowing them to drift away in order to qualify for the relative safety of a raft. This necessitated keeping a close watch on the men.

Giulio and his small band were now beginning to start trouble. Giulio, who was still on a floater net, kept insisting that he deserved some time on a raft. This request was not granted, and he continued to complain.

During the early part of this second day, some of the men swam over to Ensign Donald Blum and reported that the food had been broken into. Blum swam back with them to take a look and saw men eating and drinking. This was immediately reported to Redmayne, who then ordered that all food and water be placed on one raft and guarded at all times by the officers and chiefs. Later in the day there were reports that Giulio was again stealing food, but it was not clear whether food was being taken from the guarded raft or all the food had not been handed in. Ensign Harlan Twible, who was on a floater net about forty feet from Giulio, yelled out in a loud, clear voice, "The first man I see eating food not rationed I will report if we ever get in." He further told them that they were acting like a bunch of recruits and not seamen.

As far as can be ascertained, there were no deaths in this group during the second day, and everyone appeared to be in fairly good shape. The only problem was Giulio and his gang. The next day would be a different story.

At 10:00 A.M. on Tuesday, one hour before the *Indianapolis* was due in, Rear Admiral Lynde McCormick, commander of Task Group 95.7 and the specific unit *Indianapolis* was to join, gave the order to hoist anchor and leave the gulf for a routine training exercise. If everything had gone according to schedule, on his way out of the gulf he should have passed the *Indianapolis* coming in. McCormick didn't know this though, because, as we have seen, the admiral's staff didn't decode (nor ask for a repeat of) CinCPac's message informing him that the cruiser was joining the group for ten days' training. Admiral McCormick did, however, receive Waldron's dispatch telling him the ship had left Guam with a destination of Leyte. McCormick recalls that because of this dispatch, he made a mental note that the *Indianapolis* should be in when he returned.

Prior to the group's leaving, McCormick told Rear Admiral I. C. Sowell, the next senior officer in the gulf, to take care of any matters which had to be handled in his absence. He made no mention to Sowell that he assumed *Indianapolis* would be coming in to join his task group, and, consequently, Sowell did not check on the arrival of the ship.

McCormick claimed that Rear Admiral A. E. Smith, Service Squadron 10, should have been aware of the missing ship since he was responsible for handling repairs and services, and assigning anchorages to all ships of the Pacific Fleet entering the gulf. "I was not what you might call the bookkeeping agent in connection with incoming vessels," pointed out McCormick, and "in connection with the *Indianapolis*, I did not consider her my responsibility at the time. . . ."

McCormick's superior, Vice Admiral Jesse Oldendorf, who had received CinCPac's dispatch but not Waldron's, and who was supposed to receive a message from McVay that morning saying the cruiser had arrived safely, was not alarmed when he didn't hear from the ship or her captain. As a matter of fact, even if Oldendorf had received Waldron's dispatch, the admiral would not have been alarmed if the *Indianapolis* did not report since he would have assumed that she had been diverted to some other task while at sea. The *Indianapolis* was unusual in this respect, because she constantly operated under special orders as flagship of the Pacific Fifth Fleet. Admiral Spruance was forever changing her orders to suit his needs and, after a while, many senior officers in the Pacific were skeptical of all movement reports on the *Indianapolis*.

Even though total blackness surrounded them, because of the choppy sea the men were having a very difficult time sleeping. In this inky isolation, some of the weaker members of the crew, who could not face what they thought must be ahead of them, gave up all hope; they silently slipped out of their life jackets and committed suicide by drowning. Numerous deadly fights broke out over life jackets, and about twenty-five men were killed by their shipmates. At dawn, Dr. Haynes saw that the general condition of the men was not good, and the group appeared to be smaller.

Haynes later recalled that basically two factors, other than lack of water, contributed greatly to the high mortality: the heat from the tropical sun and the ingestion of salt water. The drinking of salt water in his group was generally not deliberate but occurred during bouts of delirium or from the accidental swallowing of water in the choppy sea. The constant breaking of waves over the men's heads the first two days, particularly when they tried to rest, caused most of them to develop a mechanical sinusitis. The swallowing of small amounts of seawater and fuel oil could not be avoided, and the sun caused intense headache and photophobia. The combination of these factors resulted in many deaths.

During the latter part of the day, the sea grew calmer. The men's thirst, however, had become overpowering as the placid water became very clear. As the day wore on, the men became more and more exhausted and complained of their thirst. Dr. Haynes noticed that the younger men, largely those without families, started to drink salt water first. As the hot sun continued to beat down on them, an increasing number of survivors were becoming delirious, talking incoherently, and drinking tremendous amounts of salt water. They started becoming maniacal, thrashing around in the water and exhibiting considerable strength and energy compared to those who were exhausted but still sane. These spells would continue until the man either drowned or went into a coma. Several brave men, wearing rubber life belts, tried to support maniacal men and also drowned, for during the struggles the belts developed punctures or rips and deflated.

Haynes kept swimming from one huge huddle of sailors to another, desperately trying to help. All during this time, people were getting discouraged and calling out for help, and he would be there to reassure and calm them down.

There were sharks in the area again. The clear water allowed the men to look down and see them. It seems that during this second day, however, the sharks were going after dead men, especially the bodies that were sinking down into the deeper ocean. They didn't seem to bother the men on the surface.

Things became progressively worse from sundown on the second day. The men's stories become mixed up, and some accounts are totally incoherent, making it difficult to piece together what actually happened. Haynes remembered that shortly after sundown they all experienced severe chills, which lasted for at least an hour. These were followed by high fever, as most of the group became delirious and got out of control. The men fought with one another, thinking there were Japanese in the group, and disorganization and disintegration occurred rapidly. Captain Parke worked until he collapsed. Haynes was so exhausted that he drifted away from the group.

Some of the men attempted to help their shipmates. They swam outside the group, rounding up stragglers and towing them back in. The kapok jackets had a brass ring and also a snap on the back. At night, people who had these jackets on would form a circle and hook them all together. The rest of the men would get in the middle. The corrallers themselves were worried, however, since the jackets had lost so much buoyancy that the feeling of security they provided was rapidly ebbing.

By nightfall, more and more people were removing their preservers and throwing them away. Most of these men died. Haynes swam from one batch of crazed men to another, trying to calm them down. He would locate the groups by the screaming of the delirious men. From this night on, what happened in the water can only be described as a nightmare.

Prior to leaving Mare Island on her voyage, the flagship of the Pacific Fifth Fleet had been outfitted with a new type of communication system known as RATT (Radio Teletype). Early Tuesday morning, a test of this new gear was to take place. The testing authority was Commander, Amphibious Forces, Pacific, who did indeed send a message to the *Indianapolis* over the RATT system. When he didn't receive a reply, he contacted Radio Guam and asked them to raise the ship. When Guam couldn't get through, Amphibious Forces became worried and sent the following dispatch to the headquarters of the Commander in Chief, Pacific Fleet:

UNABLE TO CONTACT INDIANAPOLIS X
ON HF RATT OR CUE CIRCUIT EITHER
DIRECTLY OR BY RELAY THROUGH
RADIO GUAM X REQUEST INDIANAPOLIS

ADVISE AT WHAT TIME SHE WILL BE
READY FOR FURTHER TEST X WILL
DISCONTINUE CUE CIRCUIT UNTIL
THAT TIME

This message was sent at 9:08 A.M., two hours before the
ETA of *Indianapolis* in Leyte Gulf and thirty-three hours
after this heavy cruiser rested in her grave at the bottom of
the Philippine Sea.

The headquarters of the United States Pacific Fleet told
Amphibious Forces to forget about it, and there it died. Captain Paul Anderson, Admiral Nimitz's assistant communications officer, was not at all concerned when the *Indianapolis* did not reply to the test message. He was fully aware of the
interruption and knew that nothing further was being done
to contact the ship.

Anderson later stated that radio teletype was a recent
development aboard ship, very technical, and it was to be
expected that the *Indianapolis* would experience some difficulty with the equipment on the first test. All of this is reasonable, except for the fact that this was not the first test.
Unfortunately, no one had told Captain Anderson that the
RATT system had been tried out and found to be in excellent
working order on the trip from San Francisco to Pearl
Harbor.

Lieutenant J. J. Greksouk, of the Mare Island Naval Shipyard had sailed to Pearl with the *Indianapolis* and there left
the ship, on his own advice, telling Captain McVay that the
radio teletype was satisfactory in every respect. According to
Captain Anderson, CinCPac headquarters may have had
the results of this early testing, but if it did the information
was never passed down to him.

The U.S.S. *Indianapolis* in May 1934, with the crew "manning the rail" for review by President Roosevelt.*(U.S. Navy)*

The U.S.S. *Indianapolis* at sea in September 1939. *(U.S. Navy)*

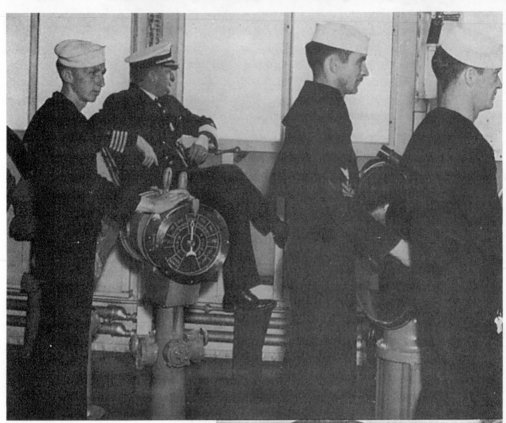

Captain Henry Hewitt, Commanding Officer, on the bridge of the U.S.S. *Indianapolis*, November 1936, while carrying President Franklin D. Roosevelt on a "good neighbor" cruise to South America. *(U.S. Navy)*

Fleet Admiral Ernest J. King, Chief of Naval Operations, for reasons known only to him, did not feel it was necessary to change the standard route from Guam to Leyte (in spite of a known Japanese submarine in the area) and who later insisted that Captain McVay be court-martialed. *(U.S. Navy)*

▲ Three days before the *Indianapolis* disaster, on the Okinawa to
Leyte route, the U.S.S. *Underhill* rammed a Kaiten (manned
Japanese torpedo), split in two, and sank.

▼ Diagrams of Kaiten. Lieutenant Commander Hashimoto was
planning to use Kaiten against the *Indianapolis* if the regular
torpedoes did not score a hit. *(U.S. Navy)*

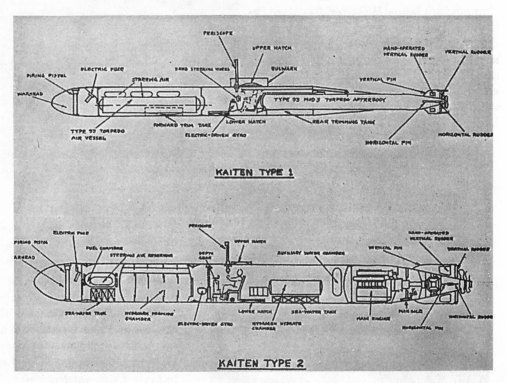

Some felt that Fleet Admiral Chester W. Nimitz, Commander in Chief, Pacific Fleet, was responsible for the delay in rescuing the crew of the missing *Indianapolis*, as his staff did nothing upon intercepting a Japanese message stating that an American ship had been sunk where the *Indianapolis* was sailing. *(U.S. Navy)*

Commodore James B. Carter, Assistant Chief of Staff to Admiral Nimitz, who didn't feel it necessary to inform Captain McVay that a submarine had sunk the *Underhill* or that there were three additional subs on offensive missions, with one of them on the Okinawa to **Leyte** route. *(National Archives)*

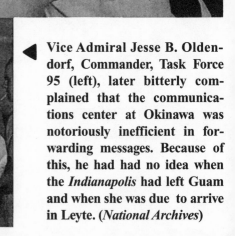

Vice Admiral Jesse B. Oldendorf, Commander, Task Force 95 (left), later bitterly complained that the communications center at Okinawa was notoriously inefficient in forwarding messages. Because of this, he had had no idea when the *Indianapolis* had left Guam and when she was due to arrive in Leyte. *(National Archives)*

▲ The communications staff of the U.S.S. *Idaho*, flagship of Rear Admiral Lynde D. McCormick, never bothered to finish decoding CinCPac's message giving the *Indianapolis*'s orders because it was erroneously decoded as belonging to someone else and because it was merely rated "restricted" and therefore not important.

◀

Commodore Norman C. Gillette, Acting Commander of the Philippine Sea Frontier. Certain members of his staff (and of his subordinate command, the Leyte Gulf Naval Base) knew of the nonarrival of the *Indianapolis* at Leyte and did not report it. He admitted later that he was concerned about Japanese submarine activity in the area but felt combat ships were not the responsibility of the Sea Frontier. *(National Archives)*

Captain Alfred Granum, Operations Officer, Philippine Sea Frontier was immediately under Commodore Gillette. Granum was aware of the submarine menace, but later said that was only a normal hazard of war. *(National Archives)*

On the fourth day after the sinking, Lieutenant (jg) Wilbur C. Gwinn flew in his Ventura on a regular day reconnaissance patrol. He happened to look down, spotted the oil slick from the *Indianapolis*, and, following it, discovered the first survivors. *(National Archives)*

Lieutenant Commander George Atteberry, Gwinn's superior and Commanding Officer on Patrol Bombing Squadron 152, responded to Gwinn's alert and flew to the area at once. He was able to circle around the survivors and give comfort by his presence until other planes arrived. *(National Archives)*

A Ventura bomber (PV-1) of the type flown by Gwinn and Atteberry.

After Lieutenant R. Adrian Marks dropped the emergency equipment from his Catalina, he landed the plane in the water to rescue individual survivors, whom he thought were being menaced by sharks. *(National Archives)*

Because Marks's plane was badly damaged in landing, the *Cecil J. Doyle* had to pour eighty rounds of 40 mm gunfire into it. Marks's Catalina is seen on fire just before going under. This photo was taken from the deck of the *Doyle*. *(Courtesy of William Stuckart)*

▲ A PBY Catalina of the type flown and landed at sea by Lieutenant Marks. *(U.S. Navy)*

▼ The U.S.S. *Bassett* arrived on the scene about an hour after the *Doyle*. This high-speed transport rescued the Redmayne group.

▲ Another high-speed transport, the U.S.S. *Ringness*, picked up Captain McVay and his small group.

▼ Although the U.S.S. *Madison* was the ship in charge of the rescue operation, it took a while before the destroyer learned that the survivors were from the *Indianapolis*.

The U.S.S. *Helm* (above) and the U.S.S. *French*, along with other ships, had the gruesome task of finding, identifying, and burying the dead. It was from the *Helm* that riflemen had to be posted to shoot sharks attacking the bodies.

After Lieutenant Richard B. Redmayne, Chief Engineering Officer on the *Indianapolis*, received reports of stealing, he ordered all food and water in his group be placed on one raft and guarded at all times. *(Courtesy Captain Richard Redmayne)*

Lieutenant Commander (Doctor) Lewis Haynes valiantly attempted to calm many of the crazed men during their four-day ordeal in the open sea and was finally able to treat some of the sickest men in the water with the emergency medical supplies dropped from the planes. *(National Archives)*

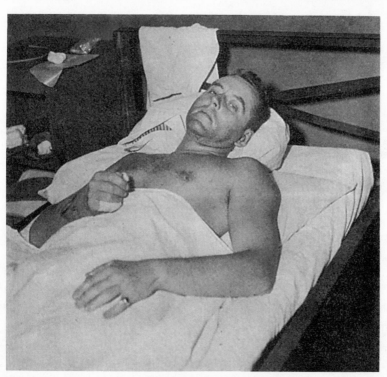

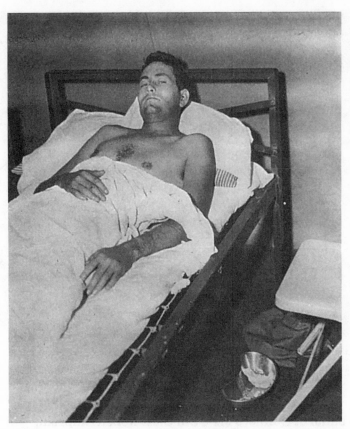

Near the end of Lieutenant (jg) Charles McKissick's watch on the *Indianapolis*, he had been ordered to stop zigzagging and resume their base course. *(National Archives)*

Chief Gunner, Cecil Harrison, whose smile and cheerful exhortations in the water kept his group of survivors united. *(National Archives)*

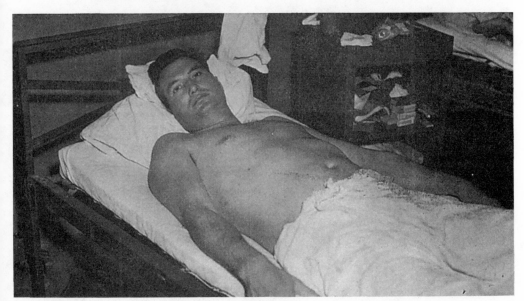

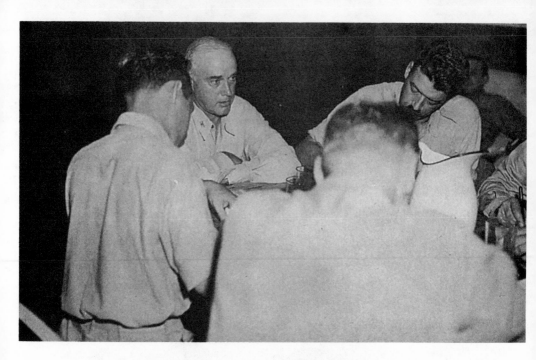

▲ Captain Charles Butler McVay, III, holding a news conference shortly after his rescue. *(National Archives)*

▼ The burial of Gunner's Mate 3rd Class Robert Shipman, on Guam. *(U.S. Navy)*

▲ The burial of Fred Harrison, Seaman 2nd Class, on Guam. *(National Archives)*

▼ Three survivors. Left to right: Bernard Bateman, A. C. King, and Erick Anderson. *(National Archives)*

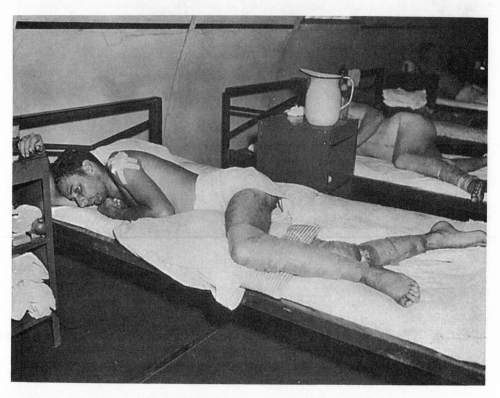

Survivor Clarence McElroy was badly burned on the legs. *(National Archives)*

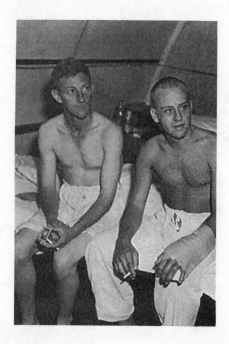

Survivors Willie Hatfield and Cozell Smith, who suffered a shark bite on his left hand. *(National Archives)*

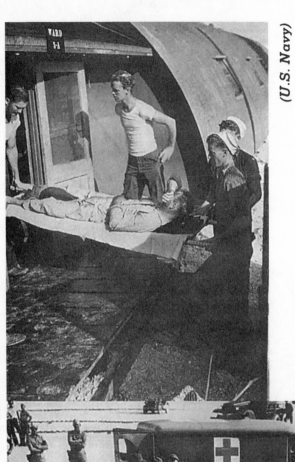

Transfer of survivors from the hospital on Peleliu to ambulances that will carry them to the U.S.S. *Tranquillity*.

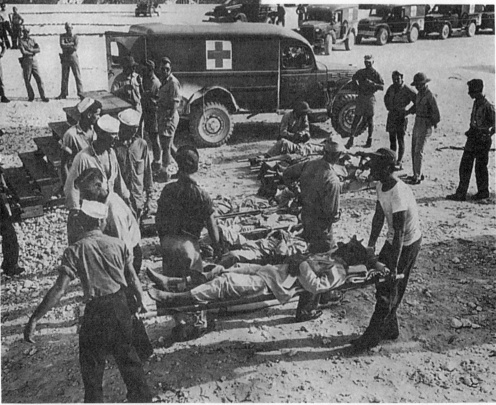

Transfer of survivors from ambulances to landing craft, to take them to the ship. *(National Archives)* ▶

(U.S. Navy)

Survivors on the landing craft for the short trip to the hospital ship.

(National Archives)

▲ The hospital ship U.S.S. *Tranquillity*. *(National Archives)*

Survivors being hoisted from the landing craft to the *Tranquillity*.

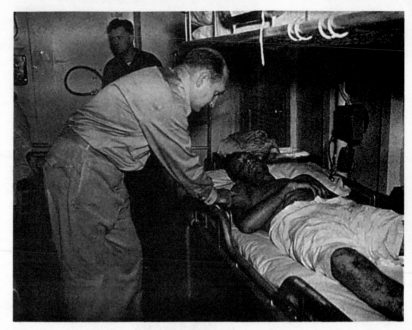

A survivor aboard the U.S.S. *Tranquillity.*
(National Archives)

The president of the Court of Inquiry, Vice Admiral Charles Lockwood, opened the proceedings on August 13, 1945, ten days after the rescue, but the news of the navy's greatest sea disaster was not released to the public until the next day. *(National Archives)*

Rear Admiral Lynde D. McCormick, Commander, Task Group 95.7 (elbows on the table), told Admiral Nimitz that his staff's error in not decoding CinCPac's message was not as great as many errors made throughout the navy. Within months of the error, he was promoted from Rear to Vice Admiral. (*National Archives*)

The fact that Vice Admiral George Murray was one of the judges of the Court of Inquiry made a mockery of the impartiality of the investigation, since his command was intimately involved in the disaster. (*National Archives*)

▲ Vice Admiral George Murray (seated) accepts Lieutenant
General Shunzabura Magikura's surrender of the Caroline
Islands, aboard the U.S.S. *Portland* (sister ship of the *Indianapolis*). The officer at Admiral Murray's left is Captain
Oliver Naquin, who testified during the Court of Inquiry that
he felt that submarine danger along Route "Peddie" was "practically negligible." *(National Archives)*

▶

Admiral Louis Denfeld,
Chief of Naval Person-
nel, didn't want McVay
court-martialed and later
recommended that the
sentence be remitted.
(National Archives)

James Forrestal, Secretary of the Navy, who agreed (together with Admiral King) to court-martial Captain McVay on failure to zigzag and failure to order Abandon Ship in time. *(National Archives)*

Admiral Raymond Spruance pinning the Purple Heart Medal on Radioman 1st Class Joseph Moran, who keyed out the distress signal from Radio I. *(National Archives)*

A group picture of some of the survivors, taken about three weeks after they were rescued. (*U.S. Navy*)

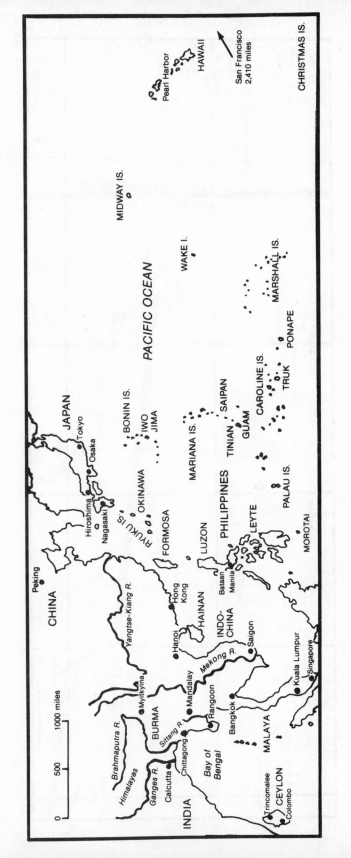

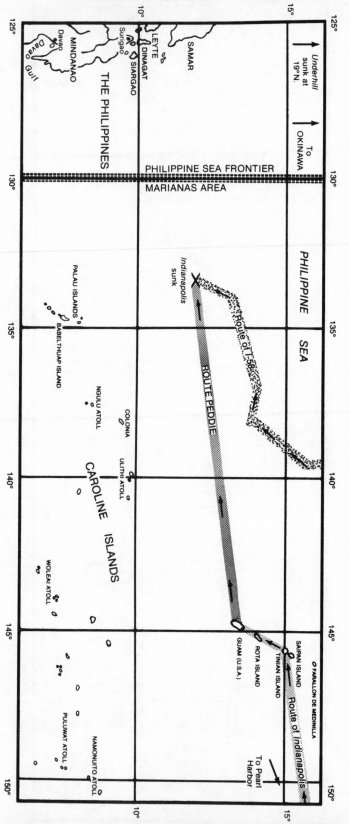

Routes of the U.S.S. *Indianapolis* and the submarine *I-58*

7.

In the Water the Third Day

Wednesday, August 1, 1945

THE captain and the men with him were continuing to fare relatively well. McVay still believed that his ship went down with all hands and that, at most, there could only be thirty survivors.

From the opening of this day, the central thought on the minds of the men was to kill the shark; it was big, it kept circling closer and closer, and they were frightened. This monster could easily rip the raft apart with one swift motion of his enormous jaws. But the only weapon they had was a knife from the fishing kit, with a one-inch blade, and there was no way they could tackle this massive creature with a blade that small. So the day passed with the men sitting and staring at the shark, annoyed that a larger weapon was not in the kit and further chafed that not one man had a sheath knife, an implement customarily carried by many of the sailors aboard ship.

Just before first light, a plane flew over, and two star shells were fired. Again at 1:00 P.M., a bomber, heading toward Leyte, passed above. They tried to attract this second plane with mirrors, yellow signal flags, and splashing, but to no avail. They were becoming more and more depressed since it didn't seem possible to them that somebody they could see so plainly could fail to see them. Stoically, McVay remarked, "It's the same old thing; if an aviator doesn't expect to see anything, he doesn't see it. He's too busy trying to fly his plane." The captain had little hope of being seen by a plane. He believed they would be found by ships.

Many aircraft flew close to the area where the ship sank. Each day planes were seen but they all failed to spot the survivors. The glassy sea made it almost impossible to see something as small as a man's head, and the chance of life rafts being picked up by radar was negligible unless the rafts were equipped with metal corner reflectors, which the rafts of the *Indianapolis* were not.

Most planes seen by the survivors were on antisubmarine patrol out of Peleliu, and the pilots were not briefed on or told to report the sighting of friendly surface vessels in their patrol area. Their sole function was to seek out, report, and attempt to destroy Japanese submarines. Consequently, aircraft had no reason to look for a steaming cruiser, much less its survivors, and another day limped by for Captain McVay and his bevy of lost sailors.

Although the order had been given the day before to bring all food to the command raft, there was still a certain amount of hoarding going on. This morning, however, several more rafts handed their cached rations over to Redmayne. During the day, one cracker, a malted-milk tablet, and a few drops of precious water were allocated to each man. Some survivors tried their luck at fishing but, as with the McVay group, the numerous sharks in the area kept stealing the bait.

Not everyone realized there was safety in numbers. Some men swam away. Attempts to stop them failed, and soon after leaving the security of the group these sailors were usually dragged beneath the surface by the sharks.

The appearance of the planes put an additional strain on

everyone and, because "they hadn't seen us, and we started to get a little worried," Lieutenant Redmayne ordered that one raft leave the group and head south toward Ulithi or Palau to get help. Ensign Donald Blum and three other men were assigned this almost impossible task and, as support, were given one water breaker (with salt water in it) and a tin of emergency rations, which was three-quarters empty. In the raft was a tarpaulin, which they managed to rig up as a makeshift sail, and at 8:00 P.M. they took off. They had hardly gone more than a mile, however, when they gave up. Along the way, they had spotted many men floating alone and they brought aboard ten of these stragglers. This rescue so overloaded the raft that they had to call a halt to their southern journey.

Toward late afternoon, some of the sailors started becoming delirious again. More and more men were drinking salt water. Chief Benton (Redmayne's assistant) attempted to talk to these half-crazed men in a calm, reassuring voice, but it wasn't much use. Fights broke out, men started swimming away, and people committed suicide by drowning themselves. A sailor yelled to Redmayne that things were getting very bad on his raft, and Ensign Eames was sent over to investigate. Upon returning, Eames reported that some of the men were making homosexual advances toward one of the other men. Upon hearing these reports, the chief engineer's reaction was to have the people around him recite the Lord's Prayer.

Giulio had been on a net for the previous two days, but this morning the pharmacist's mate decided to transfer him to a raft because Giulio complained that his eyes were bothering him. Shortly thereafter, it was noticed that Giulio and the people with him were eating and drinking. Upon checking the stored rations on the command raft, it was discovered that two of the four water breakers were missing, plus several cans of rations. The officers and chiefs ordered Giulio to return everything immediately, but he ignored them. Some of the senior people then swam over to the mutineers and tried to grab the food and water away, but they were unsuccessful since Giulio and his small band were much stronger than the tired officers. Throughout the day, he and his gang had themselves a veritable Roman feast while others suffered and died.

The breakdown in discipline was contagious. In the afternoon, Ensign Twible swam over to a raft and found the occupants eating. Twible asked them if they had not heard the order to turn in all food, and they replied that if Giulio could eat why couldn't they? Next, Twible swam to a second raft, where Giulio was. He found the hoarded and hidden rations. Twible retrieved a can of food and a water cask from Giulio and then went back to the first raft and took away their food and water. Everything Ensign Twible recovered he kept under his own guard to make certain that at least from that point onward any water consumed was rationed.

Lieutenant Redmayne, Ensign Blum, Ensign Twible, and Chief Benton were all extremely upset. The insubordination and basically mutinous action was something these officers were not going to forget, and they were determined that if they ever got out alive they were going to make Giulio pay.

Shortly after darkness cast its veil over this isolated party of dying men, Lieutenant Redmayne became delirious. Whether from fear or exhaustion, no other officer took over. When questions were asked, the standard reply remained to check with Lieutenant Redmayne. "He is in charge." At this point, however, the lieutenant was not even in charge of himself.

The Leyte Naval Base made up the Expected Arrivals and Departures List for Thursday, August 2, 1945, and, knowing she hadn't arrived on Tuesday or Wednesday, posted the *Indianapolis* on that list as an expected arrival for Thursday. The base knew the cruiser hadn't sailed into the gulf because the Ships Present List did not include *Indianapolis*. Therefore, the assumption was that if she wasn't in she should be rescheduled for the next day. By the time the list for Thursday was made up, however, the ship was thirty-six hours overdue.

Lieutenant James D. Brown, an officer on the staff of the base commandant, was responsible for preparing the Ships Present List, and knew the *Indianapolis* should have been in. Unfortunately he was not in the least concerned. Lieutenant Brown felt that the mere nonarrival of a vessel did not place upon him any actual duties or responsibilities. Furthermore, unless he was specifically requested by an interested command to tell them of the whereabouts of a particular ship, Brown didn't think he had an obligation to advise anyone of the missing *Indianapolis*. A great number of ships due to arrive in his port were being constantly diverted somewhere else without Lieutenant Brown being informed; consequently, this lone cruiser was not considered an exception, and no questions were asked.

As we have seen, Lieutenant Edward Henslee, plotting section of Headquarters, Philippine Sea Frontier, was aware on Tuesday that the *Indianapolis* had not arrived. As Wednesday wore on, Henslee remained fully aware that the cruiser had not reported in. He continued to discount the information and not relay it to his superiors.

At 4:30 A.M. Wednesday morning, another controller at the plotting board of Frontier Headquarters also became aware of the missing *Indianapolis*, and he, too, did nothing.

Lieutenant William A. Green's thoughts ran the same way as Lieutenant Brown's at the Naval Base—if she's not in, she must have been diverted. The *Indianapolis* was seventeen and a half hours overdue when Green realized she was missing. He did not deem it necessary to take any action, and he didn't.

As Captain McVay thought, so, too, did Lieutenant Redmayne and Commander Haynes probably think that their respective groups were the sole survivors of the *Indianapolis*. Redmayne didn't know that further away the enormous "swimmer" group existed, and Haynes, conversely, wasn't aware of Redmayne and his men. Although McVay and his small bunch stayed very close together, and the Redmayne group did so relatively well due to the magnetism of the life rafts and food, the Haynes group totally disbanded during the night. Scattered batches of swimmers, some large and some small, began to break away from the core and fan out over all points of the compass. Many subgroups of this once huge mass of floating humanity now existed.

The early morning hours found Doctor Haynes with a large pack of swimmers headed by Captain Parke of the Marines who, through willpower, strength, and sheer determination, kept the group under control.

Before dawn Haynes twice became delirious. At one point, he remembered, "The waves kept hitting me in the face, and I got the impression that people were splashing water in my face as a joke, and I pleaded with them that it wasn't funny and that I was sick. I begged them to stop and kept swimming furiously to make them stop, and then my head cleared."

Most of the men had become hysterical, and some were quickly going mad. A few of the sailors got the idea that people were trying to drown them and that there were Japanese in the group. The cry would circulate, "Get the Jap! Kill him!" Fights broke out, knives were drawn, and several men were brutally stabbed. Mass hysteria reigned.

The doctor did his best to calm them down but was unsuccessful and at one point he himself was held underwater by an insane crewman and had to fight his way back up. Captain Parke desperately tried to regain control but finally became delirious himself and eventually died. Once Parke was gone, the mass madness forced the subgroup to further dissolve, and the men scattered. They wanted to be alone, for no one trusted anyone else.

Under a cloudless sky and full moon, Haynes drifted, isolated but totally alert. A man floated by, and they instinctively backed away from each other. Everyone was crazy. Haynes hated being alone, however, and not very far away he heard the noises that the irrational members of another group were making and began swimming toward the sound. Only a few yards short of this band of men, his strength gave out, and he screamed for help. Breaking off from the pack, his chief pharmacist's mate, John Schmueck, grabbed him and towed him to the safety of their numbers.

Supported by Schmueck, who put his arm through the back of Haynes's jacket and lifted the doctor's body so that it rested on his own hip, Doctor Haynes fell asleep for a few hours. Schmueck himself was not in good shape and was having a difficult time with his rubber life ring. It was defective, and for two days—until he finally got a kapok jacket—he had had to hold his finger over the valve. When the ring would deflate too much, he would have to blow it up again and then hold his finger on it some more.

The new group was well organized and ably led by Ensign Moynelo. Someone in the group suggested using the leg straps on the kapok jackets to snap the men together. This worked very well and prevented them from drifting apart.

By daybreak the sea was mirror calm, but the condition of the men was becoming critical. They had difficulty thinking clearly, and most of them talked incoherently and had hallucinations. By this time, the kapok jackets just kept the men's heads out of the water. There was a great deal of anxiety within Moynelo's group concerning the buoyancy of the preservers since the Navy Manual stated that jackets would remain buoyant for only two days, and they were now well into their third. However, the kapok preservers maintained fair buoyancy, even after one hundred hours, and the mental distress that the men felt on this account turned out to have been uncalled for.

As a matter of fact, there were two aviators with them who wore Mae West jackets, and both of them complained to the doctor that they couldn't rest. The Mae West had a tendency to throw them forward, face down, and both flyers asked Commander Haynes for kapoks.

Preservers were, unfortunately, fairly easy to obtain. When a man died (and they were now dying en masse), Haynes would remove his jacket and add it to a pile in the middle of the group. This became their reserve when somebody's jacket went on the "fritz."

Sanity, as we know it, virtually disappeared on this third day. The few men who retained some semblance of sense tried to help their weaker shipmates, but it was a losing battle. Chief Gunner Harrison recalled that "Doctor Haynes's conduct throughout the time he was in the water was, in my opinion, above his normal call of duty. The comfort the men got from just talking to him seemed to quiet them down and relieve some of their worry."

Haynes felt that what kept him going was taking care of the men. They constantly asked him questions about whether the water was salty all the way down and when he thought the planes were coming.

Gunner Harrison remembered, "Early one morning somebody woke me up and wanted to know why we did not stop at an island that we passed. That story caused a great deal of trouble. Several of them believed that those islands were there—three islands. Lieutenant McKissick even dreamed he went to the island and there was a hotel there and they would not let him on the island. The first time I heard the story was, this kid woke me up and wanted to know why we did not stop there." All day long, small numbers of men broke off from the gathering and swam for the "island," never to be seen again.

The endless day was continually interrupted by questions of "Doc, if I dive down real deep will the water be less salty?" and the majority of men, including Haynes, imagined they saw their ship just below them. The cry would travel across the bobbing heads that fresh water was aboard the vessel, seemingly suspended like a hot-air balloon, not very deep beneath their dangling feet, and some would dive down to drink from the water fountains, removing their jackets to do so. Many were drowned in this manner, and the group was much smaller by sundown. Oil-stained faces kept popping up in front of Haynes, joyously proclaiming how refreshed they were from filling themselves with clear, fresh water. The doctor could only spend the day watching them drink and die.

Noticing a line of men stretching for some distance, Commander Haynes curiously swam to it and asked what was going on. He was told to be quiet for there was a hotel up ahead but it only had one room, and when it was your turn to get in you could sleep for fifteen minutes. Haynes turned and swam away from this procession of patient survivors.

Stragglers were continually being rounded up and herded back to the group. Sometimes the job would take up to an hour but Haynes knew that they had to stay together in order to be found.

On this Wednesday afternoon, Ensign Moynelo disappeared with the group who were going to swim to Leyte. It all started out when some quartermaster claimed to have figured out the current and the wind, and how long it would take to swim to Leyte. Approximately twenty-five men joined him. They anticipated that it would take them a day and a half to reach the Philippines, based upon a two-knot current and swimming at one knot per hour. Once this large party disappeared from sight, it was never seen again. This was the largest single group of men lost during the days in the water.

All of the strong leaders were now dead, except for Gunner Harrison and Commander Haynes. The doctor recalled that "Gunner Harrison and I were about the only ones left who were well enough to think, and he was just like the Rock of Gibraltar. He always had a smile and kept the group together. He used to say to the fellows, 'If that old broken-down Rickenbacker can stay out on the ocean for a week, we can stay for a month.'" Because of Harrison's leadership, "we managed to keep together. His morale was high, and his cheerful exhortations kept everyone united."

The doctor continued to pronounce men dead. He would remove their jackets, recite the Lord's Prayer, and release the bodies. The water was very clear, and Doctor Haynes remembered the bodies looking like small dolls sinking in the deep sea. He watched them until they faded from sight. A cloud of death hung over everyone, and rescue was no longer discussed. By early evening, all was calm—it was no longer a question of who would die, but when.

Now that they all felt the end was near, God seemed very close. Father Conway prayed with the sailors, moving from one group to another. The priest wasn't a very strong man, however, and eventually he had to be held up by the others. Haynes was the last man to support the now delirious and thrashing young priest, listening to him pray in Latin, until he lapsed into a coma and died in the doctor's arms. Saying a short prayer of his own, Commander Haynes released Father Conway and watched him silently drift away.

Before entering their fourth day in the water, Radioman

3rd Class Ralph Rogers wondered, as many of his surviving shipmates did, why there was no one looking for them. They were due in Tuesday morning and now Wednesday night was creeping up on them, and still they hadn't been found. Where were the rescue ships?

8.

In the Water the Fourth Day

Thursday, August 2, 1945

WITH Lieutenant Redmayne delirious, Ensign Twible tried to command the group until he became totally exhausted and his effectiveness limited. Chief Benton was in a little better shape, however, and issued many orders on his own. During the morning, a man swam over to Twible's raft with cans of crackers and said Giulio sent them. No reason was given, and it is not known whether this was in response to a direct order or a limited act of charity.

More and more people were losing touch with their rational selves. For example, there were plenty of good kapok jackets available, but an insane sailor went up to a man wearing one of the rubber rings, ripped it off his body, and swam away. Unnecessary and foolish acts of this type were taking place throughout the groups. As Freud said, "The primitive stages can always be reestablished; the primitive mind is, in the fullest meaning of the word, imperishable."

The pharmacist's mate in this group, Harold Anthony, worked as hard as humanly possible to aid men in the water and became extremely fatigued. During the night he mentioned to one of his friends that he couldn't keep this pace up much longer and would probably be dead shortly. Twelve hours later, with the relentless Pacific sun beating down on

129

this lonely spot of ocean, the lifeless body of the corpsman was permitted to drift away.

Doctor Haynes's group disbanded again. Small groups were continually forming and breaking up. The night had been particularly difficult, and most of the men suffered from chills, fever, and delirium. These lonely people were now dying in droves, and the helpless physician could only float and watch. By Thursday morning, August 2, the condition of most of the men was critical. Many were in coma and could be aroused only with exceptional effort. The group no longer existed, with the men drifting off and dying one by one. This isolation from the companionship of another human was cataclysmic. Herman Melville brought this severing of fellowship into stark focus when he wrote, "To swim in the open ocean is as easy to the practiced swimmer as to ride in a spring-carriage ashore. But the awful lonesomeness is intolerable."

At dawn, a sailor in a life jacket was seen bent over with his face in the water. Thinking him asleep, a shipmate swam over to waken the man. On attempting to rouse him, the body flipped over, and from the waist down there was nothing. He had been sawed clean in half by a shark.

At 9:00 A.M., on Thursday, August 2, securely strapped in the pilot's seat, Lieutenant (jg) Wilbur C. Gwinn pushed the throttles forward, brought the motors of his twin-engine Ventura bomber to an ear-splitting roar, and raced down the Peleliu runway. His mission was a regular day reconnaissance patrol of Sector 19V258. He was to report and attempt to sink any Japanese submarine in his area. The route for the outward leg of his journey just happened to have him flying directly over the heads of the dying men of the *Indianapolis*.

At the very rear of a Ventura is an antenna that trails

behind the aircraft. It is used primarily for navigation. In order to keep the antenna from whipping around in the wind, which would make it useless, a weight (known as a "sock") is secured to the end. Once Gwinn gained enough speed to get airborne, he pulled back and the nose of the bomber pointed up toward the blue sky. At the same time, he lost the weight from his navigational antenna. With this "trailing antenna sock" gone, he had two choices: turn around and get it fixed, or continue on patrol and navigate by dead reckoning. Because the weather was excellent, Lieutenant Gwinn decided to go on, took the plane up to 3,000 feet, and over a glassy sea began looking for enemy submarines.

Dead reckoning navigation is not very accurate, and over the Pacific Ocean it is neither a very comfortable nor enviable position to be in. At 11:00 A.M., about an hour and forty-five minutes out of Peleliu, Gwinn figured that since caution is the better part of valor, the whipping antenna being pulled behind the plane should somehow be anchored down. Because the radioman was busy with something else and his co-pilot was concentrating on filling out a weather report, Gwinn resolved to repair it himself. Crawling through the after tunnel of the Ventura, he reached the narrow end and stared at the long, slender, thrashing piece of metal, wondering how to fix it. While attempting to come up with some creative solution to his problem, Gwinn happened to look down from his 3,000-foot perch into the Philippine Sea. At that precise moment, he saw it. The thin line of oil could only have come from a leaking submarine, and the startled pilot rushed back to his left-hand seat and began flying the airplane.

At 11:18 A.M., he changed his course so as to follow the snake-like slick. Not being able to see very well, he brought the bomber down to 900 feet. Mile after mile the slick continued, never seeming to reach an end. Five miles later, he suddenly saw them—thirty heads wrapped in a twenty-five-mile orbit of oil. Many were clinging to the sides of a raft, while others floated and feebly made motions to the plane.

Gwinn had a funny feeling in his gut—the slick was enormous but he had no report of a large ship having gone down. Who in the world could these people be? At 11:20 A.M., about two minutes after sighting what had looked like black balls on the water, the pilot dropped down to a wave-skimming 300 feet.

He ordered his radioman to get a message off, and at 11:25 A.M., the following transmission was sent:

SIGHTED 30 SURVIVORS
011-30 NORTH 133-30 EAST
DROPPED TRANSMITTER AND
LIFEBOAT EMERGENCY
IFF ON 133-30

Monitored by his squadron duty officer, the word was passed on to the commander of the Western Carolines Sub Area (a subordinate of Vice Admiral George Murray, Commander, Marianas).

Now that he had positioned the thirty survivors, there was nothing more Gwinn could do so he decided to spread out his search. Following the slick on a northerly course, six miles farther on he found forty more men. Continuing on, four miles more had him pass over another fifty-five to seventy-five people—and still further north, he found scattered groups of twos and threes. After an hour of flying and looking, Lieutenant Gwinn estimated that there were 150 men in the water.

The survivors were dispersed along a line about twenty miles long. He noticed a group so crowded on rafts that he was unable to tell the exact number of rafts they had. He could barely spot a lone oil-covered man, even at his low altitude, unless he was splashing the water.

Gwinn's antenna problem now had to be solved—quickly. The position he sent out in his first message was calculated by dead reckoning and couldn't possibly be accurate. He had to fix the whipping antenna, and once again he crawled through the dark tunnel to reach the end of the bomber. Once there, he put his hand out the tail, grabbed the long rod, and pulled it inside. Taking a rubber hose, he tied it around the tip of the antenna and pushed the length back out, hoping, while crawling back to the pilot's seat, that there would be enough weight to stop the shaking and get a decent fix. They tried, and it worked.

One hour and twenty minutes after sending his first message of thirty survivors, a second dispatch from the bomber was transmitted:

> SEND RESCUE SHIP
> 11-15N 133-47E 150 SURVIVORS
> IN LIFE BOAT AND JACKETS
> DROPPED RED RAMROD

Meanwhile, Gwinn received orders to stick around:

> DUMBO* EN ROUTE ETA 1500
> REMAIN ON STATION

Doctor Haynes saw the thing and prayed it was real. Flying very low, the bomber zoomed over his head and as quickly as it came, it passed and soon was a dot on the opposite horizon. At that moment, Haynes knew he and his fellow survivors were dead men. Their last ounce of strength

---

*A large seaplane.

was giving out, and this plane was like all the others—blind
to the living hell beneath it.

After scouting the area, there was no doubt in Gwinn's
mind that these were American sailors below him. Turning
the plane, he looked for a group which appeared to be alone
and without rafts, and began dropping everything in the
plane that floated.

When Doctor Haynes saw the distant dot suddenly reverse
course and come back toward them, low over the water, he
then knew that they had been sighted. Like a sudden tropical
squall, things began falling from the sky. Two life rafts were
dropped, together with cans of fresh water. The water cans
ruptured on landing but the most important thing was that
Gwinn saw them, and those fortunate enough to be still alive
knew rescue was near.

Once there was nothing left to drop to the splashing, oil-
covered men, Gwinn released dye markers and smoke bombs
so as not to lose the position.

At 1:15 P.M., the circling sentry dropped a sonobuoy. This is
a piece of equipment used in antisubmarine work, and
although it cannot receive anything it does transmit. Gwinn
was hoping that someone would get on the thing and identify
himself, but no one in the water knew how to use the appara-
tus. It would not be until the next day that the Navy finally
discovered that these were survivors from the *Indianapolis*.

By this time, the entire Pacific was curious as to who these
people were. Ashore, many people thought that they had
Japanese in the water and weren't in too big a rush to get
things moving. A short time before, in this same area, escorts
from a convoy had reported they had attacked a Japanese
submarine. However, after the second report citing "150 survivors" came in, all hell broke loose. Because submarines
don't carry 150 men, Pacific Fleet knew they had a surface
vessel to contend with, and if a Japanese warship had been

sunk they would have known about it. It finally dawned on CinCPac that they might have an American ship down, and panic started to set in. Shortly after Gwinn's second message was received, CinCPac (now in a state of agitation) began radioing ships to report their positions. The aircraft carrier *Kuajalein* (CVE-98), for example, received the following message:

BREAK RADIO SILENCE X
REPORT YOUR POSITION

For an hour after his second dispatch, Gwinn was all alone, attempting to comfort the dying men beneath him as best he could. Then another plane, on transport duty to the Philippines, appeared. It stayed with the Ventura for about an hour and dropped three of its rafts.

Back at Gwinn's base, the communications officer decoded the first message concerning the thirty survivors and quickly passed it on to his (and Gwinn's) boss, Lieutenant Commander George Atteberry, commanding officer of VPB-152. This was the Peleliu unit of the Search and Reconnaissance Command of Vice Admiral Murray, Commander, Marianas. The unit was under the command of Rear Admiral W. R. Greer.

Atteberry calculated the fuel supply of the lone, circling bomber and estimated that Gwinn would have to leave the scene by 3:30 P.M. in order to land with a small amount of reserve fuel. Not wanting to leave the survivors alone, Commander Atteberry started making some fast decisions.

Not far from the Ventura Squadron was a squadron of seaplanes (Dumbos), and Atteberry picked up the phone and told the duty officer of VPB-23 to get a seaplane out to the area by 3:30 P.M. Not having intercepted Gwinn's message, "23" was skeptical about the whole thing and not eager to cooperate. Not liking this attitude, Atteberry drove over to their unit to ascertain the ready status personally. Once there, he decided they couldn't get a plane up in time to relieve Gwinn, so he quickly drove back to his own unit and ordered his plane and crew to get ready for take off. At exactly the same moment Gwinn's second message came in, Atteberry, whose call sign was "Gambler Leader," was lifting his bomber off the Peleliu runway.

During the hour and a half flight out, "Leader" was in constant contact with his squadron office and was happy to hear that "23" finally had gotten airborne and on the way. At 2:15 P.M., Atteberry spotted Gwinn, together with the PBM, the large seaplane on transport duty, and immediately established voice contact with both. The commander was given a quick tour of the groups in order to size up the situation. Finally, so that the men in the water wouldn't think they were being deserted, the pilot of the PBM was ordered to circle the southwest half of the huge slick while "Gambler Leader" ranged the northeast portion.

Gwinn's fuel supply was running low, and twenty minutes after Atteberry arrived, he sent Gwinn on his way. Lieutenant Gwinn's third and final message read:

> RELIEF BY 70V [Atteberry]
> RETURNING TO BASE

The PBM also had to go, and for forty-five minutes Commander Atteberry was all alone, circling and comforting those below by his presence. Then out of his cockpit window, he saw the big, lumbering Dumbo waddling toward him from the distant southern horizon.

Patrol Bombing Squadron 23 was told that Atteberry and his planes were going to remain on the scene until "23" got one of their Catalinas out there. Lieutenant R. Adrian Marks happened to be the duty pilot at the time, and 1,400 gallons of gas were loaded into his seaplane. While this was taking place, Marks, together with his air combat intelligence officer, went to group operations to see if they could gather any more information than what Commander Atteberry had given them. Operations had nothing to offer and, unable to believe that there were so many men (i.e., thirty men as per Gwinn's first transmission) in the water, Marks assumed he was going out to pick up a ditched pilot. With a full tank of gas and extra air-sea rescue gear, Lieutenant Marks shoved his mammoth down the Peleliu runway and, once airborne, turned north. The time was 12:45 P.M.

On the way out, "Playmate 2" (Marks's call sign) received word that instead of thirty men in the sea there were now about 150.* This was absolutely incomprehensible to Marks, and he assumed that the message must have been garbled in transmission. However, he "thought it would be a good idea to get to the scene as quickly as possible." At 3:03 P.M., he began picking up radio signals from Atteberry, and a little over three hours from take off, at 3:50 P.M., "Playmate 2" made visual contact and established communications with the commander.

Marks was dumbfounded—how did all these people get here? "Gambler Leader" instructed "Playmate 2" not to drop a single thing—there was much more than met the eye. For a half hour, Atteberry gave Marks the tour. Then the Dumbo dropped everything it had (saving only one small raft for itself), concentrating on those floaters who had only jackets. VPB-23 Operations Report reads, "Observed 100 to 200 survivors, some on rafts and clustered in large groups, many in

---

*Actually, there were 320 living crewmen of the *Indianapolis* awaiting rescue at this time.

singles without rafts; dropped following gear to those without floatation gear: 2 Mk-VII rafts, 1 Mk-IV raft, 1 shipwreck
kit, 1 emergency ration kit; of these, 1 Mk-VII and 1 Mk-IV
raft were opened by survivors and used, other raft ripped on
striking water, kits were useless because survivors too weak
to use."

With everything out of the plane, Marks wondered what he
could do next. Looking down at the bobbing mass of humanity, he knew they were in horrible shape but also just as
important—and maybe more so—he saw the sharks. Therefore, at "about 16:30 I decided a landing would be necessary
to gather in the single ones. This decision was based partly
on the number of single survivors, and the fact that they were
bothered by sharks. We did observe bodies being eaten by
sharks." Marks told "Gambler Leader" he was going in, and
Atteberry notified his base that the Dumbo was landing and
that he himself needed relief.

Preparations were made inside the Catalina for landing,
while Marks looked for a spot where he thought the floating
plane would do the most good. Never having made a landing
at sea before, he was a little nervous. However, "At 17:15 a
power stall was made into the wind. The wind was due North,
swells about twelve-feet high. The plane landed in three
bounces, the first bounce being about fifteen feet high."
"Playmate 2" was down safe—but not very sound.

The hull was intact, but rivets had sprung loose and seams
ripped opened from impact. While rivet holes were plugged
with pencils and cotton shoved into the seams, the radio
compartment was taking on water and was being bailed out
at the rate of ten to twelve buckets per hour. In the meantime,
the co-pilot went aft and began organizing the rescue effort.

Because of the high swells, Marks couldn't see anything
from his cockpit seat. Atteberry stayed in direct communication with him, however, and guided the Dumbo toward the

survivors. Both pilots made the decision to stay away from men on rafts, since they appeared to be in better shape than those floating alone. There were problems, however, for although every effort was made to pick up the single ones it was necessary to avoid passing near the men on life rafts because they would jump onto the plane.

The side hatch had been opened, and the plane's ladder was hung out. Standing on the rungs was a crewman and, when they passed a swimmer, he would grab him and pull him aboard. This was very unsatisfactory though, because the people in the water were too weak to hang on. Furthermore, when a burned survivor, or one whose arm or leg was broken, was snatched, the pain was excruciating. They tried throwing out their remaining raft with a rope attached for a swimmer to grab (they were too frail to jump in). Then they would reel the raft back in. This proved to be impractical, because Marks continually kept the plane taxiing and anyone hanging on was dragged through the water. Finally, they settled on going up to a man, cutting the engines, bringing him aboard, and then starting up again and going to another swimmer. Once the engines were cut, silence enveloped the area except for the terrifying cries for help heard by the crew of "Playmate 2."

Before night fell, Marks had picked up thirty people and crammed them into the body of his leaking seaplane. All were in bad shape, and they were immediately given water and first aid. Naturally, as soon as the first man was plucked from the sea, Lieutenant Marks learned the *Indianapolis* had gone down. There was no way, however, that he was going to transmit this word in the clear and "I was too busy to code a message of this nature." So it would not be until Friday, August 3, that the U.S. Navy finally learned that one of their heavy cruisers had been sunk just after midnight on July 30.

Meanwhile, all Marks and his crew could do was listen to

tales. The survivors gave Marks varied details of the ship's sinking, and because they were delirious few of their stories made any sense. He and his crew were told that a landing craft had picked up thirty men the day after the sinking and left the rest to drown; or that a seaplane had landed and picked up a few people and then flown away without helping anyone else. The crew listened to these irrational accounts all night long.

In the sky above the drifting Dumbo, Atteberry was busy directing Marks and telling other planes coming into the area where to drop their gear in order "to obtain the best possible distribution among them." Between the first sighting and midnight, planes continually flew in, and, at one point, there were eleven aircraft on the scene.

Atteberry was also in contact with rescue ships heading for the scene, and he kept them apprised of what was going on. As darkness settled over this drama in the Philippine Sea, there was nothing more Commander Atteberry could do. So, at 7:50 P.M., "Gambler Leader" turned his Ventura southward and headed home.

With night upon him, it was impossible for Marks to pick up any more individual swimmers, and he therefore taxied toward a large assembly of men who had had rafts dropped to them earlier in the day. This was Commander Haynes's group. Survivors were packed like sardines inside the hull of the Dumbo, so Marks ordered these men to be laid on top of the wings, covered with parachutes, and given water. This damaged the wing fabric, and it became doubtful whether the Catalina would ever fly again.

In the black of this Pacific night, things began to settle down; the stillness was interrupted only by the occasional pained moans of the *Indianapolis* crew. Marks couldn't move the plane for fear of running people down, so they drifted and waited for rescue. Just before midnight, a searchlight on the far horizon pierced the onyx sky, and at the same time a circling plane dropped a parachute flare over "Playmate 2." The ship changed course and steered toward the beat-up PBY and her precious cargo of fifty-six former *Indianapolis* crewmen.

It was 4:55 P.M. when 1st Lieutenant Richard Alcorn, U.S. Army Air Corps, 4th Emergency Rescue Squadron, forced his Catalina into the air over Palau. Two hours and twenty minutes later, he arrived, and after quickly surveying the situation tossed three of his eleven rafts out the door. He also saw Marks's plane already on the water picking up survivors.

Noticing that the swimmers didn't have enough strength to pull themselves into the rubber boats, Alcorn decided not to throw anymore out. Instead he landed at 7:30 P.M., bringing his plane down two miles north of Marks.

Within minutes his crew saw the first survivor and pulled him into the aircraft. Then they taxied a few feet, stopped; taxied again, stopped—and kept this up until darkness without seeing another living soul. When Alcorn stopped and searched, they found a tremendous amount of debris in the area, most of it having fallen from the sky during the day. They also saw bodies, dead bodies everywhere.

In the dark, they floated silently with their lone passenger. Soon they heard cries for help from a group of men and sergeants Needham and Higbee volunteered to take one of the rafts, pick them up and bring them back. Alcorn agreed, but with one provision—they could only go as far as the rope attached to raft and plane would take them. Unfortunately, the umbilical cord was not long enough, and the men returned disappointed.

Overhead, planes circled all night. Marks's Dumbo was totally out of commission, but Alcorn continued to signal to the flyers and they reassuringly flashed back to the two PBYs floating on the black-shrouded Philippine Sea.

When he came on duty at 8:00 A.M., Lieutenant Green, surface control officer at Frontier Headquarters, routinely checked over the Expected Arrivals Report for this Thursday and noticed the *Indianapolis* still listed but not yet in. Figuring that if she wasn't in by now she wasn't coming at all, he wrote a short memo to the plotting section requesting permission to remove the ship from his board. Five hours later, Green received a reply telling him not to touch a thing; messages were coming in of men in the water.

Captain Alfred Granum, operations officer of the Philippine Sea Frontier, received a report that an aircraft had sighted men in the water. He made an immediate check to determine what ships were in the vicinity at the time and discovered that the *Indianapolis* should have occupied that spot three and a half days ago and that she still had not reported in. At the same time, Granum's superior, Commodore Norman C. Gillette, acting commander of the Frontier, also received the news of survivors and checked the plotting board. He saw that the *Indianapolis*, the *Westward Ho*, and an LST were sailing in that area. Upon further investigation, Gillette discovered that the *Indianapolis* had not arrived.

Mid-afternoon saw a frantic message from Frontier Headquarters transmitted to Guam:

INDIANAPOLIS (CA 35) HAS NOT
ARRIVED LEYTE X ADVISE

Copies of this dispatch were rushed to Admirals McCormick, Oldendorf, Murray, and Nimitz; Commodore Carter—and, lastly, to the *Indianapolis*. The reply was not encouraging:

INDIANAPOLIS (CA35) DEPARTED
GUAM 2300Z 27 JULY IN
ACCORDANCE OUR 280032Z
OF JULY XXX

Another message was forwarded directly to McCormick (CTG 95.7):

HAS INDIANAPOLIS REPORTED
TO YOU

and the admiral's reply was simply: "Negative."

By the end of the day, still no one on shore knew for certain who the people in the water were. Finally, Frontier sent a bulletin out to all ships speeding to the area:

1ST VESSEL ON SCENE ADVISE
IDENTITY OF SHIP SURVIVORS
ARE FROM AND CAUSE OF
SINKING

Subsequent to completing its training cruise, the powerful battleship *Idaho,* with Rear Admiral McCormick on the bridge, steamed into Leyte Gulf. He made a mental note to look for the heavy cruiser, but as he was approaching the anchorage Thursday afternoon he received the message from Frontier Headquarters asking if the *Indianapolis* had reported, to which he replied no.

McCormick, however, was not upset since Vice Admiral Oldendorf (CTF 95) off Okinawa recently had had two cruisers taken from his force, and the *Portland,* a sister ship of *Indianapolis*, had been called in to replace one. It was assumed the *Indianapolis* was diverted to replace the other. Furthermore, at the time, McCormick was not alarmed about the *Indianapolis* because, as he said, "The disappearance of a ship like her would certainly be a most unusual event. ..."

Off Okinawa, Oldendorf recalled that "My personal thought in the matter was that I wondered why her non-arrival at Leyte had not been recorded by the port director." What this vice admiral didn't know was that it was recorded and that the people at Leyte were aware of the fact that she wasn't in but had done nothing about it.

After Gwinn's second frightful message was received, one of the largest rescue operations in U.S. Naval history began.

The *Cecil J. Doyle* (DE 368) was heading home after an unsuccessful submarine hunt, when she suddenly received orders from the Western Carolines Sub Area to reverse course and steam north to pick up survivors. This was immediately after Gwinn's first transmission. Once the second message came in, the destroyer escort increased speed to 22.5 knots because the skipper had received word:

> ESTIMATED NUMBER OF
> SURVIVORS NOW 150—
> KEEP ORIGINATOR ADVISED
> OF SITUATION

At 2:35 P.M., *Doyle*'s radio room made voice contact with Commander Atteberry, and they were kept informed of what was going on. The ship was asked to rush but replied that there was no way they could make it to the area until after midnight.

Initially, the *Doyle* was the only ship ordered to the scene, but ten minutes after the second message was decoded Admiral Murray instructed Western Carolines that in addition to *Doyle*:

ORDER 2 DESTROYERS AT
BEST SPEED TO [area]
RESCUE 150 SURVIVORS
IN LIFEBOATS

The destroyers *Ralph Talbot* (DD 390) and *Madison* (DD 425), both on separate patrol off Ulithi, at 4:00 P.M. turned their sleek bows northward and hastened to the scene at 32 knots. Meanwhile, *Doyle,* who took off a few hours before, received word that:

2 DDS EN ROUTE FROM ULITHI
TO ASSIST IN RESCUE X
8 PLANES WILL DROP MORE
THAN SUFFICIENT BOAST [sic]
AND LIFE RAFTS BETWEEN 1800 AND
2000K X LATEST POSITION
REPORTED TO BE LATITUDE
11-45 NORTH LONGITUDE
133-35 EAST XXX

It was 6:56 P.M. when the *Madison* made contact with the *Doyle* and pointed out that she wouldn't be able to help until 3:00 A.M. the next morning, and the *Talbot* announced that her ETA wasn't until 4:00 A.M.

At 9:49 P.M., *Doyle*'s lookouts spotted their first star shell, and from that moment on flares were always visible. An hour later, the ship's giant 24-inch searchlight was switched on and pointed skyward to give the guarding planes an idea of where she was. Instead of seeking individual people in the water, the destroyer escort headed straight for Marks's Dumbo and, shortly after midnight, the first survivor from the incredibly luckless *Indianapolis* was pulled aboard a rescue ship.

At Philippine Sea Frontier, Western Carolines, Marianas, Pearl Harbor, and throughout the Pacific, stunned officers waited anxiously for word on who these people were. Some months later, Vice Admiral George Murray verbalized what had to have been going through the minds of men at various headquarters as the fourth day of an unbelievable ordeal drew to a close: "I think the last thing that would occur to anybody—would be that all of the conditions would unfortunately be coordinated to the point that the ship disappeared, no station around the world ever picked up a trace of a message, and the survivors remained in the water for such a long period of time before they were sighted. . . . I still am mystified as to how the whole series of events possibly could have culminated in the loss of that ship."

It was noon when they noticed the circling plane far to the south of them. An hour later, there was another, and as the day wore on the planes swarmed over the line separating sky from sea. Frantically the men signaled, but they were too small to be seen. They ripped the kapok out of jackets, threw the silky fiber into an empty 40-mm ammo can, and set it afire, hoping the rising smoke would draw attention to their plight. It didn't work.

Captain McVay was confused and couldn't imagine what was going on. If the men in his group were the only survivors of the ill-fated cruiser, what was going on ten miles to the south of them? They began to feel discouraged, for as darkness blanketed their isolated spot of ocean the search seemed to be moving further away. McVay was almost certain they were not going to be found and ordered all rations cut in half.

Midnight saw them staring at the tiny pinprick of *Doyle*'s light piercing the black sky, and now they were certain of other survivors. They were also certain, though, that the search area didn't extend north to their position and that it would be a long time, if ever, before they were found. No one slept, and, as the night wore on, this lonely group was very frightened.

The planes had no problem spotting the large Redmayne group and in the afternoon rafts, rations, and other emergency gear showered downward. With the security of sentinals circling above them, the men calmed down and patiently waited for rescue.

After Gwinn dropped the two rafts, they were quickly inflated, and, while the men held onto the side, Haynes was pushed in to investigate. The doctor ordered the sickest men put on the raft. He found an 11-ounce can of water and doled it out in a plastic cup at the rate of one ounce per man.

An enormous amount of equipment was dropped to this "swimmer" group including a ten-man boat that soon had thirty people in it. But, during the day, it became so hot in the rafts that a great many men jumped back in the water to cool off.

Once the supplies were delivered, the group had almost everything they needed to keep them relatively comfortable until rescue ships arrived. Included in this bonanza were fresh water, rations, emergency medical supplies, and sun helmets. Dr. Haynes greatly appreciated the helmets for, when properly used, not only did they protect the wearer from the roasting sun but they also had a screen which dropped down in front of the face and prevented water from getting in the eyes and up the nose. As for the food, they found it impossible to eat the meat and crackers, but the malted-milk tablets and citrus candies went down easily.

Even though so much was dropped to them, the men's deteriorating physical condition made it essential that they be taken out of the water and given rudimentary first aid and medication; otherwise they wouldn't be alive when the ships came. Commander Haynes decided to swim for the plane. He told the group to stay where they were and explained what he was going to do. Then he swam toward Marks's plane and, after what seemed like two hours, finally reached it. His group still didn't have enough water, and he asked the crew of the plane to swing closer and give them some. They did so, and an emergency kit containing K-rations and a quart of water. Fresh water was still a problem, but at sundown Haynes found a saltwater converter in one of the rafts. He treat burns and administer morphine to the more seriously wounded.

When nightfall came, they were in much better shape and had enough rafts so that all but four or five were out of the water. Fresh water was still a problem, but at sundown Haynes found a saltwater converter in one of the rafts. He spent all night trying to make fresh water out of salt water. Because he was so exhausted, the directions didn't help and the effort was a failure. He eventually made two batches of water which tasted horrible, but which the men drank. They even asked for more, but it had taken almost four hours to make the first batch and Haynes had had it. The doctor, who had worked so hard over the last four days, finally surrendered. He took the converter, flung it into the hated sea, and began to cry.

On Thursday morning, August 2, 1945, Commander Hashimoto and the crew of I-58 received the following message:

HEAVY ENEMY W/T TRAFFIC
INDICATING LARGE ENEMY
WARSHIPS SEARCHING FOR
WRECK

9.

In the Water the Fifth Day

Friday, August 3, 1945

TEN minutes after midnight, in a rough sea with a north-northwest wind blowing between 8 and 10 mph, the *Cecil J. Doyle* lowered her heavy motor whaleboat. It headed directly for the closer of the two Dumbos. Twenty minutes later, it returned with eighteen former crewmen of the *Indianapolis*, taken from Marks's plane. As soon as the first man was lifted aboard, he was asked, "Who are you?" Minutes later, an urgent secret dispatch was sent to the Commander of the Western Carolines:

> HAVE ARRIVED AREA X
> AM PICKING UP SURVIVORS
> FROM U.S.S. INDIANAPOLIS
> (CA 35) TORPEODED [sic]
> AND SUNK LAST SUNDAY
> NIGHT

Between 12:30 and 4:45 A.M., *Doyle* raised from the brutal sea ninety-three men,* which included all survivors aboard

---

*The deck log of the *Cecil J. Doyle* for August 3, 1945, however, reports (probably incorrectly) ninety-six men plucked out of the water, as follows:

Marks's plane and the lone man on Alcorn's. In addition about forty men were retrieved from the water and the rafts. While the whaleboat shuttled back and forth, the mother ship slowly cruised the area, sweeping the watery expanse with her hugh searchlight and following the flares dropped from the circling planes. The crew of the whaleboat, meanwhile, had a tough time removing men from the plane and bringing them aboard ship. Transfer was difficult because of the condition of the survivors, some of whom were badly burned from the fires on board the ship, one of whom had a broken leg, and they all were terribly weak from thirst and exposure.

At 1:10 A.M., the *Doyle* saw a searchlight to the north and soon discovered it to be the high-speed transport U.S.S. *Bassett* (APD 73), sent by Philippine Sea Frontier to assist. Two hours later, the destroyer escort U.S.S. *Dufilho* (DE 422) also appeared. Until dawn, the *Doyle, Bassett,* and *Dufilho* worked independently, hoisting men to the safety of their steel decks. Sunup brought the two destroyers *Madison* and *Ralph Talbot* (who had been steaming since yesterday afternoon) on the scene, and, with five ships now in the area, *Madison* took charge.

First light allowed Marks to inspect his Catalina, and he

Time		Number of Men
0007	Arrived in area	
0030	Motor whaleboat returned with	18
0135	Motor whaleboat returned with	22
0235	Motor whaleboat returned with	17
0300	Picked up two rafts holding	10
0400	Motor whaleboat returned with	1
0445	Motor whaleboat returned with	6
0445	Ship brought alongside two rafts with	22
	Total	96

All other sources show ninety-three.

quickly determined that it would never fly again. At 6:00
A.M., *Doyle* sent her boat over to the Dumbo and transferred
the crew and all salvageable gear to the ship.

Lieutenant Alcorn was relieved of his lone survivor by
Doyle at 4:00 A.M. and, with the sun rising over the eastern
horizon, he had to decide whether or not to take off. The sea
was very rough and a heavy wind was blowing, but, fortunately, his Catalina was not nearly as beat up as Marks's. He
resolved to try it, and at 7:30 A.M., with no trouble at all, he
powered his way down the endless runway and lifted off.* At
almost the same time, *Doyle* poured eighty rounds of 40-mm
gunfire into Marks's abandoned plane, and she sunk in the
same area as the ship whose men she had so valiantly
rescued.

After sinking the seaplane, *Doyle* secured from general
quarters, and all of her survivors were logged in, treated, and
put to bed. The crew of the *Doyle* were extremely helpful to
their fellow sailors who had so recently suffered through a
living hell. Men moved out of their bunks to make room for
the former crewmen of the *Indianapolis* and constantly
hovered around them, waiting for the slightest request that
they could fill. The men were all given baths, and the oil was
removed from their tired bodies. Every thirty minutes, a half
glass of water, hot soup, hot coffee, and fruit were served to
them, and this continued throughout the night and into the
next day. The *Doyle*'s doctor examined everyone and listed
them all in medical condition ranging from serious to acute.

At one point during this Friday, while Dr. Haynes was
sitting in the wardroom he noticed that Marks had a slew of
forms in front of him. The pilot was worried because he had to

---

*He landed at 9:40 A.M. Between August 2 and August 7, Lieutenant
Alcorn continued to fly over the area, spotting for ships, and in total logged
fifty-one hours, ten minutes over the cruiser's graveyard.

explain why he had made a hazardous landing, and, more important still, why, after making it, he lost an expensive airplane. Looking at Haynes, Marks asked, "Doc, can I quote you as saying my open-sea landing was necessary to save you fellows?"

As it searched for the living, *Doyle* passed by the bodies of twenty-five to fifty dead sailors floating in life jackets. At 12:20 P.M., *Madison* ordered *Doyle* to take off for Peleliu, and this, the first ship on the scene, was now the first to leave, heading south at 22.5 knots.

All McVay and his isolated band could do was watch the distant searchlights, the falling flares, the circling planes. When the sun rose over the horizon, they were in despair. The entire morning was spent staring at the activity very far away. It did not seem to be coming closer.

At 11:30 A.M., they spotted a plane making a box search. It was a very wide pattern, and on each leg it came closer. They found it extremely depressing, for the plane gave no recognition sign. Captain McVay contended that they were never spotted from the air. But they were, for this plane, flown by Marks's squadron leader, Lieutenant Commander M. V. Ricketts, saw them and reported that he sighted two rafts, with five survivors in one and four in the other. By voice radio, he directed the U.S.S. *Ringness* (APD 100) to pick them up.

Like *Bassett, Ringness* was a high-speed transport sent by Philippine Sea Frontier,* and it had just arrived. After receiving Ricketts's message, *Ringness* headed for the spot,

---

Ringness and *Bassett* were the only two ships ordered to take part in the rescue by the Philippine Sea Frontier. All other ships were under the authority of Commander, Marianas, since the *Indianapolis* was sunk—and the survivors were—in his area of responsibility.

and at 4,046 yards she picked McVay up on radar.* On the rafts, the spell of isolation and despair was suddenly broken when somebody cried, "My God, look at this! There are two destroyers bearing down on us. Why, they're almost on top of us." The two destroyers were both transports, *Ringness* and the newly arrived *Register* (APD 92). *Register* turned north to pick up another small group while *Ringness* headed for McVay.

Everyone made it aboard under his own power, and all were immediately given first aid. They had lost about 14 percent of their body weight, and during the afternoon they were given ice cream, coffee, and as much water as they could drink. During the entire four and one-half days on the rafts, no one in the group asked for a drink. This was surprising to McVay, since he had assumed people couldn't go that long without water—but they did.

Captain McVay was asked what happened, and a dispatch was quickly drafted to Admiral Nimitz at Pearl Harbor:

PICKED UP CAPT. McVAY, CO,
WHO BELIEVES SHIP HIT 0015,
SANK 0030, ZONE MINUS NINE
ONE-HALF, 30 JULY. POSITION
ON TRACK EXACTLY AS ROUTED
PD GUAM. SPEED 17, NOT
ZIGZAGGING. HIT FORWARD
BY WHAT IS BELIEVED TO BE
TWO TORPEDOES OR MINE
FOLLOWED BY MAGAZINE EXPLOSION.**

---

*The radar zeroed in on the 40-mm ammo can in one of the rafts.
**At this time, McVay was a little confused. The ship did not hit a mine nor did the magazines blow up.

While *Doyle* was taking care of the "Haynes group," *Bassett* took care of Lieutenant Redmayne and his men. Lowering her four landing craft at 2:30 A.M., *Bassett*'s boats picked up most of Redmayne's people. A head count was taken, and a little over eighty sailors were collected from the original group of 150. *Bassett* next sent a message to Frontier Headquarters:

SURVIVORS ARE FROM USS
INDIANAPOLIS (CA 35) WHICH
WAS TORPEDOED 29 JULY [sic] X
CONTINUING TO PICK UP
SURVIVORS X MANY BADLY
INJURED

Ralph Talbot (DD 390) picked up twenty-four survivors and then spent most of the afternoon sinking eight rafts and a small boat with her 20-mm guns. Later she transferred her survivors to *Register*.

As soon as *Madison* arrived in the area, *Bassett* reported that she had 150 survivors aboard and desperately needed a doctor. Shortly thereafter, at 5:15 A.M., *Madison*'s physician, Lieutenant (jg) H. A. Stiles, was transferred to the transport. It was at the time the landing craft from *Bassett* came over to pick up Doctor Stiles that *Madison* first learned the survivors were from the *Indianapolis*.

At 5:40 A.M., *Bassett* was released, and *Madison* informed Western Carolines that the transport was going to Leyte with her people. An hour later, *Madison* was instructed to hold *Bassett* and have her sail to Peleliu so "that proper accounting and reports of survivors" might be taken, but it was too late—*Bassett* was long gone. All other survivors were brought to Peleliu.

During the day scouting lines were formed with the planes

bird-dogging, but nothing was seen except for the dead, and they were generally left where they were. The unpleasant task of recovery and identification was postponed until the next day. The last living man plucked from the Philippine Sea was Captain McVay, who was the last man to enter it.

By nightfall, more ships were ordered on the scene; the disaster was bigger than anyone had imagined. *Alvin C. Cockrell* (DE 366) left Peleliu; *Helm* (DD 388) was detached from picket duty to "assist in the search for survivors of a sunken ship;" and *Aylwin* (DD 355), on patrol off Ulithi, cut in all her boilers and at 4:40 P.M., was also speeding northward at 28 knots.

The hospital ship *Tranquillity* was ordered by Admiral Nimitz to leave Ulithi and go to Peleliu at top speed for the embarkation and treatment of survivors, then to set sail for Guam where they were to be discharged.

That afternoon, after receiving *Bassett*'s message, Philippine Sea Frontier sent the following order to all port directors under its command:

> ALL COMBATANT SHIPS 5 HOURS
> OVERDUE SHALL BE REPORTED
> TO ORIGINATOR . . .

During the early morning hours, Admiral Nimitz sent to his superior, Fleet Admiral King, the following:

> SURVIVORS BEING PICKED UP . . .
> STATE THAT INDIANAPOLIS
> (CA 35) WAS TORPEDOED AND
> SUNK 29 JULY [sic] WHILE
> EN ROUTE GUAM TO LEYTE X
> FRAGMENTARY REPORTS INDICATE

> AT LEAST 200 SURVIVORS MANY
> OF WHOM INJURED X MANY
> RESCUE SHIPS IN POSITION X
> NO REPORT THUS FAR OF CAPT
> McVAY X WILL FORWARD FURTHER
> INFORMATION AS RECEIVED

Later in the day, Nimitz ordered his commands to check the log books of all shore-based radio stations to ascertain whether any of them picked up during the night of July 29/30 a distress message on 500 or 4235 kilocycles.

During the afternoon, CinCPac instructed that:

> UNTIL FURTHER ORDERS ALL
> SHIPS WITH 500 OR MORE TOTAL
> PERSONNEL ON BOARD SHALL BE
> PROVIDED WITH AN ESCORT
> BETWEEN ULITHI AND LEYTE
> REGARDLESS OF SPEED

By the time the blazing Pacific sun reached its zenith on this day, not another living person from *Indianapolis* was to be found in that enormous ocean. She had sailed from San Francisco with 1,196 young men, was torpedoed, and about 800 of her crew escaped from the sinking ship. Of these 800, 320 were rescued; two later died in the Philippines, and two on Peleliu. Because of complacency and carelessness, approximately 500 U.S. sailors (no one will ever know the exact number) died in the waters of the Philippine Sea.

10.
Search

FOR miles around, the sea carried corpses. The many
destroyers on the scene served as funeral directors.
Because the sharks had been at work, identification was next
to impossible.

The search lasted six days, covering hundreds of square
miles of ocean. The result was always the same—bodies,
bodies, and more bodies.

In his Action Report, Commander A. F. Hollingsworth,
Captain of the U.S.S. *Helm,* brought into stark reality how
hideous the discovering of bodies really was:

> All bodies were in extremely bad condition and had been dead
> for an estimated 4 or 5 days. Some had life jackets and life
> belts, most had nothing. Most of the bodies were completely
> naked, and the others had just drawers or dungaree trousers
> on—only three of the 28 bodies recovered had shirts on. Bodies
> were horribly bloated and decomposed—recognition of faces
> would have been impossible. About half of the bodies were
> shark-bitten, some to such a degree that they more nearly
> resembled skeletons. From one to four sharks were in the
> immediate area of the ship at all times. At one time, two sharks
> were attacking a body not more than fifty yards from the ship,

157

and continued to do so until driven off by rifle fire. For the most part it was impossible to get fingerprints from the bodies as the skin had come off the hands or the hands lacerated by sharks. Skin was removed from the hands of bodies containing no identification when possible, and the Medical Officer will dehydrate the skin and attempt to make legible prints. All personal effects removed from the bodies for purposes of identification. . . . After examination, all bodies were sunk, using two-inch line and a weight of three 5"/38 cal. projectiles. There were still more bodies in the area when darkness brought a close to the gruesome operations for the day.

All the other ships of the scouting flotilla were performing the same revolting task as *Helm*. Initially, some of the captains brought the bodies on board in order to offer a formal—and decent—burial service at sea. The condition of the bodies was so horrible, however, that this idea was scratched almost immediately. After being identified, the corpses were sunk on the spot.

The sharks had been having a feast. When a boat reached a body, it was common to see a hand missing, or foot gone, a part of the head ripped off, or a chunk of meat torn from the torso. It was also usual to find nothing but bones.

In two days, the U.S.S. *French* examined twenty-nine bodies but could not identify eighteen (62 percent) of them. The *French*'s report monotonously repeated over and over again: "Impossible to take fingerprints"; "Body badly decomposed"; "Very badly mutilated by sharks."

As the evening sun dropped over the western horizon on Wednesday, August 8, 1945, the ships sailed for home, leaving in their wake the graveyard of the U.S.S. *Indianapolis* and the final burial ground of 73 percent of her young crew.

One day before the search for survivors came to an end,

Fleet Admiral King, Chief of Naval Operations, sent a harsh, Top Secret dispatch to Fleet Admiral Nimitz at Pearl Harbor:

> IF PERIODICAL ENEMY SUBMARINE ESTIMATES ARE BEING BROADCAST TO FORCES [under] YOUR COMMAND, AS WAS DONE IN THE ATLANTIC, DESIRE COMINCH [i.e., King] BE MADE REFERENCE ADDRESSEE IN FUTURE. [I] ASSUME THAT UNESCORTED SHIPS OR CONVOYS ARE NOT BEING ROUTED OVER KNOWN POSITIONS OF ENEMY SUBS WITH ASSIGNED OFFENSIVE MISSIONS BUT RECENT LOSS OF INDIANAPOLIS APPEARS TO BE A CASE IN POINT

Lieutenant Commander Hashimoto and the crew of I-58 celebrated the death of *Indianapolis* with a dinner of beans, corned beef, boiled eel, and sake. On August 10, I-58 unsuccessfully launched a pair of Kaiten against a convoy of American ships, and two days later released another manned torpedo which grazed the hull of the LST *Oak Hill*. The *Oak Hill* attack was the final Kaiten operation made by the Japanese Navy in World War II.

I-58 returned home on August 16, and as soon as she tied up the skipper was handed the Imperial Order to cease fire; the war was over. In the middle of November, after destroying all the boat's official papers and documents, the newly promoted Commander Hashimoto surrendered his submarine to U.S. forces at Sasebo.

Exactly two weeks after the ships quit their fruitless search for the living, Admiral Nimitz cut new orders to the Pacific Fleet:

> ALL NAVAL VESSELS PROCEEDING INDEPEND-

ENTLY WILL BE CONSIDERED OVERDUE WHEN
THEY FAIL TO ARRIVE AT DESTINATION WITHIN 8
HOURS. . . . THE PORT DIRECTOR AT DESTINATION
WILL REPORT IMMEDIATELY ALL OVERDUE VES-
SELS TO HIS SEA FRONTIER OR AREA COMMANDER
WHO WILL TAKE APPROPRIATE STEPS TO REQUEST
NEW ETA FROM THE SUBJECT VESSEL, NOTIFY
PORT DIRECTOR AT PORT OF ORIGIN, COMMAND-
ERS OF AREAS THROUGH WHICH VESSEL WAS
ROUTED AND ARRANGE FOR NECESSARY AIR AND
SURFACE SEARCHES

Orders not withstanding, the Navy felt that the numerous
circumstances which surrounded the *Indianapolis* disaster
would not happen again:

The Bureau of Ships considers that a recurrence of the circumstances of the survivors of the *Indianapolis*, their lack of sufficient rafts with attached supplies and the long delay in their
rescue, is not likely. It is unlikely that some generated power
supply will not be available to the ship for distress signals, but,
in that event, two battery-powered TCS will be available in
large combatant ships to start rescue vessels to the scene.
Emergency distress transmitting radio units as part of the
life-raft equipment will assure communication after sinking.
The lack of authorized automatic release devices and the failure to release toggles or to cut the lashing of the rafts during
the 30 minutes [sic] elapsing between the torpedoing and the
sinking need not be repeated in any future disasters. The
failure and unsatisfactory condition of abandon ship supplies
and equipment was due in large measure to the overcrowding
of the few rafts floated and the circumstances noted above.

It will never be redundant to state that the sinking of this

heavy cruiser was (and remains) the largest disaster, in relation to human life, of a ship at sea, in the annals of U.S.
Naval history. Many people, when questioned about loss of
life aboard a combat ship, will generally mention *Houston*
(800 dead), *Franklin* (772 dead), or *Juneau* (684 dead), but not
the 880 of *Indianapolis.**

About 400 men went down with the ship. The other 500,
instead of being reported as Killed in Action, should have
been reported as Killed by Inaction. The cause of those
deaths was not Hashimoto nor the speed with which the ship
sank, nor anything even remotely related to battle. It was
caused by (and was the fault of) the United States Navy.
Admiral Morison, when briefly discussing this tragedy in
The Two-Ocean War, ends his hasty review of the subject by
saying, "From this tale of routine stupidity and unnecessary
suffering it is pleasant to return to (a discussion of aircraft
carrier operations)."

Radarman 3rd Class Ralph Rogers was one of the lucky
survivors, and he summed up what had to be on the minds of
all the living: "We lost an awful lot of good men. We were all
wondering. Now I don't even think about it anymore myself,
because I am all right." The suffering, mutilation, and death
of the crew of the *Indianapolis* was over. All of these men
could return to their families and begin to lead normal lives.
All, that is, except one.

"I was in command of the ship and I am responsible for its
fate. [Therefore] I hope they make their decisions soon and do
what they want to with me." Captain Charles Butler McVay,
III, was about to be arrested, court-martialed, and have the
full blame for the sinking of the *Indianapolis* placed on him.

---

*Arizona had 1,104 dead but she was tied up to a pier during the Pearl
Harbor attack.

11.
Court of Inquiry

A17-24

UNITED STATES PACIFIC FLEET
AND PACIFIC OCEAN AREAS
HEADQUARTERS OF THE COMMANDER IN CHIEF

Serial 006444

c/o Fleet Post Office,
San Francisco, California

9 AUG 1945

From: Commander in Chief, U.S. Pacific Fleet and Pacific Ocean Areas

To: Vice Admiral Charles A. Lockwood, junior, U.S. Navy

Subject: Court of Inquiry to inquire into all the circumstances connected with the sinking of the U.S.S. *Indianapolis* (CA-35), and the delay in reporting the loss of that ship.

1. A court of inquiry consisting of yourself as president and

of Vice Admiral George D. Murray, U.S. Navy, and Rear Admiral Francis E. M. Whiting, U.S. Navy, as additional members, and of Captain William E. Hilbert, U.S. Navy, as judge advocate, is hereby ordered to convene at the Headquarters of the Commander Marianas, at 10 o'clock A.M., on Thursday, August 9, 1945, or as soon thereafter as practicable for the purpose of inquiring into all the circumstances connected with the sinking of the U.S.S. *Indianapolis* (CA-35), on or about July 29, 1945, the rescue operations, and the delay in connection with reporting the loss of that ship.

2.   The court will thoroughly inquire into the matter hereby submitted to it and upon the conclusion of the inquiry will report the facts established thereby, the causes thereof, the damages resulting therefrom, the losses incurred thereby, and the responsibility therefor.

3.   The court will further give its opinion as to whether any offenses have been committed or serious blame incurred, and, in case its opinion be that offenses have been committed or serious blame incurred, will specifically recommend what further proceedings should be had.

4.   The attention of the court is particularly invited to Section 734, Naval Courts and Boards.

5.   Commander Marianas is hereby directed to furnish the necessary clerical assistance for the purpose of assisting the judge advocate in recording the proceedings of this court of inquiry.

C. W. NIMITZ
Fleet Admiral, U.S. Navy,
Commander in Chief, U.S. Pacific Fleet
and Pacific Ocean Areas

It was very bad timing. Nimitz was rushing into the court of inquiry like a bull into a china shop because, as he later claimed, they had a war to run and he wanted to get this over with as quickly as possible. Preparations for the invasion (and, hopefully, surrender) of the Japanese home islands were in full swing, and the Russians complicated the situation further by declaring war on Japan. Therefore, the president of the court, Vice Admiral Charles Lockwood, who was commander of all Pacific Fleet submarines, (and many of the other officers present) had better things to do during early August, 1945, than get locked up in a room for a week, trying to piece together an enormous tragedy.

One of the members of the court, who was ordered to determine whether any wrongdoing took place, was Vice Admiral George Murray. It was he who had not diverted the *Indianapolis* and within whose jurisdiction the ship was sunk and 880 lives lost. And, most important, he was responsible for the actions (or inaction) of his operations officer, Captain Oliver Naquin. The fact that Admiral Murray was one of the judges made a mockery of the impartiality of the investigation, since his command was intimately involved in the disaster.

Captain William Hilbert, the Judge Advocate (prosecutor), summed up everything by candidly stating that they "were starting the proceedings without having available all the necessary data."

On Monday morning, August 13, 1945, the closed-door inquiry into the Navy's greatest sea disaster began.* Since this was a secret proceeding, spectators were not permitted, and therefore Captain McVay asked to be entered as an "interested party," which allowed him to remain in the room,

---

*The court of inquiry transcript has always been a secret document until this publication.

hear all of the testimony, and cross-examine witnesses. This request was granted, and the first witness was McVay himself. A total of sixty-seven questions were asked of the captain, primarily concentrating on who was on the bridge, what did they do, etc. It was also asked if he were zigzagging and his simple reply was, "No, sir." Throughout this short interrogation no mention was made of the fact that the captain's orders gave him discretionary power to cease the zigzag maneuver whenever he thought conditions permitted. McVay related to the court that the poor visibility on the night of the sinking, and the lack of any hard intelligence warning him about the submarine menace justified his increasing speed and sailing in a straight line.

When Joseph Waldron, the routing officer on Guam, was called, he was asked thirty questions and dismissed. The lieutenant was queried about Route "Peddie" and his routing instructions in general, but not one question was asked about the attached, worthless intelligence report.

Next, Captain Oliver Naquin was quizzed. He was the key to a major mystery; how could a ship be torpedoed by a submarine in an area where there wasn't supposed to be a submarine? The court asked him only ten questions. Within the framework of the questions, however, he was asked to give his estimate of the submarine danger along Route "Peddie" at the time the *Indianapolis* sailed. Captain Naquin's answer was that he thought the risk was "practically negligible." The court took this as gospel and dismissed this senior officer under Admiral George Murray, Commander of the Marianas, and, coincidentally, one of the judges. The court never asked Naquin why, if the danger was negligible, the *Indianapolis* was sunk. Captain Naquin kept this terrible secret to himself. After about ten minutes on the stand, he walked out of the inquiry, leaving them totally in the dark.

Lieutenant Stewart Gibson related to the Court that he did,

indeed, know of the missing *Indianapolis* by dusk on Tuesday (the day she was due in) and did not report it. Once Gibson told them this, he was made an "interested party," which permitted him to remain and call witnesses in his own defense. He was informed of his rights, and the lieutenant immediately stated that he wanted an attorney.

The cover-up began on the second day of the inquiry and snowballed onward from that point. It was August 14, sixteen days after the sinking, when the public heard the following:

NAVY DEPARTMENT

IMMEDIATE RELEASE   AUGUST 14, 1945
PRESS AND RADIO

NAVY DEPARTMENT COMMUNIQUE
NUMBER 622

1. The U.S.S. *Indianapolis* has been lost in the Philippine Sea as the result of enemy action.

2. The next of kin of casualties have been notified.

However, at the same moment, President Truman was announcing to the world Japan's surrender. The report of the demise of the heavy cruiser was apparently timed to be released when it would do the least harm.

During the week, many officers and crew members of the ship were called upon to relate their experiences, and through this testimony the court obtained a clear insight into the horror these men witnessed, both during the sinking and in the course of their subsequent four days in the water. If the function of the inquiry was to hear individual tales of bravery and terror, it succeeded. If, on the other hand, the members were to follow their orders, as outlined by Admiral Nimitz, to wit, inquire thoroughly into the causes of the sinking "and the responsibility therefor," they failed dismally.

The court did spend a great deal of time on the officers at Leyte Gulf and the question of why that command did not report the missing ship. Gibson's superior, Lieutenant Commander Jules Sancho, was asked if he knew of the nonarrival of the ship, and his response was "No, sir." Obviously, he didn't know because Gibson didn't tell him, but all of the information Gibson had was readily available to Sancho if he wanted to check up on his subordinates. In his own defense, Commander Sancho pointed out that he did take two or three turns around the office every day, asking how things were going, and neither Gibson nor anyone else reported anything new to him.

Sancho's boss, Commodore Jacob Jacobson, commandant of the Leyte Gulf Naval Base, stated to the court that they had no duty to announce the nonarrival of a combat ship, unless that ship were reporting directly to them. In the case of the *Indianapolis*, she was reporting to Admiral McCormick, who received a daily copy of the base's Ships Present List. According to Jacobson, if McCormick had read the list, he would have noticed the absence of the *Indianapolis*. Unfortunately, McCormick, who assumed the cruiser was reporting to him because of Guam's sailing dispatch, wasn't quite sure since, as we have seen, his staff never decoded Nimitz's original orders to the ship.

Captain Alfred Granum, operations officer for the Philippine Sea Frontier, told the members of the court that his office assumed that the *Indianapolis* had arrived, without investigating the matter further. He implied that if 10CL-45 were properly drafted by CinCPac in the first place, they wouldn't have had to make assumptions since an investigation would have been necessary in order to report the nonarrival.

The acting commander of the Philippine Sea Frontier and Captain Granum's superior, Commodore Norman C. Gillette, pointed out that the Frontier was not overly concerned about combat ships since they generally operated under task force commanders and were constantly diverted by them. Consequently, a missing combat vessel was the responsibility of the task force commander and not the Sea Frontier.

Commodore James Carter, the author of 10CL-45, told the court that both Admiral McCormick and the Port of Leyte should have felt a responsibility to notify someone of the missing cruiser. Although Carter indirectly admitted that his order was poorly drafted, he maintained that a "moral obligation still remains for an established authority to keep his seniors informed when he has evidence to the effect that something appears to be amiss."

On Wednesday, August 15, Lieutenant Redmayne, Ensigns Blum and Twible, and Chief Benton, ripped into Giulio. They all felt that Giulio should be subject to a special censure for his actions, and the court immediately made Giulio an "interested party" to the inquiry. Giulio introduced Commander Frank E. Bollman as his counsel.

The first thing Giulio did was make a motion to strike out all the testimony regarding him, since it was hearsay. This was denied. He next moved to strike the words "the ringleader seemed to be a man by the name of Giulio," which words were used by Lieutenant Redmayne. This also was denied. Therefore, on Thursday, August 16, Giulio introduced four witnesses in his behalf, each of whom testified that he did no wrong. Finally, Giulio himself took the stand and said he was innocent of all charges. After testifying, he asked the court to withdraw him as an "interested party" on the grounds that the evidence so far produced in no way involved him. Once again, this was denied.

During this inquisition, Admiral McCormick and his chief of staff, Commander Thomas Langen, were called. The two officers pointed out that since they received CinCPac's dispatch in garbled form (which is incorrect; it was garbled in the decoding process) they were not aware of the pending arrival of the cruiser and, therefore, had no responsibility toward her.

Seven days and forty-three witnesses after the inquiry began, it ended, with the members knowing just enough about the fiasco to be dangerous.

Captain McVay chose not to make a closing argument. Apparently, he felt that, based upon the testimony, nothing had been introduced to implicate him in any wrongdoing. In a certain sense he was absolutely correct. The court of inquiry had scrambled all over the place, with an emphasis on the delay in reporting the nonarrival of the ship in Leyte.

Gibson, who was involved in that delay, made a very long closing argument. His entire statement revolved around the thesis that he had no directive calling for the reporting of nonarrivals. Therefore, he argued that he had neither the duty—nor a moral obligation—to make such a report.

Giulio, too, closed with an argument. He pointed out to the members that he was a leader of men aboard the cruiser and asked how all his leadership qualities could evaporate so quickly, especially with the same men he had worked with. He felt that the evidence was too nebulous to make such a fact believable and, therefore, he should be dropped as an "interested party."

The Judge Advocate closed the proceedings by saying that the proximate (or legal) cause for the delay in reporting the missing cruiser was the failure to take notice of the non-arrival of the vessel at Leyte.* He further stated that if the court found any of these officers negligent, they should be punished. As far as Giulio was concerned, the prosecutor told the court that he didn't think they had a case. He pointed out that much of the testimony was hearsay and contradictory, and given by persons under severe mental strain at the time. He doubted whether such a case could be proved beyond a reasonable doubt. Most important, the Judge Advocate did not once in his closing argument mention McVay's name, nor did he imply that any blame for this disaster be placed on him.

After the closing statements by the various parties, the court came up with a *Finding of Facts*, which was broken down into four sections.

The first section was a "Narrative" of what happened. It was only one and a half typewritten pages and said little except that the ship was sunk and not reported overdue.

The second section was entitled "Facts" and was fairly correct as far as it went—except for the first fact. This "fact," in part, stated categorically that the *Indianapolis*, prior to sailing from Guam, was informed by Lieutenant Waldron "of recent submarine and mine contacts made along her assigned route." This simply is not accurate, and any conclusions based on this "fact" would be erroneous.

The third section of the *Findings* was the "Opinions" of the court, and in this part it is most apparent why they shouldn't have been in such a rush. For example, they formed the "Opinion" that Captain Naquin's estimate of submarine

---

*Actually, a number of officers at Leyte (which, for the sake of argument, includes the Philippine Sea Frontier) knew the ship did not come in but nothing was done about it, and that is evidently what the Judge Advocate meant.

activity ("practically negligible") was correct. Obviously, if that was the situation in that area of the Pacific at the time, then what was the reason for zigzagging?

Another "opinion" was that the visibility on the night in question was good. However, in their previous "Facts" section of the *Findings,* they stated that the testimony regarding visibility was conflicting, as was testimony on whether or not the sky was overcast. When the *Indianapolis* was sinking, there had been men on the bridge, the bow, and other parts of that doomed vessel who couldn't see their hands in front of their faces. Though there had been intermittent moonlight, the court's "opinion" of good visibility on the night of the cruiser's torpedoing seems unjustified.

A third "opinion" the court held was that Fleet Doctrine and sound operational practice required McVay to zigzag. This is false. Fleet Doctrine did not contain this mandate for the conditions under which the *Indianapolis* was sailing, and whether the captain should have zigzagged because it would be sound operational procedure is highly debatable. However, they prefaced this "opinion" with the phrase "in view of all the attendant circumstances" McVay should have zigzagged. What attendant circumstances? The captain was told he could stop zigzagging at his own discretion. Captain McVay had no intelligence stapled onto his Routing Orders informing him of enemy submarines; it was strictly a routine voyage.

Another erroneous "opinion": there was a delay in sending a distress message, and this delay was caused by damage to the radio installations and uncertainty as to what frequency was to be used. This conclusion is unwarranted. There was absolutely no delay in getting out a signal. In addition, the transmitting room (Radio II) was not damaged, and there was never a doubt as to what frequencies were to be used.

The members of the court were persuaded that Giulio did

nothing wrong because they felt his four witnesses, plus his own testimony, refuted everything stated by the officers. Therefore, there were to be no further proceedings in Giulio's case.

Incredible as it may seem, the court of inquiry stated that it had "been unable to establish the fact that the ship was torpedoed." The members were of the "opinion," however, that it probably was and, consequently, the "failure of the ship to be zigzagging at the time the explosions occurred was a contributory cause of the loss of the ship."

The fourth and last section of the *Finding of Facts* was the list of "Recommendations" to CinCPac. They advised Admiral Nimitz to send a Letter of Admonition to Lieutenant Gibson, and to instruct Admiral McCormick to take disciplinary action against his communications staff. They also advised that first-aid kits be made watertight, that ships without escort zigzag at all times (why this "Recommendation" if it was Fleet Doctrine and sound operational procedure to do so?), and other fairly minor things. Of the seven "recommendations" made, however, it was the first one which would generate headlines around the world:

1. The court recommends that further proceedings be had as indicated below:

    A. That Captain Charles B. McVay, III, U.S. Navy, be brought to trial by general court-martial on the following charges:

        I *Culpable Inefficiency in the Performance of His Duty* under Article 8, Section 10, Articles for the Government of the Navy

        and II *Negligently Endangering Lives of Others* under Article 22, Articles for the Government of the Navy.

It seems quite obvious that McVay was to be made a scapegoat; a breathing body had to be hung—a living victim shown to the American people. Someone had to shoulder the blame publicly: why not the captain of the ship? As a matter of fact, the inquiry brought to light the names of some (but not all) of the other officers involved in this tragedy but ended with the curt statement that there wasn't "sufficient interest" in any of these other people* to either "make them defendants or interested parties or to warrant further proceedings against them."

Chester Nimitz didn't like the recommendation of the inquiry, and on September 6, 1945, wrote a letter to the Judge Advocate General of the Navy stating that he wasn't going to follow its advice:

> The Commander in Chief, U.S. Pacific Fleet, does not agree with the court in its recommendation that Captain Charles B. McVay, III, U.S. Navy, be brought to trial by general court-martial. He did incur blame for failure to order zigzag courses steered on the night in question, and for failure to send a distress message immediately after the explosions [sic]. His failure to order a zigzag course was an error in judgment, but not of such nature as to constitute gross negligence. Therefore, a letter of reprimand will be addressed to Captain McVay in lieu of a general court martial.

It is a very rare instance, indeed, when an order given by a fleet admiral is countermanded, but that is precisely what happened. On September 25, Chief of Naval Operations Ernest King addressed a memo to Secretary of the Navy Forrestal stating that "I cannot agree with the opinion of Com-

*Except, as noted earlier, Gibson and McCormick's communications staff.

mander in Chief, U.S. Pacific Fleet, that the failure of Captain McVay to order a zigzag course was an error in judgment of such nature as not to constitute culpable negligence." Therefore, "I further recommend that the Secretary of the Navy direct the following action:"

CAPTAIN CHARLES B. McVAY BE BROUGHT TO TRIAL BY GENERAL COURT MARTIAL IN ACCORDANCE WITH RECOMMENDATION I.A. OF COURT OF INQUIRY IN THIS CASE

About a month after the court of inquiry ended, Admiral McCormick received a direct order from Fleet Admiral Nimitz "to take necessary disciplinary action with regard to blame incurred" on the part of his staff for the foul-up. The Pacific Fleet Commander wanted someone punished, but McCormick told Nimitz, "While I do not condone the error, I believe that the individual mistake was not as great as many which are made frequently throughout the Navy."

In October, 1946, well over a year after the disaster, the new chief of naval operations, Fleet Admiral Chester Nimitz, wrote a memo to the Secretary of the Navy which, in essence, absolved McCormick of all responsibility. "The dispatch ordering the ship to report to the Commander Task Group 95.7 for training was received by him with a garbled address and was not decoded by his staff, since its classification was 'Secret' and the garbled address, as received, did not include his command. He therefore had no reason to inquire into the whereabouts of the *Indianapolis*. It is the opinion of the Chief of Naval Operations, therefore, that there is no matter of interest [which] relates to the record of Vice Admiral Mc-Cormick."

The only thing wrong with this memo is that Nimitz

doesn't have his facts straight. First of all, the dispatch was not classified "Secret" but bore the much lower classification of "Restricted." Secondly, it did include his address (i.e., 95.7) in correct form, not "garbled," but upon decoding, McCormick's staff garbled it, turning the correct 95.7 into 75.8. And third, of course, because the dispatch held such a low security classification, the communications people aboard the *Idaho* didn't feel it had a high enough priority to request a repeat.

Within months after this careless error on the part of McCormick's staff, he was promoted from Rear to Vice Admiral.

On September 25, 1945, in the same memo in which Admiral King told Forrestal that he didn't agree with Nimitz and wanted McVay court-martialed, he also told the secretary that he was not at all satisfied with the evidence developed by the court of inquiry, and that the men essentially did not do the job expected of them. They certainly did go into the command structure at Leyte Gulf and their reasons for not reporting the missing ship, but there was so much more to this disaster than that. King wanted to know who picked Route "Peddie" and if there were other routes available;* why the *Indianapolis* was not furnished with an escort; why only four of the fifteen surviving officers were called as witnesses; why no lookouts or radarmen testified, and so on. In conclusion, he told the secretary "that valuable amplifying information for reviewing authorities could have been obtained had more witnesses" been called. Therefore, he suggested to Forrestal that "an investigating officer of appropriate rank" be chosen to perform a thorough, in-depth review of the total disaster.

---

*As we have seen, he personally had the opportunity to rectify that situation, but didn't. See chapter 2, pp. 18-19.

For a little over a week, Forrestal sat on King's recommendation for appointing an investigation unit to dig into the disaster. This annoyed Admiral Louis Denfeld, Chief of Naval Personnel, and on October 4, Denfeld wrote his own memo to Secretary Forrestal urging him to heed the request. Denfeld stated that he felt "it most expedient that the investigation recommended be initiated" and that the Naval Inspector General be appointed to perform this task.

On October 8, King wrote Forrestal, agreeing with Denfeld and noting that "if the Secretary of the Navy approves the recommendation . . . and so desires, I am prepared to instruct the Naval Inspector General to conduct the further investigation recommended into the sinking of the U.S.S. *Indianapolis* and the delay in reporting the loss of that ship."

Ten days later, the Naval Inspector General received his orders to get to work. He was given complete authority, money, and personnel to get to the bottom of the *Indianapolis* disaster. There would be no objections to questions, no courtroom procedures, and everyone called had better show up and answer questions, no matter how many stars he had on his shoulder. The NIG simply took each person into a room, closed the door, and pumped away.*

Aware that the NIG would bring to light new facts in the case which most likely would absolve McVay of any wrongdoing, the Chief of Naval Personnel wrote the following memo to King:

---

*A great deal of this book's previously unknown facts about the *Indianapolis* disaster are based upon the interrogations, exhibits, and reports of the Naval Inspector General. The testimony alone came to 616 legal-size, single-spaced pages. There were also close to 1,000 additional pages of documents and reports. The secret Court of Inquiry testimony came to only 131 pages. All of the NIG's documents were classified "Secret" and, to the best of this author's knowledge, have never been made public until now.

SECRET   November 8, 1945

Subject Court of Inquiry is this day being forwarded by [me] to
the Secretary of the Navy, [through you]. It is being recommended to the Secretary of the Navy that trial of Captain
McVay be withheld, pending completion of the supplemental
investigation now being conducted by the Inspector General
of the Navy. The Office of the Inspector General advises that
completion of the supplemental investigation may consume
approximately one month, possibly involving a trip to Guam.

At the same time, the personnel director addressed a similar
letter to Forrestal:

SECRET   November 8, 1945

[I recommend] that action upon the recommendation of
[Admiral King] that Captain Charles B. McVay, III, USN,
Commanding Officer of the USS *Indianapolis* at the time [she
sank], be brought to trial before a general court martial, be
withheld pending completion of the supplemental investigation now being conducted by the Inspector General of the
Navy.

Two days later, King supported Denfeld's proposed halt to
the proceedings by sending off his own note to Forrestal:

SECRET   November 10, 1945

In view of the information expected from the supplemental
investigation by the Inspector General of the Navy and its
possible relation to the evidence which may be expected in this
case, I concur in the recommendation of the Chief of Naval
Personnel that Captain Charles B. McVay, U.S. Navy, not be

brought to trial before a general court martial until the completion of the supplemental investigation.

This particular missive was written on Saturday morning, November 10. By the afternoon, however, someone, or something, got to Fleet Admiral King and he pencilled a short note to Admiral C. P. Snyder, the Naval Inspector General: "Comment on the feasibility of bringing C.O. *Indianapolis* to trial *now*."* By the time evening was closing over the nation's capital, King received Snyder's reply:

10 November, 1945

Memorandum for Fleet Admiral King:

1. With reference to your pencilled memorandum on my memorandum to you (attached hereto) regarding the progress of the *Indianapolis* case, preliminary talks with Captain McVay lead me to believe that he will introduce into our record when interrogated certain information in his interest which was not brought out by the Court of Inquiry. Further, Captain McVay feels that due to the exhaustive manner in which this office is conducting its investigation, additional facts favorable to his case may be developed. In so far as known to me, it is for this reason that Captain McVay desires that his trial be deferred until the record of my investigation has been submitted.

2. Should you desire to bring Captain McVay to trial before my investigation is completed it is, in my opinion, entirely feasible to do so. In this event, a resume of the case as completed to date could be prepared and submitted to the Bureau of Naval Personnel together with a list of witnesses still to be called in my investigation and a brief summary of the reason for calling them. These witnesses could then be called either by

---

*The emphasis is King's.

the prosecution or defense during the conduct of the court martial and the information which it is expected that they will give before my investigation could be developed at that time.

C. P. Snyder

Why would King, in a few hours, undergo a 180° turn in attitude? Was it because of the small but strong lobby of families insisting that responsibility had to be placed somewhere? Or was it that Admiral King, as a junior officer in the Asiatic Fleet, had served under McVay's father and been reprimanded by him? Could this possible old wound plus public pressure combine to make King change his mind and, in effect, put McVay on trial as a scapegoat?

James Forrestal walked into his office Monday morning, November 12, read King's memo of the tenth requesting a hold-up of the court martial while the NIG gathered all the data, and signed his approval.

Sometime during the day, Admiral King cornered Forrestal. We will never know what happened, but just hours after giving his concurrence to postponing the proceedings, Forrestal, too, changed his mind and ordered that McVay be immediately brought to trial. King, in his own hand, wrote the following memo that evening:

12 Nov 45

The Secretary directs that General
Court Martial of C.O. *Indianapolis*
be proceeded with at once—the
G.C.M. to comprise selected officers.

12.
Court-Martial

THE trial of Captain McVay was slated to begin on Monday, December 3, 1945. Four days before it was to begin, the Navy still did not know what charges to bring against him. On November 29, Rear Admiral O. S. Colclough, the Judge Advocate General, wrote a lengthy memo to Forrestal, outlining his predicament. He said that his office considered everything based upon the Court of Inquiry and up-dated NIG transcripts in their possession, including:

Failure to insure that the communication department was maintained in a proper condition of readiness for emergency transmission;

Failure to procure and read secret dispatch 290442 and take any action in regard thereto;

Failure to procure and read a secret dispatch addressed to all ships and stations on July 29, 1945;

Failure to keep a sufficient lookout for enemy submarines;

181

Failure to issue and cause to be
effected orders needed to maintain
watertight integrity;

Failure to issue and cause to be
effected orders needed to insure
proper distribution and use of
life belts;

Failure to release a sufficient
number of rafts and floater nets;

Failure to give proper attention to
the water breakers and other emergency
equipment on the life rafts.

But, the Judge Advocate General continued, unfortunately not one of the above contemplated charges could be proved—and, in fact, were disproved by the documents on hand.

Having to court-martial McVay for something, however, the JAG and Forrestal agreed that "failure to zigzag" could easily be proved, and, therefore, McVay was charged with that fault. But, if that were the only indictment, the travesty would be over before it began since the captain admitted he wasn't zigzagging. Alone, the charge was insufficient.

After burning the midnight oil, the JAG and Forrestal agreed to also charge McVay with failing to order Abandon Ship in time. The only problem with this is that they concurred that he did, in fact, order it in time and if ordered any earlier they would have had to fault him for giving up the ship prematurely.

Admiral Colclough explained to the secretary that the second charge "alleges a failure to issue timely orders to abandon ship. In order to support a finding of guilty it must appear that the accused did not use due care in deciding that more time was needed to ascertain the extent of the damage, after receiving a report about 12:10 A.M. that the vessel was badly damaged forward. The order to abandon ship was allegedly given about 12:12 A.M., and during this interval the accused was awaiting further information. It is noted that, almost immediately after the explosion occurred, the officer of the deck, on his own initiative, ordered all hands to come topside, but this was merely a preliminary order. The earlier issuance of orders to abandon ship prior to making an investigation, or at the time of the topside order, could have prompted disciplinary action (against Captain McVay)." So why the charge?

The JAG's reasoning, as related to Forrestal, was that "this specification is [still] recommended, however, on the ground that its use will permit Captain McVay to clear himself of criticisms made in the press." In addition, "A further ground for its use is that it will prevent any adverse remarks suggesting the impropriety of determining the sufficiency of the evidence by administrative action." Finally, "Full justification for ordering a trial on Charge II springs from the fact that this case is of vital interest not only to the families of those who lost their lives but also to the public at large."

"Justifications" for public relations purposes are, of course, inappropriate to a court-martial proceeding. Such proceedings must follow rigid rules. Any questions—or answers—not connected to specific charges will generally be omitted from the record. The charges relate to what happened aboard the ship prior to the torpedo attack and during the time she was going down. It therefore would be difficult to introduce testimony concerning any other subject which contributed to the loss of the *Indianapolis*. Furthermore, since the newspapers printed only what was furnished them by the Navy, there were essentially no criticisms made of Captain McVay in the press. Consequently, why would he have to clear himself—and of what?

It appears that the primary reason for the trumped-up second charge and the court-martial itself (since McVay could plead guilty to the first charge of not zigzagging and bring the trial to a halt before it began) was to placate the public. The American people were astonished at the number of fatalities, and demanded that they receive answers about the cause of this disaster and who was to blame. The Navy decided to point to Charles McVay as the culprit.

In closing his memorandum to Forrestal, the Judge Advocate General told the secretary that "it is, therefore, respectfully submitted that Charge II (failure to order Abandon Ship in time) should not be omitted, despite the fact that the evidence may be held insufficient."

The next order of business was to arrest Captain McVay:

29 Nov 1945

To: Commandant, Potomac River Naval Command.

Subject: McVay, Charles B., 3rd, Captain, U.S. Navy, trial of by general court-martial.

1. You will deliver the enclosed certified copy of the charge and specification to the subject-named officer, place him under arrest in conformity with article 44 of the Articles for the Government of the Navy, and direct him to report to Rear Admiral Wilder D. Baker, U.S. Navy, at the time designated for his trial before the general court martial of which that officer is president.

2. You will inform the accused that the limits of his arrest are hereby fixed as the area within a hundred-mile radius of

the place where the court is directed to meet, and that, in the event the court adjourns to some other place, the assigned limits of arrest will change accordingly.

Forrestal

Enclosed with this memo were the formal charges and specifications:

NAVY DEPARTMENT
WASHINGTON, D.C.

29 Nov 1945

To: Captain Thomas J. Ryan, Jr. U.S. Navy,
         Judge Advocate, General Court-Martial,
         Navy Yard, Washington, D.C.

Subject: Charges and specifications in case of
          Captain Charles B. McVay, 3rd, U.S. Navy

1. The above-named officer will be tried before the general court-martial of which you are judge advocate, upon the following charges and specifications. You will notify the president of the court accordingly, inform the accused of the date set for his trial, and summon all witnesses, both for the prosecution and the defense.

Charge I

*Through Negligence Suffering a Vessel of the
Navy to Be Hazarded*

Specification

In that Charles B. McVay, 3rd, captain, U.S. Navy, while so

serving in command of the U.S.S. *Indianapolis*, making passage singly, without escort, from Guam, Marianas Islands, to Leyte, Philippine Islands, through an area in which enemy submarines might be encountered, did, during good visibility after moonrise on 29 July 1945, at or about 10:30 P.M., minus nine and one-half zone time, neglect and fail to exercise proper care and attention to the safety of said vessel in that he neglected and failed, then and thereafter, to cause a zigzag course to be steered, and he, the said McVay, through said negligence, did suffer the said U.S.S. *Indianapolis* to be hazarded; the United States then being in a state of war.

Charge II

Culpable Inefficiency in the Performance of Duty

Specification

In that Charles B. McVay, 3rd, captain, U.S. Navy, while so serving in command of the U.S.S. *Indianapolis*, making passage from Guam, Marianas Islands, to Leyte, Philippine Islands, having been informed at or about 12:10 A.M., minus nine and one-half zone time, on 30 July 1945, that said vessel was badly damaged and in sinking condition, did then and there fail to issue and see effected such timely orders as were necessary to cause said vessel to be abandoned, as it was his duty to do by reason of which inefficiency many persons on board perished with the sinking of said vessel; the United States then being in a state of war.

James Forrestal

November 29 was a Thursday, and the accused had until Monday morning to prepare his defense.

A half world away, Captain Henri Smith-Hutton, USN, an intelligence officer stationed in Tokyo, received a message from Admiral King's office ordering him to find Hashimoto and have him in Washington before December 1st—he was to be a witness for the prosecution at the trial. Smith-Hutton immediately contacted Rear Admiral Nakamura of the Demilitarization Section of the Japanese Navy, and instructed him to have the submarine commander brought to Tokyo from his country home. Nakamura rushed to Smith-Hutton's office, considerably agitated, fearful that Hashimoto was to be tried as a war criminal and probably put to death. He was calmed down and guaranteed that the commander would be returned to Japan in good shape; he was simply going to be a witness against the captain of the ship he had sunk. Obviously in a state of shock, for this was unheard of in the history of the world, Admiral Nakamura promised to have Hashimoto in Tokyo within forty-eight hours.

A few days later, the commander reported, and transportation was arranged via Naval Air Transport Command, together with an escort. Just before leaving, Smith-Hutton gave the witness $100.00 to buy presents for his wife and children while in the United States.

About two weeks after the sinking, *The New York Times* editorialized on the demise of *Indianapolis*, saying, "Her loss just a month before the dawn of peace, with nearly nine hundred dead, marks one of the darkest pages of our Naval history." This certainly is true, but what was about to happen can also be included in this statement. Never before in U.S. Naval history had a captain of a combat ship been court-martialed for losing his vessel to enemy action. Yutaka Yakota, a former Kaiten pilot aboard the Japanese submarine I-36, said, "I-58 crewmen would have been amazed, when they sank this big enemy ship, if they had known it would give the commanding officer the strangest experience any naval officer ever had."

On Monday morning, December 3, 1945, in a third-floor ordnance classroom of the Washington Navy Yard, which was especially remodeled to accommodate the press and public, the participants in the trial of Captain Charles Butler McVay, III, Commanding Officer of the U.S.S. *Indianapolis*, assembled:

The seven members of the court were:

Rear Admiral Wilder D. Baker, President
Commodore Paul S. Theiss
Commodore William S. Popham
Captain Homer L. Grosskopf
Captain John R. Sullivan
Captain Charles B. Hunt
Captain Heman J. Redfield

The Judge Advocate was Captain Thomas J. Ryan, and McVay's counsel was Captain John P. Cady.

The Judge Advocate asked the accused if he was ready for trial, and McVay said no, stating that he did not feel he had been given sufficient time in which to prepare his defense. He had received the charges and specifications only a few days earlier, and he requested an adjournment until the next day, when he would be ready to proceed. This was granted, and on Tuesday, December 4, they began in earnest to destroy the naval career of Captain McVay.

In order to prepare the public for the shocking appearance of a Japanese Naval officer as a witness, the Navy issued the following statement:

NAVY DEPARTMENT

IMMEDIATE RELEASE
PRESS AND RADIO   DECEMBER 12, 1945

Memorandum to the Press

Commander Iko (also spelled Machitsura) [sic] Hashimoto of the Japanese Navy is scheduled to appear as a witness tomorrow in the General Court Martial of Captain Charles B. McVay, III, U.S.N., former commanding officer of the USS *Indianapolis.*

Commander Hashimoto, former commanding officer of the Japanese submarine I-58, was summoned from Japan by the Navy Department. He was unable to bring with him any official documents from the submarine because, he said, they had all been destroyed before the surrender of I-58 to United States forces at Sasebo about the middle of November.

Commander Hashimoto will be asked to take two oaths when he appears in court. The first oath will be the one usually taken by witnesses, as provided by Article 41, Articles of the Government of the Navy, with the word "affirm" substituted for the word "swear," and the words "This you do under pain and penalty of perjury" substituted for the words "So help me God."

The Japanese oath, administered in Japanese court martials, follows: "I swear to tell the truth, neither adding thereto nor concealing any matter whatsoever."

Commander Hashimoto had been in command of the I-58 from the time of her commissioning in September, 1944, until her surrender. He described the submarine as about 300 feet long, with maximum surface speed of 16 knots and maximum speed submerged about seven knots. The I-58's complement was 119 men and 11 officers.

The I-58 at first carried one aircraft but it was never used. Commander Hashimoto said the I-58 later discontinued carrying it.

The Japanese Commander said that his submarine was never under attack from surface craft, but was bombed by American planes at Kureiti in the middle of June, 1945. He said the bombs fell fairly close, but the submarine was not seriously damaged. He said that he never suffered personal injury at any time during the war.

Commander Hashimoto is 36 years old, married, with three children, all boys, ages six, four and two. His home is at Kure. The Commander was graduated from Eta Jima Naval Academy in 1931. He then served on a destroyer and a cruiser, and in the so-called China incident in 1937, saw service aboard a gunboat and minesweeper. In 1939, he went to a gunnery and torpedo school for three months, then entered the submarine service where he remained throughout the war.

The Commander, who does not speak English, had never been in the United States before. He described his visit as "pleasant."

On December 13, Hashimoto, wearing an ill-fitting blue-black suit and white shirt with the collar turned up, walked into the packed courtroom. Commander Hashimoto bowed low to his two American interpreters, Commander John R. Bromley and Francis R. Eastlake, a civilian, then turned and bowed again to Admiral Baker, the president of the court. Immediately, McVay's counsel objected.

Captain John Cady was angry. How could anyone, he asked the court, come up with the idea of bringing a Japanese officer into a United States Navy courtroom to testify against an American Naval captain. He pointed out that during the war, the Japanese, as a nation, were guilty of every despicable treachery, infamous cruelty, and barbarous practice one could imagine. He said that the American people were disgusted at this spectacle, and that our lawmakers could never have imagined, through centuries of Anglo-Saxon law, any such grotesque proceedings. Furthermore, Captain Cady told the court that the ability of the Japanese, as a race, to tell the truth was highly questionable and consequently, he asked, what good would it do to have him take an oath.

Captain Thomas Ryan, the Judge Advocate, deeply regretted Cady becoming so emotional. Ryan stated that Hashimoto was being called solely to explain to the court what caused the explosions that led to the sinking of the *Indianapolis*, and nothing else. He said that he had no intention of asking the witness any questions other than where he was at the time of the incident, what he saw, what he did, and how he did it. Concerning the pains to be suffered by Hashimoto if he perjured himself, Ryan countered by proposing that the submarine commander be given two oaths: the first oath administered according to U.S. law, and the Japanese oath, which would make him subject to punishment under Japanese law if he lied. In this manner, Ryan concluded, if Hashimoto didn't tell the truth, he could be punished both in the U.S. and in Japan.

Cady was not going to take this lying down, however, and requested that he be permitted to question Hashimoto on his *voir dire* prior to testifying, and the court concurred.

Commander Hashimoto took the stand and stated that he was a Shintoist and was fully aware of the difference between the truth and a lie. He further explained that if he did lie he would be punished, not in the hereafter but during the remainder of his life on earth. After death, there would be forgiveness.

When Cady was finished questioning Hashimoto, the court announced that they felt he understood the taking of an oath and was competent to testify as a witness at the trial.

A total of seventy-eight questions was asked of Hashimoto by prosecution and defense, and the only interesting thing to come out of it was that there was nothing interesting. It was simply a submarine commander's view of what he did technically in order to sink a ship. Actually, based upon his answers, there was no reason to have him there at all, since his testimony didn't relate to the charges. He couldn't possibly testify on the second charge of failure to abandon ship in time, and, as far as failure to zigzag, McVay admitted that. The whole thing was a sad affair. Possibly the only point to be made (and in McVay's favor) is that Hashimoto implied that even if the ship had been zigzagging, it would have gotten hit anyway.

Congresswoman Edith Rogers of Massachusetts was furious. Four days after Hashimoto gave his testimony, she took the floor of the House of Representatives and vented her anger at the U.S. Navy.

She told her colleagues that not only was she profoundly shocked over what the Navy had done in bringing Hashimoto to the U.S. to testify against McVay, but she was also very much alarmed. She said that no other country would have done this, and it was unprecedented in a military court of any nation. Mrs. Rogers pointed out that mothers of sons in the armed forces were very much concerned over the establishment of this precedent, for if their sons got into some difficulty it was now quite possible for a Japanese, or Nazi, to be brought in to testify against them. Hashimoto's presence, she told Congress, was an outrage against justice and something better be done about it.

She next introduced a Concurring Resolution calling Commander Hashimoto's testimony incompetent and therefore, lest the ends of justice be prejudiced, demanding that his testimony be stricken from the records of the Court.

Rogers ended by stating that Japan was a barbarous and inhuman country and that the citizens of the United States would not stand for one of their officers being convicted on the testimony of an enemy alien. If something wasn't done at once, the entire country would rise up in protest against such a proceeding.

The Concurring Resolution was not acted on by the House or Senate, and the testimony of Lieutenant Commander Hashimoto remains, to this day, in the record of Captain McVay's court martial.

On December 19, 1945, after thirteen working days, thirty-nine witnesses for the prosecution and eighteen for the defense, the court-martial of Charles McVay was over. During the morning, both sides made closing arguments and then the members retired to deliberate.

Two and a half hours later, the Judge Advocate was called into the deliberating room and directed to record the following findings:

> The specification of the first charge (i.e.,
> failure to zigzag) proved.
> And that the accused, Charles B. McVay, 3rd,
> Captain, U.S. Navy, is of the first charge
> guilty.
> The specification of the second charge not
> proved.
> And that the accused, Charles B. McVay, 3rd,
> Captain, U.S. Navy, is of the second charge,
> not guilty; and the court does therefore
> acquit the said Charles B. McVay, 3rd,
> Captain, U.S. Navy, of the second charge.

Back in open court, both parties had no further evidence to

offer and the jury retired once again. Shortly thereafter, Captain Ryan was called in again and ordered to record the sentence of the court:

> The court, therefore, sentences him, Charles
> B. McVay, 3rd, Captain, U.S. Navy, to lose
> one hundred (100) numbers in his temporary
> grade of Captain and to lose one hundred (100)
> numbers in his permanent grade of Commander.

The future naval career of Captain McVay was ruined.

The findings and punishment of the court had to be reviewed and approved by higher authority, i.e., King and Forrestal, and, in closing, all the members, who were performing a very unpleasant duty and probably would have given their right arms to be a thousand miles away, signed the following statement:

> In consideration of the outstanding previous
> record of the accused and our belief that no
> other Commanding Officer who lost his ship
> as a result of enemy action has been subjected
> to a court martial, we strongly recommend
> Charles B. McVay, 3rd, Captain, U.S. Navy,
> to the clemency of the reviewing authority.

After that, "The court, having no more cases before it, adjourned to await the action of the convening authority."

As noted, the court-martial concentrated solely on two points: did McVay zigzag, and did he order Abandon Ship in time. By law, all questions and answers during the trial had to relate to the charges, and any other subject brought up was objected to and the objection sustained. Therefore, through the trial proceedings alone, the entire picture of what happened to the *Indianapolis* could not possibly be drawn for the public. On the other hand, the court of inquiry and, more importantly, the Naval inspector general were not constrained by rigid rules of procedure and the transcripts of their investigations piece together all the components of the disaster. Unfortunately, the inquiry and NIG investigations were labeled "Secret" and kept from the American people for over thirty years. Therefore, the families of those killed on the *Indianapolis*, together with the press and public at large, knew only what the Navy wanted them to know, which was essentially what they learned from the trial of Captain McVay. Zigzagging or not zigzagging, however, cannot be included as one of the reasons for the cruiser going down nor for the death of 880 men.

Still, during the trial, a strange thing took place. Although McVay admitted that he stopped zigzagging at dusk, an in-depth probe at the trial as to why he stopped (aside from his discretionary power to do so) never was made by Captain Cady, his defense counsel. McVay's lawyer never brought out the fact that he sailed a straight line because he was never informed of Japanese submarines on offensive missions along his route. And Cady had a perfect opportunity to do so when Captain Oliver Naquin was called to the stand.*

Defense Counsel:
Q. What is your estimate of the risk of enemy submarine activity at that time, at the end of July, along the route the *Indianapolis* was to proceed?

*Recall that Naquin knew of the submarines through "Ultra Secret" information, but never passed this data down to Lieutenant Waldron at the routing office in Guam.

Captain Oliver Naquin, Surface Operations Officer, Commander, Marianas:

A. I would say it was a low order.

Q. I am sorry; I didn't understand.

A. I would say it was a very low order.

Q. That means your estimate was of a low order?

A. My estimate is that the risk was very slight.

But, just a few days *before,* locked up in a room with the inspector general, Naquin gave an entirely different picture:

Secret

Naval Inspector General:

Q. Were you informed that four enemy submarines were, during the month of July, operating on offensive missions in the general area of the Western Pacific, bounded by Guam, Palua [sic], the Philippines, and the Southern Islands of the Japanese Group?

Captain Oliver Naquin:

A. Yes, I had such information.

Q. While there was only one sinking [*Underhill*], you know there were four submarines operating in the area; is that more submarines than normally operating in there, or less, or approximately the same number?

A. I would say that would be more than average.

Captain Cady asked Naquin only twenty-two questions, which took about ten minutes, then let him go. Captain Naquin did not relate to the members of the court everything he knew, and it appears that Captain Cady did not sweat this crucial information from him.*

---

*According to the documents in the author's possession, Captain McVay and his counsel, Captain Cady, were furnished with the court of inquiry transcript and, more importantly, with a transcript of the Naval Inspector General's investigation to date, to aid in the preparation of the defense.

A second opportunity was presented to Cady when Captain Alfred Granum, operations officer at the Philippine Sea Frontier, was called. About a month prior to this officer taking the stand at McVay's trial, he, too, was interrogated by the NIG. During the questioning, he admitted that he was aware of the sinking of *Underhill* and knew of enemy submarines along the Leyte/Okinawa route and Guam/Okinawa route. Furthermore, Granum's immediate superior and close associate, Commodore Norman Gillette, acting commander of the Philippine Sea Frontier, admitted to the NIG on December 12, 1945, that there was an increase in submarine activity in the Western Pacific in late July, 1945, and that he and his senior officers, were concerned about it. In fact, Gillette told the NIG that he was "unusually concerned" and "especially concerned with the submarine menace at that time."

On December 17, only five days after Gillette pronounced to the NIG his Frontier's concern over submarine activity, Captain Granum was called to the stand by McVay's counsel. Eleven questions were asked of him, the main one being: "Was there any enemy activity at that time within the Philippine Sea Frontier which caused you to have any concern over vessels which might be approaching from Guam?" This senior staff officer for the Frontier simply replied, "No more than a normal hazard that could be expected in wartime."

Why didn't Cady force the whole truth out of Naquin and Granum? Was Naquin not to divulge "Ultra Secret" information in open court? Why didn't Cady ask either officer about *Underhill* and the circumstances surrounding her sinking? The worthless intelligence report attached to McVay's routing instructions wasn't shown to Naquin nor was he questioned about its accuracy. Why not? Why wasn't Captain Naquin's or Captain Granum's testimony used to prove that the *Indianapolis* was sailing into extremely dangerous waters, while neither her captain nor her crew was made privy to this vital data prior to leaving Guam? Every day the trial of Captain McVay was reported in the nation's newspapers. Would someone in a very high position verbally have passed an order down to the court that no participants in the case were to divulge ultra secret information?

Captain Cady had a sworn responsibility to defend McVay to the best of his ability. He was, however, inexperienced,* which could account for his letting an opportunity to vindicate his client slip from his fingers after twenty-two (Naquin) and eleven (Granum) questions. Furthermore, Naquin and Granum obviously were not the only officers who knew of the four dangerous submarines on the prowl, and any number of others could have been called to the stand to give this fundamental testimony, but they weren't.

It would seem that the Navy preferred that the public not know the entire truth about their greatest sea disaster ever. The cover-up could be said to have begun with McVay's trial, and this blanket of silence was given the highest blessing on February 23, 1946. On that date, there was issued to the press and radio a nine-page report entitled "Narrative of the Circumstances of the Loss of the USS *Indianapolis.*" This was the Navy's final word on the sinking. Generally, everything in the "Narrative" is true. The problem with the document is not what it contains but what it does not.

Vice Admiral Forrest Sherman was the author of the "Narrative," and on February 20, three days prior to publication, he submitted the final draft to his superiors for approval. What he wrote and what was printed, however, are two different things. Words were changed, sentences deleted, and paragraphs omitted. One of the most startling cuts is the

---

*Graduated from Annapolis in 1922, and he received his law degree from George Washington University in 1932, but as a line officer he had had little or no trial experience.

following paragraph which was in the draft but cut from the final "Narrative":

> Secret intelligence had been received in the Headquarters of the Commander in Chief, United States Fleet and in the Headquarters of the Commander in Chief, Pacific Fleet that there was considerable Japanese submarine activity to the westward of Guam in the Philippine Sea, in June and July, 1945. There were indications that at least four Japanese submarines were reported operating at sea on offensive missions. This specific information, however, although known to Captain Naquin, the Operations Officer on the staff of Commander Marianas, did not reach the Operations Officer or the Routing Officer at the Naval Operating Base, Guam. For this failure, Captain Naquin has been held responsible.

The lid was on. It was hoped that it never would be removed.

On the third day of January, 1946, the Judge Advocate General of the Navy gave his official sanction to the court martial:

> The proceedings, findings, and sentence of the general court-martial in the foregoing case of Captain Charles B. McVay, 3rd, U.S. Navy, are, in the opinion of this office, legal.
>
> Referred to the Chief of Naval Personnel for comment as to disciplinary features.

Next, Vice Admiral Denfeld put the ball in Forrestal's lap:

> 1. Forwarded, recommending approval of the proceedings and findings in the attached general court-martial case of Captain Charles B. McVay, 3rd, U.S.N.

2. In view of his excellent war record and the unanimous recommendation for clemency by the members of the court, it is recommended that the sentence be remitted and that Captain McVay be restored to duty.

The secretary, however, wasn't that quick to furnish his stamp of approval and went back to Admiral King, the man who started the action.

The next day, King replied to Forrestal:

1. The record of proceedings of the subject General Court-Martial is returned herewith.

2. I concur in the recommendation of the Chief of Naval Personnel that the sentence awarded Captain McVay be remitted on the ground of his excellent record and the unanimous recommendation to clemency made by the members of the Court.

Finally, the dean of the Navy Department closed the case:

The record of proceedings in the foregoing court-martial case of Captain Charles B. McVay, 3rd, U.S. Navy shows that he was acquitted of (II) Culpable Inefficiency in the Performance of Duty, and convicted of (I) Through Negligence Suffering a Vessel of the Navy to be Hazarded. He was sentenced to lose one hundred (100) numbers in his temporary grade of Captain and to lose one hundred (100) numbers in his permanent grade of Commander.

The proceedings, findings and sentences are approved. In view, however, of the recommendations of the Chief of Naval Personnel and Fleet Admiral E. J. King, based upon the outstanding record of Captain McVay, which clearly evidences his long and honorable service, performance of duty of the highest order including combat service in World War II,

numerous commendations, and the award of the Expeditionary China Service, Silver Star and Purple Heart Medals, and
further, in view of the unanimous recommendation to clemency signed by all the members of the court, the sentence is
remitted in its entirety.

Captain McVay will be released from arrest and restored to
duty.

James Forrestal
Secretary of the Navy

After six months of putting McVay through hell and of
going through the vast expense of a general court-martial
(conceived and instigated by the Chief of Naval Operations
and Secretary of the Navy), King and Forrestal essentially
said, "Now let's forget about the whole thing."

On February 23, 1946, the new chief of Naval operations,
Chester Nimitz, scheduled a news conference that was to be
the final word on the disaster. The meeting with reporters
was to have three purposes:
1) Nimitz was to answer any general questions the press
   might have.
2) Distribution of the "Report on Court-Martial of Captain
   Charles B. McVay, III, U.S.N., Commanding Officer, USS
   Indianapolis."
3) Distribution of the nine page "Narrative of the Circumstances of the Loss of the USS *Indianapolis*."
The newsmen entered the Navy Building on Constitution
Avenue, jammed into Nimitz's office, and were immediately
handed two releases, one being the "Narrative," the other the
"Report of Court-Martial." Nimitz then read what he termed
a "typical" letter received by him from a family of one of the
men who died on the cruiser:

Dear Sir:

We have searched the press and other publications diligently for acknowledgment, by you, for your part in the mistake and inefficiency connected with the sinking of the USS *Indianapolis*. To date [2/6/46] we have seen nothing. . . . We hold the Navy responsible for the loss of our son, which they refuse, so far, to do. When does the Admiral and officers at Guam and Leyte go on trial, or is this being whitewashed?

E. Connelly
Burlingame, Calif.

The admiral "profoundly" shared Mr. Connelly's sorrow and said, "As Commander in Chief of the Pacific Fleet and Pacific Ocean Areas, I carried the broad responsibility for all operations of the Pacific Fleet in the areas under my command. This included, of course, responsibility for both successes and failures. To the extent that a commander in chief should be held responsible for failures or errors of judgment on the part of subordinates, I must bear my share of responsibility for the loss of *Indianapolis*."

In closing, Nimitz made a dishonest statement: "There is no thought of exonerating anyone in the Navy who should be punished for his performance of duty in connection with the sinking of the *Indianapolis* and the attending loss of life." Furthermore, "We have no desire or intention to deny any of our mistakes."

The "Narrative" distributed at Nimitz's press conference had, of course, been significantly altered. As reported earlier, the entire paragraph concerning the fleet's knowledge of enemy submarine activity in the Western Pacific and the fact that it was not being funneled down to the people who needed it was censored from the final draft. The following paragraph was also cut from Sherman's original draft:

On 27 July, Captain C. B. McVay III, USN, Commanding Officer of the *Indianapolis*, visited the Advance Headquarters of the Commander in Chief, Pacific Fleet and discussed general matters connected with his voyage to Leyte. He was, at this time, given no information regarding enemy activity to the westward of Guam and was informed that he would be routed by the Port Director, Guam. At the Office of the Port Director, Guam, he discussed with an officer from the routing office, details of his routing and of limited enemy activity in the area through which he was routed. He was not informed of the presence of the four Japanese submarines to the westward.

Obviously, the Navy did not want the public to know that they had failed to inform McVay of submarines for this information would have created an indefensible scandal.

Commodore Norman C. Gillette, acting commander of the Philippine Sea Frontier and his operations officer, Captain Alfred Granum, both received Letters of Reprimand in connection with the delay in reporting the missing ship. In addition, Lieutenant Gibson of the Leyte Port Director's Office received a Letter of Reprimand while his superior, Lieutenant Commander Sancho, received a less severe Letter of Admonition. Within a short period of time, however, all four letters were withdrawn by Forrestal, and the records of these officers at Frontier Headquarters were wiped clean. In the end, no other officers in the Navy were censured for their role in the tragedy and only Captain McVay continued to live with the stigma. In the eye of the general public, he was held responsible for the sinking of the U.S.S. *Indianapolis*.

Epilogue

A very warm and special thank you must be paid to Florence Regosia (Captain McVay's housekeeper) and Al Dudley (his gardener) for sharing with us their sad reflections of a cold November day on a farm in Litchfield, Connecticut.

After the trial and cover-up, a defeated McVay was assigned to duty as chief of staff and aide to the Commandant, Eighth Naval District and Commander of the Gulf Sea Frontier, in New Orleans. For three years he marked time in this limbo and then was transferred to the retired list of the Navy on June 30, 1949, with the rank of Rear Admiral, on the basis of combat citations. Eventually he retired to Litchfield, Connecticut.

If you ask his friends about him, you hear contradictions. They say he was a fun-loving person, frequently joking, a lovely man, a perfect gentleman. But they also say he seemed to have things bottled up in him. He never forgot the boys who went down with the ship or died in the water. Every Christmas he was swamped with cards from many of the survivors.

It was said that Captain McVay confided to his close friends that he didn't understand why the young, good ones went down with the ship. He wished he had, too. Every night before retiring McVay would kneel next to his bed and plead with God to keep the boys in His safekeeping.

On November 6, 1968, the Admiral helped his gardener, Al Dudley, place rough burlap over the shrubs and plants on his property; they had to be kept alive for the following spring. The left-over burlap was then fastened to the storm fences that would prevent the coming snows from drifting toward the house.

At lunchtime Al Dudley went home as usual. McVay's housekeeper, Florence Regosia, laid out a bowl of soup and a sandwich on the dining room table. Mrs. McVay was busy in the back part of the house.

A few minutes later, Florence Regosia returned to see whether the captain was eating and found him standing in the doorway in his khaki gardening clothes. He never ate lunch in his work clothes, for it was his habit to go to play bridge at his club in Litchfield after lunch each day.

"Aren't you coming in to eat your lunch?" she asked.

"Oh yes, Florence," he replied.

She left the room, but she was bothered by the flushed look in his face and the way his eyes seemed glazed.

Meanwhile, Al Dudley, who was not only McVay's gardener but his friend, had a strange intuition that caused him to cut short his lunch and run back to McVay's house.

Florence checked back into the dining room to see whether the admiral wanted dessert. The food was untouched. She ran up the stairs to find him. In his bedroom she saw an empty holster on the night table. She ran back down the stairs, checked the garage—the car was still there. Florence put on her coat to find the admiral, when suddenly someone was making a commotion at the back door, and she found Al Dudley there.

"I'm just going to look for the admiral," she said.

But Al stopped her, begged her not to go out, for he had found McVay on the front lawn, his Labrador beside him. His left hand gripped a blue toy soldier, his right the .38 that had sent a bullet through his head from right to left.

The 881st casualty of the U.S.S. *Indianapolis* was accounted for.

Appendices

Appendix A
Orders to the U.S.S. Indianapolis from the Commander in Chief, Pacific Fleet

DATE: 26 July 1945
FROM: CinCPac Adv Hq
TO: *Indianapolis*

Upon completion unloading Tinian report to Port Director for routing to Guam where disembark Com 5th Fleet personnel X Completion report to PD Guam for onward routing to Leyte where on arrival report CTF 95 by dispatch for duty X CTG 95.7 directed arrange 10 days training for *Indianapolis* in Leyte area

Appendix B
Routing Instructions to the U.S.S. Indianapolis

PDG 1849   OFFICE OF THE
                      PORT DIRECTOR   28 July 1945

From: Port Director, Guam
To: Commanding Officer, USS *Indianapolis* (CA 35)

Subj: Routing Instructions

Encl: (A) Intelligence Report
       (B) Approach Instructions
       (C) Flight Briefing Bulletin

Encl. B

1. When in all respects ready for sea on or about 0900 King, 28 July, depart Apra Harbor, proceed Leyte via the following route positions:

Code Letter	Latitude	Longitude
MNG	13-35 N	144-00 E
BWV	13-14	143-00
CFL	12-30	138-00
DCM	11-44	132-30
EHO	11-06	128-05
PG	10-37	126-00
HN	10-41.5	125-40

Thence Leyte as directed by branch Port Director's Office on Homonhon Island.

2. Speed of advance shall be 15.7 knots. Distance to position PG 1123 miles. ETA 0800 I, 31 July. Distance Guam to ETA point (10-54 N, 125-20 E) is 1171 miles. ETA 1100 I, 31 July.
3. Friendly submarines may be observed west and south of Guam in established haven and training areas; they will be escorted by surface vessels. Your route takes you clear of these areas.
4. See Intelligence Reports (Enclosures A and C) for information of our own and enemy forces.
5. Crossing and joining traffic may be encountered in the following areas:

(a) Apra to 142-30 E   (c) 134-30 E to 131-00 E
(b) 138-30 E to 137-30 E   (d) 127-00 E to destination

6. Commanding Officers are at all times responsible for the safe navigation of their ships. They may depart from prescribed routing when, in their judgment, weather, currents, or other navigational hazards jeopardize the safety of the ship. They will return to the prescribed route as soon as safety permits. Zigzag at discretion of the Commanding Officer.
7. A Fleet Unit Commander, while carrying out a movement, is authorized to originate supplementary messages when the mil-

itary situation permits. These messages shall contain information of:

(a) Breakdown
(b) Changes in orders or corrections of erroneous information
(c) Weather conditions or any circumstances which cause a deviation from schedule of more than 40 miles in controlled waters or a delay in ETA of over (3) hours

   The messages shall be addressed (if approaching Philippine Islands) to Commander Philippine Sea Frontier.
8. Communications shall be conducted in accordance PAC 70 (B).
9. Port Director Guam will make your departure report including "Queen messages: QP 32, QPF 31, QPH 119, QN 5, QNA 37, QNH 35" held by you.
10. On arrival destroy these instructions; carry out basic orders incorporated in CinCPacAdvon 260152.

Encl. A

Operational Intelligence Section NOB, Guam, M.I.   Eix

Intelligence Brief for GUAM to PHILIPPINES
(This brief is a part of your secret routing instructions and merchant ships must turn in with same at next port of call.)

FOR _____ Date 27 July 1945.

The enemy bases within approximately 300 miles of your route are as listed below. No enemy offensive activity from any of these bases has been reported in recent months unless specifically mentioned under this heading:

ROTA	14-09	N	144-37	E
WOLEAI	07-21	N	143-53	E
SOROL	08-08	N	140-23	E
YAP	09-31	N	138-08	E
BABELTHAUP	07-30	N	134-34	E

Enemy Submarine Contacts:
22 July — Sub sighted surfaced at 10-34 N - 132-47 E at 0015K.
Hunter-killer ordered.
25 July — Unknown ship reports sighting a possible periscope at
13-56 N - 136-56 E.
25 July — Sound contact reported at 10-30 N - 136-25 E. Indications at that time pointed to doubtful submarine.

Enemy Surface Contacts:
None.

Friendly Ship Movements:
It is impracticable to attempt to enumerate all the ship movements
which might pass within visual range of your route, however, the
positions at which your route crosses or approaches regular shipping lanes is indicated in your routing instructions.

General Information:
1. Friendly submarines are operating south and west of Guam
and possibly in the vicinity of Ulithi. They should be escorted
at all times when in the vicinity of these islands.
2. Several instances of floating mines have been reported in the
Forward Area recently. A sharp lookout should be kept and a
report made if any sighted.
3. Firing Notice—Guam:
(a) There will be sleeve and drone AA firing practice from
Agat between 1000-1500, danger area 12,000 yards to sea-
ward, 235-305 degrees from Agat.
(b) Until further notice, the area in the vicinity of Santa Rosa
Reef, SW of Guam, as well as balance of area A-8, will be
used as AA ships gunnery area.
4. Menace to Navigation:
PCE 898 sighted large floating palm stump with three feet
above water at 260945Z in position 14-53 N - 132-48 E.

Appendix C
Simplified Organizational Chart on Reporting Responsibilities of Key Officers Mentioned in the Text

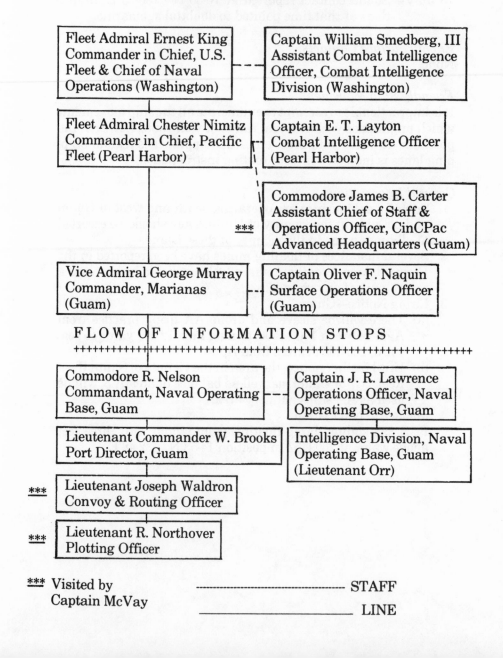

Fleet Admiral Ernest King
Commander in Chief, U.S.
Fleet & Chief of Naval
Operations (Washington)

Captain William Smedberg, III
Assistant Combat Intelligence
Officer, Combat Intelligence
Division (Washington)

Fleet Admiral Chester Nimitz
Commander in Chief, Pacific
Fleet (Pearl Harbor)

Captain E. T. Layton
Combat Intelligence Officer
(Pearl Harbor)

Commodore James B. Carter
Assistant Chief of Staff &
Operations Officer, CinCPac
Advanced Headquarters (Guam)

***

Vice Admiral George Murray
Commander, Marianas
(Guam)

Captain Oliver F. Naquin
Surface Operations Officer
(Guam)

FLOW OF INFORMATION STOPS
+++

Commodore R. Nelson
Commandant, Naval Operating
Base, Guam

Captain J. R. Lawrence
Operations Officer, Naval
Operating Base, Guam

Lieutenant Commander W. Brooks
Port Director, Guam

Intelligence Division, Naval
Operating Base, Guam
(Lieutenant Orr)

***

Lieutenant Joseph Waldron
Convoy & Routing Officer

***

Lieutenant R. Northover
Plotting Officer

*** Visited by
Captain McVay

-------------------------------------- STAFF

_____ LINE

Appendix D
Waldron's Dispatch Notifying Various Commands of the Sailing of the U.S.S. Indianapolis

DISPATCH NUMBER 280032

SECRET
PRIORITY

From: PD Guam
USS *Indianapolis* (CA-35) departed Guam
2300Z (GCT) 27 July X SOA 15.7 knots X
Route Peddie thence Leyte X ETA Position
PC 2300Z (GCT) 30 July ETA Leyte 0200Z
31 July X Chop 30 July X
QP 32 OPH 119 X QN 5 QNA 37 ONH 35 X
USS *Indianapolis* guards NPM Fox

Appendix E
Simplified Organization Chart
of Philippine Sea Frontier

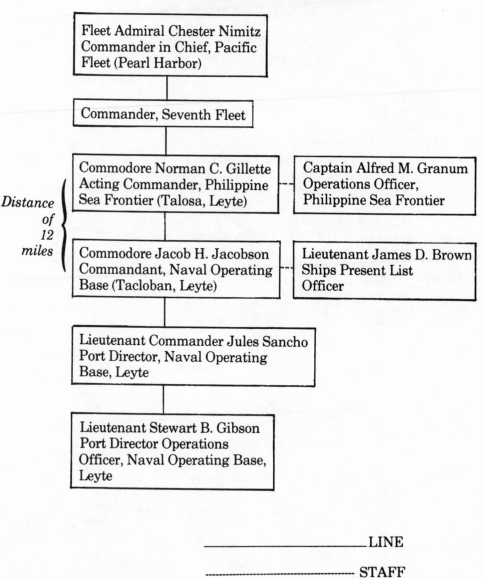

Fleet Admiral Chester Nimitz
Commander in Chief, Pacific
Fleet (Pearl Harbor)

Commander, Seventh Fleet

Commodore Norman C. Gillette
Acting Commander, Philippine
Sea Frontier (Talosa, Leyte)

Captain Alfred M. Granum
Operations Officer,
Philippine Sea Frontier

Commodore Jacob H. Jacobson
Commandant, Naval Operating
Base (Tacloban, Leyte)

Lieutenant James D. Brown
Ships Present List
Officer

Lieutenant Commander Jules Sancho
Port Director, Naval Operating
Base, Leyte

Lieutenant Stewart B. Gibson
Port Director Operations
Officer, Naval Operating Base,
Leyte

*Distance
of
12
miles*

_____LINE

-------------------------------------- STAFF

Appendix F
Original of Exhibit Offered and Received in Evidence in Case in Chief at Trial of Charles B. McVay, III, Captain, U.S. Navy

I swear to tell the truth,
neither adding thereto nor
concealing any matter whatsoever.

眞實を述べ何事をも默祕せず
又何事をも附加せざる事を誓ふ

橋本以行

Appendix G
Testimony of Commander Hashimoto
at the Court-Martial of Captain McVay
on December 13, 1945 (CM, pp. 266-76)

1. Q. State your name, rank, and present duty.
   A.* Hashimoto, Mochitsura—in Japanese they put the family name first—commander, in His Imperial Japanese Majesty's Navy, Reserve; at the present, here at the disposition of this court.

2. Q. How long have you been a commander?
   A. I have been a commander since—since September ninth of this year—since September sixth—correction, please; since September sixth of this year.

3. Q. Have you received any threats or promises of any kind which might tend to influence you to give any particular kind of testimony?
   A. I have received neither threats nor promises to put any— to try to influence me to bear witness one way or the other.

4. Q. Do you fully understand the implications of the oaths which you have taken?
   A. I fully understand.

5. Q. What duties were you performing in the Japanese Navy during the night of 29-30 July, 1945?
   A. The duty as ordered.

6. Q. What duty was this?
   A. Serving as captain of submarine I-58.

7. Q. Will you repeat the number of that submarine, please?
   A. I-58.

8. Q. What zone time was your ship keeping during the night of 29-30 July, 1945?
   A. Minus nine.

*All answers are "As given by interpreter Eastlake [or] Commander Bromley."

9. Q. In what position was your ship at or about 2305 on that evening?

   A. In position bearing 355 degrees from Palau, distance 290 miles.

10. Q. Plot that position on the chart you see there, Exhibit 2.

At this point the accused requested that the witness plot the position last above referred to on a different chart than "Exhibit 2."

The judge advocate stated that he was agreeable to this procedure, and he produced another chart.

The witness plotted the position last above referred to on a chart marked "Exhibit 9 for identification."

11. Q. What is that position as charted in latitude and longitude?

    A. This position is 12 degrees 31 minutes north; 134 degrees 16 minutes east longitude. The witness qualified this statement; it is approximate.

12. Q. If anything happened at or about 2305 zone minus nine time on the evening in question, that was of particular interest to you, tell the court what it was—to you, Commander Hashimoto—anything which happened that was of peculiar interest to you, tell the court what it was.

    A. On the supposition that at the time the visibility would have improved and the moon would be out, he brought his submarine to the surface. Thereupon, under the moon, he discerned a dark object and crash-dived immediately, and then swung his ship around to head in its direction.

13. Q. At the time he saw this dark object, did he make any estimate of the range of that dark object?

    A. At that time he estimated the range as being in the vicinity of ten thousand meters.

14. Q. And what—from his knowledge now—was the position of his ship relative to the dark object at that time?

    A. His position was established still, roughly, at ten thousand meters, bearing ninety degrees from true—with the target bearing ninety degrees true.

At this point the accused objected to the last question on the ground that the judge advocate was putting words into the witness's mouth.

The question was repeated.

The judge advocate replied, stating that he would rephrase the question.

15. Q.   Then what did you do after sighting this dark object?
    A.   He submerged and headed towards the object and prepared to fire torpedoes and launch Kaitens.

16. Q.   And then what did you do?
    A.   He then proceeded with further observation of the target.

17. Q.   How long after sighting the target did it take you to arrive at the estimate of course and speed of the target?
    A.   It took about ten minutes to swing around and steady on a course heading for the target, and at the end of that time he was, roughly—he had roughly made up his mind as to the target's course and speed.

18. Q.   And what was that?
    A.   Speed, 12 knots; course, 260.

19. Q.   Between the time you sighted the target and when you arrived at this estimate, describe, in general terms, whether your ship was approaching the target, going away from the target, or circling?
    A.   Generally speaking, the submarine was approaching the target.

20. Q.   And what speed, average speed, over this period was he making?
    A.   An average speed of about three knots.

21. Q.   You have said that you took about ten minutes to arrive at an estimate of the target's course and speed; then what did you do?
    A.   He completed preparation for firing torpedoes; he set up the problem on his director; that is, he put in the estimates and then awaited the proper time to fire.

22. Q.   Then what did you do?

A. It became apparent that the target was approaching off of his starboard bow, so he swung his ship to starboard, and when the ship had approached within a distance of 1500—1500 meters, he fired his torpedoes.

23. Q. Proceed.
   A. After firing, he put up his periscope and saw his torpedoes make three hits in the forward part of the ship between the bridge and bow. Thereafter he heard an explosion from what he took to be a fourth torpedo hit, and saw a cloud of water aft of the ship's bridge. Thereafter he swung his ship further to the right, and—he had bounced up when he fired his torpedoes, and at the same time lowered his periscope. At that time he heard—a total of ten explosions, of which several were louder than the rest.

24. Q. How do you know you scored three hits on the target?
   A. One of the three torpedo hits scored in the forward part of the ship, the center hit produced a flame which revealed three columns of water, a center column and one on either side.

25. Q. What kind of torpedoes did you fire?
   A. Type-95 torpedoes, propelled by oxygen.

26. Q. What kind of warheads were on these torpedoes?
   A. Five warheads were magnetic; one, inertia type.

27. Q. Did you fire these torpedoes independently, or did you use a spread?
   A. The torpedoes were fired with a spread of three degrees and at intervals of three seconds.

28. Q. What do you mean by a "spread of three degrees"?
   A. By a "spread of three degrees" is meant that there were— an angle of three degrees between each of the torpedoes fired, with the exception that—to be strictly accurate, between the two center torpedoes there was an angle of two degrees.

29. Q. How long after sighting this target did you fire this salvo?
   A. About twenty-seven minutes.

30. Q.   On which side of the target did your torpedoes hit?
    A.   They struck on the starboard side.

31. Q.   Did these torpedoes which you fired leave a wake which could be seen at night?
    A.   No.

32. Q.   In what part of your ship were these torpedoes before you fired them?
    A.   In the bow.

33. Q.   Why did you not use Kaitens?
    A.   Kaitens weren't used, first, because he was delayed in determining the type of target; secondly, because it was night; and, thirdly, because torpedoes were considered to be sufficient.

34. Q.   Can you draw from your memory a rough sketch showing the relative positions of the target and your ship from the time of sighting until you fired the torpedoes?
    A.   Yes, roughly.

35. Q.   Do so, and indicate thereon your position relative to the target at the time of sighting and at the time of firing.

The witness drew a rough sketch as requested.

36. Q.   Did you recognize the type of ship which was your target?
    A.   At the time when the target had approached to a distance of about three thousand yards, and at which time the foremast and main mast had separated, he recognized it as a ship of ten-thousand-ton cruiser class or bigger.

37. Q.   Did you make any further studies in relation to the type of ship which was your target?
    A.   Subsequent to the time that he fired the torpedoes, he looked into a book of silhouettes for the ship that he saw at the time of firing.

38. Q.   How did you know that this target was not a Japanese ship?
    A.   At the time the submarine left Kure, there were no Japanese vessels navigating in this area. The arrangements were made to be advised by wireless if subsequent

to the time of departure friendly vessels should navigate in this area, and as he had no advice by wireless, he knew in this instance that it wasn't a Japanese vessel.

39. Q. Did you take any prisoners from this ship you testified you torpedoed?
    A. He took no prisoners.

Cross-examined by the accused:

40. Q. Where did you depart from on this patrol?
    A. He got under way from Kure and proceeded to a base called Hirao, loaded Kaitens, and then took departure.

41. Q. When did you depart from that latter point?
    A. He departed from Hirao on the 20th of July.

42. Q. Can you trace on this chart your approximate course from then until the place that you last testified to?
    A. He can.

43. Q. Will you please do that, and will you please identify the locations by dates on there as you are able to?

The witness traced, on the chart marked "Exhibit 9 for identification," the approximate course last above referred to.

44. Q. I would like to ask you how you know and how you can remember this abrupt break, this break, in your course at the point marked "7/28"?
    A. This point represents the intersection of a line joining the approach to Leyte Gulf and Guam and another line from Okinawa to Ulithi. At this point he attacked a tanker with Kaitens. He withdrew from this point slightly to the north, and then proceeded—started to proceed to another point, the intersection of the line from Palau—the intersection of the line connecting Palau and Okinawa and the line connecting Leyte Gulf and Guam. En route, because of poor visibility, he submerged, which takes us to the point indicated on the chart.

45. Q. What can you testify as to the success of the attack that you reported with Kaitens on the 28th, I think?
    A. He cannot confirm success of that particular attack.

46. Q.   Did you report this attack?
    A.   He did not report it immediately, but reported it later.

47. Q.   What was your average speed on this track that you have shown, surface and submerged?

This question was objected to by the judge advocate on the ground that it was a double question.

The accused [Captain Cady] replied, stating that he would reframe the question.

48. Q.   Please testify as to your average surface speed on this track.
    A.   About twelve knots.

49. Q.   What was your maximum speed on the surface?
    A.   In the condition of his ship at that time, fifteen knots.

50. Q.   What was your best submerged speed?
    A.   Between two and a half and three knots.

51. Q.   His best submerged speed; his highest speed?
    A.   His highest speed, seven knots; highest submerged speed, seven knots.

52. Q.   Did you have any radar on your submarine?
    A.   Yes.

53. Q.   What was its effective range?
    A.   The effectiveness of the radar with regard to surface vessels depended upon the visibility of the vessel in question. However, for a vessel of the size of a destroyer or above, about ten thousand meters.

54. Q.   Did you have any sound detecting gear?
    A.   He had sound gear.

55. Q.   Was it operative at this time?
    A.   It was being used at the time in question, but its condition was not very good.

56. Q.   Did you use it at all in the attack about which you have testified?
    A.   Yes, it was used.

57. Q. What use was made of it?
    A. The sound gear was used to determine any change in the course of the target and any changes in determining— and in determining speed.

58. Q. How many torpedoes did you fire on this attack?
    A. Six torpedoes were fired.

59. Q. How many hits do you claim that you got on the target?
    A. Three confirmed hits on the target. The explosion from a fourth hit was—the explosion from what was believed to be a fourth hit was heard but couldn't be confirmed by observation.

60. Q. What was the speed of your torpedoes?
    A. Forty-eight knots.

61. Q. What depth setting was set on these torpedoes?
    A. Four meters.

62. Q. What do you estimate the range to have been at the time of firing?
    A. Fifteen hundred meters.

63. Q. What was the range of the torpedoes at that speed, the maximum range of the torpedoes at that speed?
    A. Five thousand five hundred meters.

64. Q. Was there a lower speed setting?
    A. Yes.

65. Q. What was the lowest speed setting?
    A. The second setting is believed to be forty-two knots, but the witness is not quite sure of the exact speed.

66. Q. Did the lower speed give an increased range to the torpedo?
    A. Yes, it did.

67. Q. What was the range for forty-two?
    A. The answer to this question, too, he doesn't clearly remember, but in the vicinity of nine thousand meters.

68. Q. Was the target zigzagging at the time you sighted it?
    A. At the time of the sighting of the target, there was an

indistinct blur, and he is unable to—was unable to determine whether or not it was zigzagging.

69. Q.   Was it zigzagging later?
    A.   There is no question of the fact that it made no radical
          changes in course. It is faintly possible that there was a
          minor change in course between the time of sighting and
          the time of attack.

70. Q.   Would it have made any difference to you if the target had
          been zigzagging on this attack?
    A.   It would have involved no change in the method of firing
          the torpedoes, but some changes in the maneuvering.

71. Q.   How long was she on the surface when you testified that
          you first sighted a dark object? You said you crash-dived;
          how long do you estimate you were on the surface?
    A.   He estimates the time that elapsed from the sighting of
          the target until the time he was completely covered as
          fifty seconds.

Reexamined by the judge advocate:

72. Q.   Did you use radar which was in your ship at any time in
          relation to the sinking of this ship about which you have
          testified?
    A.   The radar was not used from the time he submerged until
          the time—from the time he submerged, that is, until after
          the attack was completed.

73. Q.   Please repeat that.
    A.   The radar in his ship was not used from the time he
          submerged until he completed his attack.

74. Q.   Which submerging do you mean?
    A.   The reference was intended to mean from the time he
          submerged after having sighted the target.

75. Q.   Did the radar assist you in any way to pick up this target?
    A.   Prior to surfacing, the visibility was good. Because the
          visibility had improved, radar was used to search for
          planes and for a limited time to search for surface craft
          with no contacts.

The accused did not desire to recross-examine this witness.

Examined by the court:

76. Q. You testified earlier that your first estimate of the target speed was twelve knots; did you make an estimate in order to fire torpedoes?

A. He used a speed of twelve knots to fire his torpedoes, sir, a target speed of twelve knots. Subsequent to the firing, when a chart was made up, he revised his estimate of target speed down to eleven knots.

77. Q. Were any observations made of the target after crash-diving?

A. The target was observed after he crash-dived.

78. Q. By what means?

A. He made continuous observation using a night periscope.

Neither the judge advocate, the accused, nor the court desired further to examine this witness.

The witness said that he had nothing further to state.

The witness was duly warned and withdrew.

Appendix H
Brief in the General Court-Martial Case of Captain Charles B. McVay, III, U.S. Navy, Tried on 3 December 1945

Captain Charles B. McVay, III, U.S. Navy, was tried on December 3, 1945, by general court-martial at the Navy Yard, Washington, D.C., by order of the Secretary of the Navy. He was acquitted of Charge II, Culpable Inefficiency in the Performance of Duty (failing to issue and see effected such timely orders as were necessary to cause vessel to be abandoned), and convicted of I, Through Negligence Suffering a Vessel of the Navy to be Hazarded (neglecting and failing to cause a zigzag course to be steered). He was sentenced to lose one hundred (100) numbers in his temporary grade of Captain and to lose one hundred (100) numbers in his permanent grade of Commander. All members of the court strongly recommended clemency.

The single specification under Charge I alleges that the accused while serving in command of the U.S.S. *Indianapolis,* making passage singly, without escort, from Guam to Leyte "through an area in which enemy submarines might be encountered, did, during good visibility after moonrise on 29 July 1945, at or about 10:30 P.M., minus nine and one-half zone time, neglect and fail to exercise proper care and attention to the safety of said vessel in that he neglected and failed, then and thereafter, to cause a zigzag course to be steered, and he, the said McVay, through said negligence, did suffer the said U.S.S. *Indianapolis* to be hazarded. . . ."

The evidence adduced by the prosecution tends to prove that routing instructions with intelligence annex attached were issued to the navigator of the *Indianapolis* at Guam. The accused had previously held a conference with the routing officer relative to speed, course, etc. The *Indianapolis* sailed from Guam at 0910 on 28 July 1945. The ship was struck by two or more torpedoes. The first hit approximately 0005, 30 July 1945, minus 9½ zone time at a reported position, Lat. 12° 02′ N, Long. 134° 48′ E. The ship prior to being torpedoed was on a steady course of 262° true, speed 17 knots, the accused having ordered the officer of the deck on the dog watch (1800-2000) to cease zigzagging and resume the base course. Several paragraphs of Wartime Instructions concerning the navigation and safety of ships under conditions similar to have stated in the specification were introduced into evidence as well as documents indicating places where enemy submarines had been reported. The testimony as to visibility during the time with which the specification is concerned is somewhat conflicting. Moonrise was at 2230, the phase of the moon two days before the last quarter. The testimony of several witnesses indicates intermittent moonlight between 2300 and 2400—visibility good when moon not obscured by clouds and poor when clouds were in front of moon. A witness who plotted the projected route and submarine information stated that in his opinion the track would pass through an area in which enemy submarines might be encountered. (Chart is Exhibit 2.)

There was testimony that the night orders contained a definite time to cease and resume zigzagging, and that a submarine had been reported at the expected 8 o'clock position. The weight of the testimony, as to orders to resume, is to the contrary.

A Commander in the Japanese Naval Reserve testified that on 29-30 July he was commander of the submarine I-58; that at 2305 he was in position bearing 355 degrees from Palau, distance 290 miles. He plotted his approximate position on a chart as 12° 31′ N, 134° 16′ E. He surfaced at 2305 and under the moon he observed a dark object at an estimated range of 10,000 meters. He crash-dived immediately. He headed toward his target. Twenty-seven minutes after he sighted the target he fired six torpedoes at 1500-meter range and observed three hits between the bow and the bridge and later heard an explosion which he thought was a fourth. The target had made no radical change in course. From a distance of about 3,000 yards he recognized the target as a ship of 10,000-ton cruiser class or bigger.

The evidence offered by the defense indicates that there were typewritten orders pasted in the night order book which contained provision for zigzagging in submarine waters and, in fact, contained the gist paragraph 3410 of Current Tactical Orders and Doctrine (Exhibit 4). The night orders normally contained the time of moonrise, when to commence zigzagging and zigzagging plan to be used. One witness who was Surface Operations Officer, Marianas, at the time the ship sailed from Guam testified from information available to him at the time of sailing and soon thereafter that the risk of submarine attack along the course of the *Indianapolis* was very slight. Another witness who was Surface Operations Officer, Philippine Sea Frontier, testified that the danger of submarine attack along the course of the *Indianapolis* was slight. An expert witness (submarines), a Captain, U.S.N., testified that zigzagging would not preclude a successful attack by submarine. The accused testified that he was on the bridge at about 2200, July 29th, at time of moonrise, 2230, and at about 2300. Visibility was poor, night order book was delivered to the officer of the deck about 2300. In general the night orders contained data as to speed, course, and a direction to carry out the standing night orders. No specific orders were given to the officer of the deck because the accused did not think it necessary—visibility was poor and there was no moon. As far as the accused remembered the night orders contained no specific orders to zigzag; no moonlight on the night of July 29th. The officers on watch including the supervisory watch were competant [sic]. They had been brought up to call the accused in case of doubt and ship doctrine required the officer of the deck to resume zigzagging on his own initiative as conditions required. On cross examination, the accused's statement in his report of Loss of Vessel: "There was intermittent moonlight at which times the visibility was unlimited" was based on his memory as of the time he was in the water.

Testimony in mitigation indicates that the accused's record was that of an outstanding officer during his entire commission service. He holds several commendatory letters as well as the Naval Expeditionary Medal, China Service Medal, Silver Star, and Purple Heart.

Appendix I
The Naval Inspector General's Final Report on the Sinking of the U.S.S. Indianapolis

A—Short covering memo from the NIG to Admiral Nimitz
B—"Facts and Discussion of Facts"
C—Memo from NIG to Admiral Nimitz discussing "Facts and Discussion of Facts" and offering "Conclusions" and "Recommendations"

A

Navy Department Office of the Chief of Naval Operations Washington

7 January 1946

Memorandum for the Chief of Naval Operations
1. This report is submitted in duplicate in order that a copy may be supplied at once to the Secretary of the Navy, who has expressed his desire to see it as soon as it is completed.
2. The duplicate copy is supplied direct to the Secretary through the Chief of Naval Operations in order that he may secure the comments of Fleet Admiral King upon this report. It is believed that the Secretary will desire Admiral King's comments as he, King, prepared the original endorsement on the court of inquiry in this case, in which endorsement the suggestion was made that the Inspector General be directed to secure the additional information desired.

C. P. Snyder

B

"Facts and Discussion of Facts"

Historical Background
1. On 1 May 1945, the USS *Indianapolis* entered the Navy Yard, Mare Island, California, for overhaul. Her overhaul was completed and she was reported ready for sea on 16 July 1945.
2. Although all preparations had been made to give the vessel a post-repair shakedown period in San Diego, California, preparatory to her rejoining the Fleet in the combat area, assignment to a mission of greater importance necessitated the postponement of this period of refresher training until a later date.
3. While in the Navy Yard, there had been a great number of

changes among the officers attached to the vessel and a turn-over in her enlisted complement in excess of 25 percent.

4. Advantage was taken of opportunities to send both officers and enlisted men to schools and other instruction, while in the Navy Yard; and when reported ready for sea, the ship was well organized and the training of personnel was progressing satis-factorily.

5. The *Indianapolis* proceeded at high speed from San Francisco to Pearl Harbor, thence to Tinian, where special cargo (atomic bomb parts) was landed. A great many passengers were trans-ported to Pearl Harbor and a lesser number beyond that point. These factors interfered somewhat with the schedule of train-ing under way, but instruction was continued, general drills were held daily, and at least one battle problem was held during this passage.

6. Upon completion of unloading at Tinian, the *Indianapolis* was ordered by CinCPac to proceed to Guam, to discharge certain personnel and to report to the Port Director, Guam, for onward routing to Leyte, there to report by dispatch to CTF 95 for duty. CTG 95.7 was directed to arrange ten days' training for the *Indianapolis* in the Leyte area. (These dispatches have an important bearing on the case. See Facts 30, 31, 32.)

The Routing Instructions

7. The routine procedure at Guam in July, 1945, in connection with the issuing of routing instructions, was for the Command-ing Officer of the routed unit to receive his briefing from the Port Director at the Naval Operating Base, Guam. Intelligence for this briefing originated and was secured in the CinCPac Headquarters, from which it was piped through the ComMari-anas Headquarters to the Port Director, Naval Operating Base, Guam. The briefing received was supplementary to the information of enemy activity which was written in the rout-ing instructions and which originated from the same source. (NOTE: Information of all categories which flowed into CinCPac Headquarters was evaluated by the CinCPac Intelli-gence Staff and disseminated as intelligence. It was issued as a screened product, some of which had fairly broad dissemina-tion, but other parts went only to senior commanders. As it was necessary to conceal the sources of this information in order to

keep these sources in operation, intelligence was often given in general terms. The enemy frequently passed out false information and claims and made deliberate effort to confuse Allied Intelligence; therefore intelligence passed out was at best only an estimate based on available information, and could not be considered as being reliable until confirmed from other sources. A single report from an enemy source, particularly, was not given very much weight until something else confirmed it. Supplying intelligence for all operations in the Pacific Ocean Area was the function of the CinCPac Intelligence Staff. Routing Officers and Operations Officers were supplied with the information which it was believed was necessary for them to accomplish their mission.)

8. Evidence indicates that intelligence had been received in the Headquarters of CominCh and in the Headquarters of CinCPac that there was considerable Japanese submarine activity to the westward of Guam in the Philippine Sea, in June and July, 1945. It was known to Commodore J. B. Carter, USN, the Operations Officer on the Staff of CinCPac, and to Captain O. F. Naquin, USN, the Surface Operations Officer on the Staff of ComMarianas, that at least four Japanese submarines were reported operating in this area on offensive missions. This information, however, did not reach ComMarianas (Vice Admiral Murray) or the Operations Officer, Commander J. R. Lawrence, USNR, or the Routing Officer, Lieutenant J. J. Waldron, USNR, at the Naval Operating Base, Guam. The responsibility for not passing this information regarding the reported Japanese submarine activity appears to lay with Captain Naquin, the Surface Operations Officer, ComMarianas.

9. On 27 July, Captain C. B. McVay III, USN, Commanding Officer of the *Indianapolis*, visited the Advance Headquarters of CinCPac and discussed with Commodore J. B. Carter, USN, Assistant Chief of Staff for Operations, general matters connected with his voyage to Leyte. He was, at this time, given no information regarding enemy activity to the westward of Guam and was informed that he would be routed by the Port Director, Guam. Commodore Carter stated in effect that the Port Director, Guam, in his capacity as routing officer for the *Indianapolis*, was the proper officer to brief the commanding

officer for his voyage and that for this purpose, the Port Director was supplied with all necessary intelligence and other information. At the Office of the Port Director, Guam, he discussed with an officer from the Routing Office, details of his routing and of limited enemy activity in the area through which he was routed. He stated in effect that he was not informed of the presence of the four Japanese submarines to the westward and was given the impression that his voyage was being made under normal conditions and that no escort would be required or given.

10. The Operations Officer of the Naval Operating Base, Commander J. R. Lawrence, USNR, had been given no information of enemy activity which caused him any special concern. Route "Peddie," over which the *Indianapolis* was to travel, which was the only direct route between Guam and Leyte, and was the route regularly assigned vessels making passage between these islands, was considered within the acceptable risk limit for combatant vessels, by this officer. Circuitous routes were available from Guam to Leyte, but the Operations Officer felt no special apprehension regarding the use of Route "Peddie" by the *Indianapolis*, and no other route was considered.

11. The speed of advance of the *Indianapolis* was set by Captain McVay and was based upon his desire to arrive off the entrance to Leyte Gulf at daylight on 31 July in order to conduct antiaircraft practice prior to his entering the Gulf. No special consideration was given the possibility of delaying the departure of the ship from Guam in order to enable her to proceed in company with other vessels, since the route assigned was not thought to be unduly hazardous. Zigzagging was, by his routing instructions, left to the discretion of Captain McVay.

12. Prior to the departure of the *Indianapolis* from Guam, Captain McVay, his Executive Officer and his Navigator went over the routing instructions with care. No protest was made to any feature of the routing, but the remark was made to the effect that the ship was once again proceeding unescorted.

13. The policy determination with regard to the escorting of vessels in the Western Pacific was the function of CinCPac. This policy, which required the escorting of vessels in some areas but dispensed with escorts for some classes of vessels in others,

which were less active, was largely dictated by the availability of escort vessels. At the time of the sailing of the *Indianapolis*, there was a shortage in this regard and escorts were, as a rule, not given combatant vessels which were capable of "taking care of themselves." The *Indianapolis* was considered to be in this class and escort, if furnished her, would have been at the expense of other ship movements. No change had been made nor contemplated in the then current policy as a result of recent enemy submarine activity in this area, even though it should have been evident from intelligence on hand that such change should have been under consideration.

14. Upon the sailing of the *Indianapolis* from Guam, responsibility for her safety and control of her movements passed to ComMarianas, Vice Admiral G. D. Murray, USN. This officer relieved Vice Admiral J. H. Hoover, USN, four days prior to the sailing of the *Indianapolis*. Authority to divert the ship from its course, if found necessary, rested with ComMarianas. ComMarianas was assigned a similar mission to that of various Sea Frontier Commanders.

15. On 28 July, the *Indianapolis* departed from Guam for Leyte. On this same date, information was disseminated that anti-submarine warfare operations were in progress along her route but well in advance of the *Indianapolis*, as a result of a submarine contact which had been made by a merchant vessel. This information was known to CinCPac and to ComMarianas.

Testimony from Additional Witnesses (Survivors)

16. At the time of her departure from Guam, the *Indianapolis* was not at peak efficiency; but she was well organized, her personnel were well disciplined and, in the main, well versed in the performance of their routine duties. Training of personnel was continuing and her visit to Leyte was being made in order to complete her refresher training program.

17. At 0015, Zone 9½ time, on 30 July, while steaming unescorted and without zigzagging, at a speed of 17 knots, under good conditions of visibility and in a moderate sea, two heavy explosions occurred against the starboard side of the *Indianapolis* forward of frame 60, as a result of which explosions, the ship

capsized and sank at 0027-0030, Zone 9½ time, 30 July. It cannot be understood why Captain McVay was steaming on a steady course at 17 knots with partial moonlight and good visibility unless he was lulled into a false sense of security through lack of intelligence of enemy submarine activity in the general area through which he was passing. There is evidence that he was not informed of the contents of at least one message dealing with enemy submarine activity, which message was on board the *Indianapolis*, and that other intelligence of this nature which should have been received by the ship in broadcast messages, either did not reach the ship or was not brought to the attention of Captain McVay.

18. Nothing was sighted either before the explosions occurred or afterward. Watches were properly stood and good lookout was kept, both visual and radar. No extra precautions were being taken against enemy submarines. The lookouts were generally experienced men and were fully alert. The damage control party, though well organized, was unable to function properly due to the heavy personnel casualties forward, the rapid flooding and the intense fire which was started in the forward section of the ship.

19. The communication set-up and provisions made for sending emergency messages were in accordance with good practice and current instructions. There is ample evidence that distress messages were keyed and possibly transmitted on at least one (500 kc) and possibly two frequencies. No evidence has been developed that any distress message from the ship was received by any ship or shore station.

20. Orders to abandon ship were given by some officers locally, but no general word was passed through the ship to that effect. This was partly due to the disruption of all mechanical and electrical means of communication, but personnel on the bridge who were available were not employed as messengers. Word for all hands to go on deck was passed through some of the lower deck compartments by the boatswain's mate of the watch, but was heard by only a few of the survivors. No calls of any kind were sounded on the bugle, although there was a bugler available on the bridge. Many men stood by their abandon ship stations until they were forced by the listing of the

ship, to enter the water. Much lifesaving equipment went down with the ship as it was manually released and was not cast loose through failure of general word being passed to abandon ship.

21. The conduct of Captain McVay and that of practically all of the other officers and men of the ship was, in the face of this emergency, satisfactory. Captain McVay refused to order abandon ship when it was first recommended by the First Lieutenant. Shortly thereafter, the same recommendation was made by the Executive Officer. The Captain, agreeing to this recommendation, ordered the word to be passed to all hands to abandon ship. This word, if passed at all, did not reach any considerable number of the crew. In fact, no survivor interrogated can recollect having heard it.

22. While some life rafts and floater nets were available to those in the water, many men had only their life jackets and large groups floated until they drowned or were rescued, with no other means of support.

23. Correct maintenance routines for emergency equipment had been in effect. The lifesaving equipment, while not entirely satisfactory in performance, was in accordance with BuShips design and specifications and entirely similar to that supplied other vessels of the *Indianapolis* class.

24. Testimony has been received reporting serious deficiencies in lifesaving equipment and emergency supplies. These deficiencies are not attributable to the *Indianapolis*, but indicate a definite need for study by BuShips and BuMed, with a view toward improving the equipment and facilities connected with the saving of life at sea which are now furnished vessels as standard equipment.

25. Numerous acts of heroism and leadership and display of fortitude have been reported. These were in keeping with the best traditions of the service and merit suitable recognition.

CinCPac Dispatch 260152 of July and the Delayed Search for Survivors

26. In the Headquarters of ComMarianas on Guam and of the ComPhilSeaFrontier on Leyte, operational plotting boards were kept. On these boards was kept a graphic plot of the

positions at sea of all vessels in which the headquarters concerned was interested. In the case of *Indianapolis*, the departure of the vessel from Guam on 28 July was recorded on the plotting boards in each of these headquarters. Her estimated position was plotted on each board daily. On 31 July, *the date on which the vessel was scheduled to have arrived at Leyte, the* Indianapolis *was removed from the board in the headquarters of ComMarianas and was recorded on the board at the headquarters of ComPhilSeaFrontier as having arrived at Leyte. This was the routine method of handling the plot of combatant vessels.* Since, in accordance with the provisions of CinCPac letter 10CL-45, the arrival of combatant vessels was not reported, vessels of this class were assumed to have arrived at their destinations on the date and at approximately the time scheduled. *No check was made at either headquarters to confirm such arrival.*

In the departure report of vessels was included a "chop" date. This was the date on which the vessel was scheduled to cross the geographical boundary separating the sea areas over which two commanders had cognizance and responsibility. In the departure report of the *Indianapolis*, which was made by the Port Director, Guam, in his dispatch 280032 of July, 1945, the "chop" date was given as 30 July. This was the date on which the vessel was due to pass from waters under the cognizance of ComMarianas into those under the cognizance of ComPhilSeaFrontier. No hour for this transfer of jurisdiction was given in the dispatch.

27. Within sixteen hours of the actual sinking of the *Indianapolis*, there was, in the Advance Headquarters of CinCPac, information (from a single enemy source) to the effect that the Japanese had sunk something (the nature of which was unknown) in a position which was approximately the predicted position of the *Indianapolis* at the time. This information did not reach ComMarianas, to whose headquarters it should have been passed by CinCPac if evaluated as intelligence. No action was taken on this information by CinCPac nor, due to nonreceipt, by ComMarianas. Had this information been passed by CinCPac to ComMarianas as was his responsibility, the necessary investigation into the matter should have been initiated by

ComMarianas, since the position given was in the area under his jurisdiction. Had either CinCPac or ComMarianas taken immediate steps to have this matter investigated, it is probable that the survivors of the *Indianapolis* would have been located within twenty-four hours of the time of the sinking of the ship and many lives possibly would have been saved.

In passing judgment on this ommission of CinCPac, certain salient features connected with this phase of the work of his staff should be born in mind. The person who was directly responsible for the collection, evaluation, and dissemination of intelligence, particularly that of high classification, was the Combat Intelligence Officer who was charged with the general supervision of the work of the Combat Intelligence Section. Evaluating intelligence is not an exact science. It is at best an estimate, frequently it is only an intelligent assumption. In the prosecution of the Naval phase of the war in the Western Pacific, the work of this Section had been outstanding. Information developed by this Unit made possible the successful execution of several operations which were of such significance and importance at the time, as to have changed the entire course of the war against Japan. Regrettable though it was, this failure to properly evaluate a report made by a Japanese submarine had no bearing on the prosecution of the war as a whole and was actually of local significance.

This failure in the evaluation of intelligence is attributable in part to the exaggerated claims and false intelligence which had characterized many Japanese reports. It is a matter of record that enemy reports of sinking of our combatant units were constantly being made, whereas in fact the units against which these claims were made were then operating in an entirely different area. Many of our units were several times reported to have been sunk or damaged as a "feeler" on the part of the enemy. Constant investigation of such enemy claims and the generally resulting proof of their exaggeration or falsity had caused a low evaluation to be placed on this type of intelligence. Such was the case in this report, that a vessel of undetermined size and classification had been sunk in waters to the westward of Guam.

28. This intelligence was also in the hands of CominCh at about

the same time, and was passed by him to ComSeventh Fleet. ComSeventh Fleet did not pass this intelligence to ComPhil-SeaFron nor did he take any action on it himself. However, since the position given was not in an area under his cognizance or that of ComPhilSeaFron, these officers did not have the interest in this matter which devolved upon CinCPac and ComMarianas. As a matter of fact, no suspicion was created in the headquarters of ComSeventh Fleet or ComPhilSeaFron that this intelligence involved the *Indianapolis*, since that vessel was not, at the time, due to have arrived in Leyte.

29. The *Indianapolis* was scheduled to have arrived at Leyte at 0200Z on 31 July. This was at 1100, 31 July, Leyte time and date. It is probable that under normal conditions, no concern as to her nonarrival would have been felt until she was eight or nine hours overdue. Several additional hours would elapse incident to the dispatch traffic necessary to check her movements so that, in all probability, search for her would normally not have commenced until she would have been approximately twenty-four hours overdue. That would have been sometime in the forenoon of 1 August. The survivors of the *Indianapolis* were actually sighted at about 1025 Leyte time on 2 August, by a plane on routine patrol. Search action was never instituted by the Philippine Sea Frontier Command.

30. CinCPac Advance Headquarters dispatch 260152 of July in which CTF 95 (Vice Admiral Jesse B. Oldendorf, USN) and CTG 95.7 (Rear Admiral Lynde D. McCormick, USN) were information addressees, contained the sailing orders of the *Indianapolis*. It was ordered that the vessel upon its arrival in Leyte report by dispatch to CTF 95 for duty and directed to CTG 95.7 to arrange ten days' training for the vessel in the Leyte area. Neither ComSeventh Fleet, ComPhilSeaFron nor any shore-based commands in the Philippines were included in the addresees of this dispatch. This dispatch was received and understood by CTF 95 who was, at the time, at Okinawa. It was received in garbled form by CTG 95.7, who was in the Leyte area. CTF 95 noted that the actual dates of departure from Guam and of the arrival of the vessel in Leyte were not given. CTG 95.7 did not decode this dispatch since its classification was "secret" [sic—this is incorrect; i.e., he did not ask for a

repeat of the message since it had a very low security classification] and the garbled address as received, did not include his command.

31. Port Director, Guam dispatch 280032 of July included as an action addressee, CTG 95.7 and as an information addressee, CTF 95. In this dispatch, the routing of the *Indianapolis* was given, including the date of her departure from Guam and the date of her arrival in Leyte. This dispatch was not received by CTF 95 who was, therefore, still uninformed of the date on which the *Indianapolis* should have been expected to report to him by dispatch. CTG 95.7 received and understood this dispatch, but as there was nothing in its contents which concerned his group, gave it no further attention. The Port Director, Tacloban, was an action addressee on this dispatch.

32. CTG 95.7 was at sea conducting training exercises at the time when the *Indianapolis* was scheduled to arrive in Leyte. Although CTG 95.7 had left a subordinate Flag Officer in Leyte, ComBatDivFour (Rear Admiral I. C. Sowell, USN), no mention had been made to this officer of the prospective arrival of the *Indianapolis* since the Task Group Commander had, for the reason previously given, no feeling of interest or concern in the matter. ComBatDivFour did not check on the arrival of the *Indianapolis*.

33. The Acting Port Director at Tacloban, Leyte, Lieutenant Commander Jules C. Sancho, USNR, was not aware that the *Indianapolis* had not arrived as was scheduled and that she could be considered as being overdue. It, however, was his duty in his capacity as Acting Port Director, to keep himself informed of such matters.

Lieutenant Stuart B. Gibson, USNR, the Operations Officer under the Port Director, Tacloban, was the officer who was immediately concerned with the movements of the *Indianapolis*. The nonarrival of that vessel on schedule was known at once to Lieutenant Gibson, who not only failed to investigate the matter but made no immediate report of the fact to his superiors. He took no action in this matter for the reason that a directive, then current, specifically prohibited the reporting of the arrival of combatant vessels. This was interpreted by him as also prohibiting the reporting of the nonarrival of vessels of

this category. The provision of the directive in question referring to reports on the movements of combatant ships has
subsequently been clarified by ComPhilSeaFron dispatch
031406 and CinCPac dispatch 220340, both of August.

While not excusing the failure of Lieutenant Commander
Sancho and Lieutenant Gibson to use the initiative and ordinary good judgment in this connection which would have been
expected of naval officers, this dereliction may be attributed to
the weakness of an organization which has been brought on by
the exceedingly rapid expansion of the Navy to meet its wartime requirements. The need for officers of the Naval Reserve
to fill administrative positions has been so great and so press-
ing that these officers have been placed in positions of considerable responsibility with little more than training in the fun-
damentals of naval requirements. These officers are, necessarily, more or less specialists and do not have the broad naval
aspect which is acquired only through many years of active
service. They are not fully equipped, hence are generally
incapable of meeting the requirements of a difficult situation
where extensive knowledge of naval matters is essential to
proper execution.

In view of the volume of shipping which was being handled
by the Port of Tacloban, it would appear that the important
assignments of Acting Port Director and of Operations Officer
of the port should have been given to more experienced officers
than was the case.

34. The Commander in Chief, U.S. Pacific Fleet and Pacific Ocean
Areas, in his directive 10CL-45, dated 26 January 1945, made
specific provision that the arrival of combatant vessels was not
to be reported. In preparing this as well as in the preparation of
all directives issued by his headquarters, the Commander in
Chief, U.S. Pacific Fleet was mindful of the fact that these
instructions would be given general dissemination and that
officers who were relatively inexperienced in naval matters
would be charged with their execution. For this reason, every
attempt was made to insure that the wording was clear, concise
and that the meaning could not be misinterpreted. Although
PacFleet Confidential Letter 10CL-45 was prepared with
thought and care, that it *was* subject to misinterpretation is

proven by the inference drawn from it by Lieutenant Gibson. It was not the intention of CinCPac to prohibit in this directive the reporting of the nonarrival of combatant ships. However, no mention of this was made in the letter and the inference was drawn by this officer that since arrival reports were not to be made for combatant ships, by the same token neither were reports of nonarrivals to be made. (See testimony of Vice Admiral McMorris.)

The Commander in Chief, U.S. Pacific Fleet has, in his dispatch 220340, of August 1945, completely clarified this matter by making specific provisions under which the nonarrival of combatant vessels is to be reported. Had a specific directive, complete in its coverage of *all* conditions, been issued in the first place, at least one full day would have been saved in the rescue of the survivors of the *Indianapolis*.

35. Lieutenant Commander Sancho and Lieutenant Gibson were members of the Philippine Sea Frontier organization. Bearing in mind the lack of experience of these officers in naval matters, it was incumbent upon their superior officers to exercise closer personal supervision over the manner in which their duties were performed than was actually the case. At the time of the loss of the *Indianapolis*, the Commander, Philippine Sea Frontier, Vice Admiral James L. Kauffman, USN, was absent from his command since 1 July, 1945, on temporary duty status in the United States; Commodore N. C. Gillette, USN, was in temporary command, and the Operations Officer of the Headquarters Staff, Captain A. M. Granum, USN, was intensively occupied in diversion of shipping in typhoon areas and other operations. These facts do not, however, relieve these senior officers from their responsibility connected with the failure of their subordinates to take appropriate action to ascertain the whereabouts of the overdue *Indianapolis*, for the junior officers who were directly concerned with this failure were members of the organization which was being administered by these officers. For this demonstrated weakness in the organization under their control, brought on largely through their failure to give closer personal attention to the work of these inexperienced juniors, Commodore Gillette and Captain Granum (due to the absence of Vice Admiral Kauffman) must bear the

responsibility. (See testimony of Commodore Gillette and Captain Granum.)

36. CTF 95, at Okinawa, took no action to check on the arrival in Leyte of the *Indianapolis*. It was known to this officer that the *Indianapolis* was directed to report to him by dispatch upon her arrival in Leyte but, for reasons before mentioned, he was not informed of her departure from Guam or of the date of her scheduled arrival in Leyte, hence assumed that the ship was still at Guam.

37. ComPhilSeaFron (Commodore N. C. Gillette, USN, Chief of Staff, Acting) was charged with the mission of safeguarding and protecting shipping in the area under his cognizance. He maintained an Operations Board at his Headquarters at Tolosa, Leyte, on which was kept a running record of the scheduled and actual arrival and departure of vessels of all categories, in the area under his cognizance. His Headquarters had been given intelligence of all submarine activity in the Philippine Sea and was aware that the *Indianapolis* was overdue in Leyte, but no investigation as to her whereabouts was instituted until after her survivors were sighted.

38. ComMarinas, in Guam, felt no particular concern connected with the arrival of the *Indianapolis* in Leyte. He was of the opinion that the authorities at the destination of a vessel have the principal concern as to her arrival or nonarrival and assumed that, since the arrival of combatant vessels was, by directive, not reported, the *Indianapolis* had reached her destination. No action was taken by this headquarters until the survivors were sighted.

39. A not uncommon practice in the Pacific Ocean Area was the diverting of combatant units from the destinations to which they had been originally ordered without informing all interested commands, particularly that at the destination in question, of such change of orders. Due to the frequency with which this procedure was followed, a feeling of unconcern in the movements of combatant units had been built up, particularly in the shore-based commands, the tendency being to attribute all failures of these units to reach their originally assigned destinations on schedule to an uncommunicated change and there to let the matter drop.

40. Aircraft patrols which daily covered a great part of the route followed by the *Indianapolis*, and which were sighted daily by the survivors, failed:
    (a) To report the presence of the *Indianapolis* in their area before she was sunk;
    (b) To sight the oil slick or the survivors for several days after the sinking.

    Discovery by aircraft patrol of the survivors was largely accidental.

41. Investigation of these aircraft patrol failures revealed that:
    (a) Planes were flying at altitudes which were considered the optimum for searching the area for enemy craft by search radar and visual lookout. Since, at this time and in this area, enemy craft were almost certain to be submarines, this was, in effect, an antisubmarine patrol. Planes were, generally, flying too high to see the *Indianapolis* survivors whose life rafts did not have radar reflectors.
    (b) Planes had not been briefed completely on friendly vessels in the area because they were considered too numerous to give complete information regarding their movements.

    The conclusion is reached that planes on antisubmarine patrol are not effective as general lookouts for personnel adrift unless life rafts are provided with radar reflectors.

C

Navy Department Office of the Chief of Naval Operations Washington

7 Jan 1946

Op-o8/OK
(SC) A17-25
Serial: 006P08
S E C R E T

From: The Naval Inspector General
To: The Chief of Naval Operations

Subject: Investigation of the Sinking of the USS *Indianapolis*, and the Delay in Reporting the Loss of that Ship

References: (a) CNO's directive to NIG, Serial 009P03, of 18 October 1945
             (b) NIG's Confidential Memo to CNO Serial 01P08, of 19 November 1945
             (c) NIG's Secret Letter, Serial 001P08, to CNO, of 30 November 1945

Enclosure: (A) "Facts and Discussion of Facts"

1. By reference (a), the Chief of Naval Operations directed the Naval Inspector General to:
   (a) Inquire fully into the routing chosen for the USS *Indianapolis* from Guam to Leyte and considerations governing the escorting of the ship on this trip;
   (b) Take testimony from certain additional survivors;
   (c) Investigate further the matter of the receipt of the Commander in Chief, Pacific Fleet's dispatch 260152, of July, by Commander, Task Group 95.7.

2. By references (b) and (c), the Naval Inspector General reported progress in the investigation, which is now completed. During the progress of the investigation, senior assistants to the Naval Inspector General proceeded to Pearl Harbor, Guam, San Pedro, and Marietta, Pennsylvania, and have examined 50 witnesses, many of whom were brought from considerable distances to Washington. The record contains over 600 pages of sworn testimony which is exclusive of that taken by the Court of Inquiry previously held in this case. Among the witnesses interrogated have been: Vice Admiral C. H. McMorris, Chief of Staff to CinCPac; Vice Admiral G. D. Murray, Commander, Marianas; Vice Admiral Jesse B. Oldendorf, Commander Task Force 95; Rear Admiral L. D. McCormick, Task Group 95.7; Commodore N. C. Gillette, Chief of Staff, temporarily in command of the Philippine Sea Frontier; Commodore E. E. Stone, Assistant Chief of Staff for Communications, CinCPac's Staff; Commodore J. B. Carter, Assistant Chief of Staff for Operations, CinCPac's Staff—as well as key officers in various organizations concerned, including Captain C. B. McVay, eight surviving officers, and 21 key men of the USS *Indianapolis*.

3. The Naval Inspector General has reached the following conclusions in the premises enumerated in part (a) above:

"Conclusions"

(a) *Routing chosen and considerations given to the escorting of the
ship:*

(1) Route "Peddie," the only direct route established from Guam to
Leyte, and which was used in routing the *Indianapolis*, was set
up in a current directive issued by the Commander in Chief,
Pacific Fleet, which appears to take due regard of the existing
war situation and accepts certain risks as necessary. No other
route was considered. Circuitous routes were available but
were considered no more safe. The policy with regard to escorting was also set up by the Commander in Chief, Pacific, and
was based on supplying escorts where most needed. In routing, escorting, briefing of commanders of routed units, and
diverting of vessels, in the Marianas Area, the constantly
changing war intelligence situation was given consideration
by the Staffs of Commander, Marianas, and the Commander,
Naval Operating Base, Guam. In the case of the *Indianapolis*,
there appears to have been a failure on the part of the Surface
Operations Officer, Captain O. F. Naquin, on the Staff of
ComMarianas, to cause to be passed on to the Office of the Port
Director, Guam, certain information of enemy submarine
activity which was necessary in connection with the routing of
vessels and the briefing of their commanding officers. Inas-
much as this failure of Captain Naquin prevented this information from reaching the Routing Officer and Captain
McVay, it may be considered as a contributory cause to the loss
of the *Indianapolis*. (See Facts, 7, 8, 9, 10, 12, 13, 14, 17.)

(b) With regard to: (b)—*Testimony from additional witnesses
(survivors):*

(1) The *Indianapolis* was well manned and organized, her officers
were in the main experienced and competent and her crew well
disciplined and as well trained as was possible under the
conditions prevailing at the time. (See Facts, 2, 3, 4, 5, 6, 16, 18,
19, 21, 23, 25.)

(2) The Communication Department of the ship was properly

organized to meet this emergency and functioned as well as was possible under the circumstances. All reasonable means were employed to transmit distress messages but it is doubtful if these attempts met with any degree of success. (See Facts, 19.)

(3) The Commanding Officer of the *Indianapolis*, Captain Charles B. McVay, III, USN, failed to exercise due diligence to safeguard his vessel and its personnel in the following particulars:

  a. His failure to zigzag at night during partial moonlight and good visibility. (See Facts, 11, 17.)

  b. His failure to exhaust all possible sources of intelligence regarding enemy activity in the waters through which he was about to pass. There was at least one message received in his ship regarding submarine activity, with which he was not familiar. (See Facts, 9, 17.)

  c. Failure in the *Indianapolis* to use all possible means of passing emergency orders to its personnel, that is, by bugle and by the employment as messengers of all persons available on the bridge. (See Facts, 20.)

(4) There were material deficiencies in emergency equipment under the cognizance of various bureaus of the Navy Department. Examples are:

  a. Life rafts: No automatic or mechanical releases; no radar markers on rafts; no colored markers furnished.

  b. Water supply: Outmoded wooden water breakers subject to leakage and difficult to prevent contamination of fresh water with salt water.

  c. Medical supplies: Poorly packaged and in many cases water-soaked and useless.

  d. Food supplies: Poorly suited to emergency conditions.

  e. Probable cause of failure to communication [sic] distress message—failure of power to radio transmitters. (Material deficiencies covered by Facts, 19, 20, 22, 23, 24.)

(c) With regard to: (c) *CinCPac's Dispatch 260152 of July, and the delayed search for survivors:*

(1) Communication failures played a vital part in the delayed search for survivors. Some of these were due to the fortunes of

war, others were due to the rapid increase in the size of the Navy and the consequent inexperience and lack of training of personnel involved. Examples are:

a. The basic failure of the *Indianapolis* to successfully communicate to any vessel or station a distress message. This failure, while it must be ascribed to the fortunes of war, nevertheless should be considered in developing emergency radio transmitting equipment and in considering means for preventing loss of life at sea. If a distress message had been communicated, the loss of life and suffering of survivors would have been greatly reduced. (See Facts, 19.)

b. The failure to deliver to Commander, Task Force 95, Vice Admiral Oldendorf, dispatch 280032 of July, from the Port Director, Guam, which left Commander Task Force 95 not completely supplied with information concerning the movements of the *Indianapolis*. He took no action because there was none he could intelligently take. (See Facts, 31, 36.)

c. The garbled transmission or reception on the Flagship of Commander, Task Group 95.7 (Rear Admiral McCormick), of CinCPac Advance Headquarters dispatch 260152 of July, which left this officer incompletely supplied with information regarding the orders given the *Indianapolis* and no reason to inquire where she was. (See Facts, 30, 32.)

d. The faulty general practice of ordering combatant units to one destination and then diverting them to another without giving information of the change to all interested commands, which fault was aggravated by communication failures. (See Facts, 39.)

(2) The Combat Intelligence Unit on the Staff of the Commander in Chief, Pacific Fleet, failed to correctly evaluate an enemy report of an undetermined sinking in the area then being traversed by the *Indianapolis*. This report was completely processed about 16 hours after the actual sinking of the *Indianapolis*, but little credence was given the report as it was believed it was intended to deceive. There was no substantiation until the survivors of the *Indianapolis* were sighted. This Combat Intelligence Unit under Captain E. T. Layton per-

formed brilliantly during the war. Evaluating enemy reports into combat or operational intelligence is not an exact science. Errors will occur. (See Facts, 7, 27.)

(3) The Philippine Sea Frontier organization failed to follow up on the movement of an important unit of the fleet when that unit became overdue at a port under the cognizance of that command. The specific instances are:

a. The plot of vessels at sea was maintained at Tolosa, Leyte, for the Headquarters of the Philippine Sea Frontier, and at Guam for the Headquarters of Commander, Marianas. The *Indianapolis* was correctly carried on both plots and was scheduled to have arrived at Leyte at 1100, 31 July, Leyte time and date. Her marker was removed from the Guam plot when no news was heard from her and time had expired for her normal presence in the Marianas area, which is considered normal procedure with no blame attached. Under normal conditions no concern as to her non-arrival at Leyte would be felt until she was 8 or 9 hours overdue. Several additional hours would elapse incident to dispatch traffic necessary to check her movements, so that in all probability search for her would normally not have commenced until she would have been approximately 24 hours overdue—that is, the forenoon of 1 August. The survivors of the *Indianapolis* were actually sighted at about 1025 on 2 August, Leyte time and date. Search action was never instituted by the Philippine Sea Frontier Command. However, her marker was left on the plotting board as having arrived in Leyte Gulf. (See Facts, 26, 29.)

b. Lieutenant Stuart B. Gibson, USNR, the Operations Officer under the Port Director, Tacloban, was the officer who was immediately concerned with the movements of the *Indianapolis*. He was cognizant of the fact that the *Indianapolis* was overdue but made no report of the fact to his superiors. (See Facts, 33.)

c. The Acting Port Director, Lieutenant Commander Jules C. Sancho, USNR, at Tacloban, was not aware that the *Indianapolis* had not arrived and that she could be considered as overdue. This was a dereliction of duty on his part. In his capacity as Acting Port Director it was his responsibility to keep himself informed on such matters. (See Facts, 33.)

d. This lack of appreciation of responsibility in this case on the part of these two officers, was largely occasioned by a directive of the Commander in Chief, Pacific Fleet, then current, which *specifically prohibited the reporting of the arrival of combatant* vessels. This was interpreted by Lieutenant Gibson as also *prohibiting* the reporting of the *nonarrival* of vessels in this category.

e. Provisions of the directive in question, which was prepared in CinCPac's Headquarters and issued by the Chief of Staff, Vice Admiral McMorris, USN, referring to reports of the movements of combatant ships, have *subsequently* been clarified by competent authority. (See Facts, 34.)

f. While not excusing the failure of Lieutenant Commander Sancho and Lieutenant Gibson to use the initiative and good judgment expected of naval officers, the dereliction may be partly attributed to the weakness of organization which has been brought on by the exceedingly rapid expansion of the Navy to meet its wartime requirements. (See Facts, 33, 34.)

g. In view of the volume of shipping which was being handled at the Port of Tacloban, it would appear that the important assignments of Acting Port Director and of Operations Officer of the Port should have been given to more experienced officers than was the case. Bearing in mind the lack of experience of these officers, it was incumbent upon their superior officers to exercise closer personal supervision over the manner in which their duties were performed than was actually the case. (See Facts, 33.)

h. The Commander, Philippine Sea Frontier, Vice Admiral James L. Kauffman, USN, *had been absent from his command since the first of July, 1945,* on temporary duty status in the United States. Commodore N. C. Gillette, USN, was in temporary command, and therefore responsible for operations pertinent to his assignment; it was incumbent upon him to check up on the efficient operation of the organization set up by his superior whom he had temporarily relieved. The Operations Officer of the Headquarters Staff, Captain A. M. Granum, USN, was intensively occupied in diversion of shipping in typhoon areas and other operations. (See Facts, 35). These facts do not, however, relieve Commodore Gillette and Captain Granum from their responsibility connected with the failure of their subordinates to take appropriate action to ascertain the whereabouts of the overdue *Indianapolis*. The junior officers, who were directly concerned with this failure, were members of the organization which was being administered by these officers. For this demonstrated weakness in the organization under their control, brought on through their failure to give closer personal attention to the work of these inexperienced juniors, Commodore Gillette and Captain Granum must bear the responsibility, with Vice Admiral Kauffman, sharing the responsibility for any basic defects in the organization which were developed by events. (See Facts, 35.)

i. The responsibility for the ambiguous order with regard to not reporting the arrival of combat vessels (10CL-45), which was prepared in the Headquarters of the Commander in Chief, Pacific Fleet, and signed by Vice Admiral McMorris, Chief of Staff, must rest with that Headquarters. (See Facts, 33, 34.)

(4) Planes on antisubmarine patrol are not effective as general lookouts for personnel adrift unless life rafts are provided with radar reflectors. (See Facts, 40, 41.)

"Recommendations"

4. From the Facts, and conclusions drawn therefrom, there is no doubt that there were faults of omission and commission contributory to the loss of the *Indianapolis* and the subsequent suffering and loss of life due to delay in rescuing survivors. Responsibility extends from the Commander in Chief, Pacific, to the Lieutenant Operations Officer, Tacloban, and into the Bureaus of the Navy Department. It must be borne in mind that planning and preliminary work connected with impending operations of great moment were under way and occupied the attention of all senior commanders, and they could hardly be expected to personally concern themselves with the constant whereabouts of a single vessel making passage from

Guam to Leyte, although the organization and standing orders of the command and all its ramifications should have provided for all contingencies.

The undersigned has refrained from making any definite recommendations in this case as he was charged primarily with securing additional and clarifying information and amplifying the work of the original Court of Inquiry. He believes the task has been performed in an exhaustive manner and that subsequent action must be taken by high executive and administrative authority, after study of the subject matter submitted herein. They only must decide whether the exigencies of the situation require more than:

(1) That the lessons now learned be disseminated to the naval service;

(2) That the public be informed of the reasons surrounding the loss of the *Indianapolis* and the delay in rescuing her survivors; or

(3) Whether admonishment or even punitive action be taken in the case of those responsible.

In any case, it is recommended that the Facts, appended hereto, be studied carefully before action is taken. The Assistants to the Naval Inspector General who made this investigation, and who are thoroughly informed of the subject matter of the testimony, including that contained in the record of the Court of Inquiry, are available to answer questions which may be raised in the study of the case.

C. P. Snyder

Appendix J
Press and Radio Release: Narrative of the Circumstances of the Loss of the U.S.S. Indianapolis

(++   ++) = word, sentence, phrase, etc. *Put Into Final Release.*
(—   —) = word, sentence, phrase, etc. *Taken Out of Final Release.*

NAVY DEPARTMENT

IMMEDIATE RELEASE
PRESS AND RADIO   February 23, 1946

Narrative of the Circumstances of
the Loss of the USS *Indianapolis*

Adequate understanding of the circumstances under which the (++USS++) *Indianapolis* was torpedoed and sunk, and in which delays resulted in the rescue of her survivors, requires some preliminary consideration of the overall situation in the Pacific at the time.

On April 1, 1945, following the recapture of the Philippines and the capture of Iwo Jima, United States Forces landed on Okinawa. Heavy fighting ashore on Okinawa continued until the 21st of June, when organized resistance ceased.

The victory ashore on Okinawa was made possible only by the continued support of all available units of the Pacific Fleet. Throughout the spring and (—early—) summer of 1945, the fleet continued to control the sea and air in the vicinity of Okinawa, but in so doing received heavy damage. This damage was received principally by destroyers, destroyer escorts, and other types of ships normally used for escort purposes. These units, which formed screens for our forces at sea and also for the forces ashore, were the principal targets for kamikaze attack. The extent of the damage sustained in these types made it necessary to modify the escort procedures throughout the Pacific, so that damaged escorts might be returned to the navy yards for repair, and so that the escorts still available could be used in the most exposed areas and on assignments where they would contribute most to the overall safety of our forces, more particularly to the safety of the ships off Japan and the ships carrying troops.

The records for the period, from the beginning of the Okinawa operation almost until the end of the war, show clearly the concern which existed in this regard. Destroyers and destroyer escorts were brought to the Central Pacific from the Atlantic and from the North Pacific. Ships were sailed unescorted in the more remote areas. Priority was given to the repair of escort types in our navy yards and a determined effort was made to improve the escort situation in preparation for the invasion of Japan during which there could be anticipated a repetition of the conditions under which such heavy damage to escorts was sustained off Okinawa.

During July we were engaged in consolidating our position at Okinawa and in sustained attacks on Japan itself with both carrier task forces and shore-based air forces in order to create the conditions prerequisite for invasion. The Third Fleet was actively engaged in attacking Honshu. The Twentieth Air Force was bombing Honshu. Naval aircraft from the Ryukyus were ranging over the East China Sea and along the coasts of Kyushu and Southern and Central Korea. The Far East Air Force was moving its personnel and equipment up from the Philippines to Okinawa and was increasing the weight of its attack on Kyushu.

At the end of July the carrier task forces were delivering very heavy attacks which destroyed many Japanese aircraft and which practically completed the elimination of the Japanese fighting ships in their home ports. Important conferences were going on in Manila between the staffs of Fleet Admiral Nimitz and General of the Army MacArthur in connection with plans for the invasion and alternate plans for the occupation of Japan in case of an early surrender. Extensive mine sweeping operations were in progress in the East China Sea. Rescue operations for downed carrier pilots and B-29 pilots were in progress south of Japan. There were approximately 700 fighting ships and (++about++) 400 merchant ships at sea in the Western Pacific. Radio traffic in the (—Headquarters of the Commander in Chief, Pacific Fleet—) (++Joint Communications Center at Guam++) averaged 16,000 messages a day (—and in the Headquarters of the Philippine Sea Frontier . . . messages a day—). The responsible officers in the Pacific Fleet were devoting their time and energy to accelerating the tempo of the campaign and to increasing the pressure on Japan in order to bring the war to a conclusion, and specifically, to pound the Japanese into submission without the necessity for a costly invasion.

On (—1 May 1945—) (++May 1, 1945++), the USS *Indianapolis* had entered the Navy Yard, Mare Island, California, for overhaul. Her overhaul was completed and she was reported ready for sea on (—16 July 1945—) (++July 16, 1945++).

Although all preparations had been made to give the vessel a post-repair shakedown period in San Diego, California, preparatory to her rejoining the Fleet in the combat area, assignment to a mission of greater importance necessitated the postponement of this period of refresher training until a later date.

While in the Navy Yard, there had been a great number of changes among the officers attached to the vessel and a turnover in her enlisted complement in excess of 25 percent.

(++Every++) advantage was taken of opportunities to send both officers and enlisted men to schools and other instruction, while in the Navy Yard; and when reported ready for sea, the ship was well organized and the training of personnel was progressing satisfactorily.

The *Indianapolis* proceeded (++unescorted++) at high speed from San Francisco to Pearl Harbor, thence to Tinian, where special cargo (atomic bomb parts) was landed. A great many passengers were transported to Pearl Harbor and a lesser number beyond that point. These factors interfered somewhat with the schedule of training underway, but instruction was continued, general drills were held daily and at least one battle problem was held during this passage.

Upon completion of unloading at Tinian, the *Indianapolis* was ordered by the Commander in Chief, Pacific Fleet to proceed to Guam, to discharge certain personnel and to report to the Port Director, Guam, for onward routing to Leyte, there to report for duty by dispatch to Vice Admiral (++Jesse B.++) Oldendorf (++U.S.N.++) who was then off Okinawa.

The routine procedure at Guam in July, 1945, in connection with the issuing of routing instructions, was for the Commanding Officer of the routed unit to receive his briefing from the Port

Director at the Naval Operating Base, Guam. Routing Officers and Operations Officers were supplied with the information which it was believed was necessary for them to accomplish their mission.

(—Secret intelligence had been received in the Headquarters of the Commander in Chief, United States Fleet and in the Headquarters of the Commander in Chief, Pacific Fleet that there was considerable Japanese submarine activity to the westward of Guam in the Philippine Sea, in June and July, 1945. There were indications that at least four Japanese submarines were reported operating at sea on offensive missions. This specific information, however, although known to Captain Naquin, the Operations Officer on the staff of Commander, Marianas, did not reach the Operations Officer or the Routing Officer at the Naval Operating Base, Guam. For this failure, Captain Naquin has been held responsible—)

(—On 27 July, Captain C. B. McVay III, USN, Commanding Officer of the *Indianapolis*, visited the Advance Headquarters of the Commander in Chief, Pacific Fleet and discussed general matters connected with his voyage to Leyte. He was, at this time, given no information regarding enemy activity to the westward of Guam and was informed that he would be routed by the Port Director, Guam. At the Office of the Port Director, Guam, he discussed with an officer from the Routing Office, details of the routing and of limited enemy activity in the area through which he was routed. He was not informed of the presence of the four Japanese submarines to the westward—)

[The following paragraph was inserted in lieu of the previous two, which were omitted.]

(++On July 27, Captain C. B. McVay, III, U.S.N., Commanding Officer of the *Indianapolis*, visited the Office of the Port Director, Guam, in connection with his routing to Leyte. Later that day the Navigator of the *Indianapolis* also visited the Port Director's office to obtain the Routing Instructions and discuss their details. Information of possible enemy submarines along the route was contained in the routing instructions and was discussed with the Navigator++)

The route over which the *Indianapolis* was to travel, which was the only direct route between Guam and Leyte, and was the route regularly assigned vessels making passage between these islands, was considered within the acceptable risk limit for combatant vessels. Circuitous routes were available from Guam to Leyte, but no special apprehension was felt regarding the use of the direct route by the *Indianapolis*, and no other route was considered.

The speed of advance of the *Indianapolis* (++(15.7 knots)++) was set by Captain McVay and was based upon his desire to arrive off the entrance to Leyte Gulf at daylight on (—31 July—) (++July 31++) in order to conduct antiaircraft practice prior to his entering the Gulf. (++To have arrived a day earlier would have required a speed of advance of about 24 knots++). No special consideration was given the possibility of delaying the departure of the ship from Guam in order to enable her to proceed in company with other vessels, since the route assigned was not thought (++by the Port Director++) to be unduly hazardous. Zigzagging was, by his routing instructions, left to the discretion of Captain McVay. However, tactical orders then in force required zigzagging in conditions of good visibility (++in waters where enemy submarines might be present++).

The policy determination with regard to the escorting of vessels in the Western Pacific was the function of the Commander in Chief, Pacific Fleet. This policy, which required the escorting of vessels in some areas but dispensed with escorts of some classes of vessels in others, which were less active, was largely dictated by the (++limited++) availability of escort vessels. At the time of the sailing of the *Indianapolis*, there was a shortage in this regard and escorts were, as a rule, not given combatant vessels which were capable of "taking care of themselves." The *Indianapolis* was considered to be in this class and escort, if furnished her, would have been at the expense of other requirements of greater urgency.

(—On 28 July, the *Indianapolis* departed from Guam for Leyte. On this same date, information was disseminated that anti-submarine warfare operations were in progress along her route but well in advance of the *Indianapolis*, as a result of a submarine contact which had been made by a merchant vessel. Captain McVay apparently was not informed of the contents of at least one message dealing with enemy submarine activity, which message was on board the *Indianapolis*. Other intelligence of this nature which should have been received by the ship in broadcast messages either did not reach the ship or was not brought to the attention of Captain McVay—)

At the time of her departure from Guam, the *Indianapolis* was not at peak efficiency; but she was well organized; her personnel were well disciplined and, in the main, well versed in the performance of their routine duties. Training of personnel was continuing and her visit to Leyte was being made in order to complete her refresher training program.

(—At 0015, Zone 9½ time, on 30 July—) (++Early in the morning, at 12:15 A.M., on July 30++), while the *Indianapolis* was steaming unescorted, and not zigzagging, at a speed of 17 knots (++through the water++), under good conditions of visibility and in a moderate sea, two heavy explosions occurred against her starboard side forward, as a result of which explosions the ship capsized and sank (—at 0027-0030, Zone 9½ time, 30 July—) (++between 12:27 and 12:30 A.M., July 30. The ship sank 12 minutes after the torpedoes hit++).

(—Nothing was sighted either before—) (++No enemy vessel was sighted either before++) the explosions occurred or afterward. Watches were properly stood and good lookout was kept, both visual and radar. Normal precautions were being taken against enemy submarines. The lookouts were generally experienced men and (—were—) fully alert. The damage control party, though well organized, was unable to function properly due to the heavy personnel casualties forward, the rapid flooding and the intense fire which was started in the forward section of the ship.

The communication set-up and provisions made for sending emergency messages were in accordance with good practice and current instructions. There is ample evidence that distress messages were keyed (++by radio operators++) and possibly (++were actually++) transmitted on at least one (500 kc) and possibly two frequencies. No evidence has been developed that any distress message from the ship was received by any ship, (++aircraft++) or shore station.

Orders to abandon ship were given by some officers locally, but general word to that effect was not passed throughout the ship. This was partly due to the disruption of all mechanical and electrical means of communication. Word for all hands to go on deck was passed through some of the lower deck compartments by the boatswain's mate of the watch, but was heard by only a few of the survivors. Many men stood by their abandon ship stations until they were forced by the listing of the ship to enter the water. Much lifesaving equipment went down with the ship.

The conduct of Captain McVay and (—that of practically all—) of the other officers and men of the ship was, in the face of this emergency, satisfactory. Captain McVay (—refused to—) (++did not++) order abandon ship when it was first (—recommended—) (++suggested++) by the First Lieutenant. Shortly thereafter, (—the same recommendation was made by the Executive Officer—) (++the Executive Officer recommended abandoning ship++). The Captain, (—agreeing to—) (++approving++) this recommendation, ordered the word to be passed to all hands to abandon ship.

While some life rafts and floater nets were available to those in the water, many men had only their life jackets (—and large groups floated until they drowned or were rescued with no other means of support—).

Correct maintenance routines for emergency equipment had been in effect. The lifesaving equipment was the best type developed for surface ships and was identical with that supplied other vessels of the *Indianapolis* class.

Numerous acts of heroism and leadership and display of fortitude have been reported.

In the Headquarters of Commander Marianas on Guam and of the Commander Philippine Sea Frontier on Leyte, operational plotting boards were kept. On these boards was kept a graphic plot of the positions at sea of all vessels in which the headquarters concerned was interested. In the case of the *Indianapolis*, the departure of the vessel from Guam on (—28 July—) (++July 28++) was recorded on the plotting boards in each of these headquarters. Her estimated position was plotted on each board daily. On (—31 July—) (++July 31++), the date on which the vessel was scheduled to have arrived at Leyte, the *Indianapolis* was removed from the board in the headquarters of Commander Marianas and was recorded on the board at the headquarters of Commander Philippine Sea Frontier as having arrived at Leyte. This was the routine method of handling the plot of combatant vessels. Since, in accordance with orders standard throughout the Southwest Pacific Area, the Pacific Ocean Areas, and the Atlantic, the arrival of combatant vessels was not reported, vessels of this class were assumed to have arrived at their destinations on the date and at approximately the time scheduled in the absence of information to the contrary. However, since the *Indianapolis* did not arrive, the responsible officers at the office of the Port Director, Leyte who knew of her nonarrival should have instituted action to determine the reason.

Within sixteen hours of the actual sinking of the *Indianapolis*, there was in the Advance Headquarters of the Commander in Chief, Pacific Fleet an indication (from a single enemy source) to the effect that the Japanese had sunk something (the nature of which was unknown) in a position which was approximately the predicted position of the *Indianapolis* at the time. Had this information been evaluated as authentic, it is possible that the survivors of the *Indianapolis* might have been located within twenty-four hours of the time of the sinking of the ship and many (++additional++) lives might have been saved.

In passing judgment on this (++intelligence++) matter, certain salient features connected with this phase of the work of intelligence personnel should be borne in mind. The person who was directly responsible for the collection, evaluation, and dissemination of intelligence, particularly that of high classification, was the Combat Intelligence Officer who was charged with the general supervision of the work of the Combat Intelligence Section. Evaluating intelligence is not an exact science. It is at best an estimate; frequently it is only an intelligent assumption. In the prosecution of the Naval phase of the war in the Western Pacific, the work of this Section has been outstanding. Information developed by this Section made possible the successful execution of several operations which were of such significance and importance at the time as to have changed the entire course of the war against Japan. Regrettable though it was, failure to evaluate accurately a report made by a Japanese submarine (—had no—) (++did not necessarily have a++) bearing on the prosecution of the war as a whole and was actually of only local significance.

This failure in the evaluation of intelligence is attributable in part to the exaggerated claims and false intelligence which had characterized (++so++) many Japanese reports. It is a matter of record that enemy reports of sinking of our combatant units were constantly being made, whereas in fact, the units against which these claims were made were then operating in an entirely different area. Many of our units were several times reported to have been sunk or damaged as a "feeler" on the part of the enemy. Constant investigation of such enemy claims and the generally resulting proof of their exaggeration or falsity had caused a low evaluation to be placed on (—this—) (++the++) type of intelligence (—Such was the case in this—) (++represented by the++) report, that a vessel of undetermined size and classification had been sunk in waters to the westward of Guam.

This intelligence was also in the hands of the Commander in Chief, United States Fleet in Washington at about the same time, and was passed by him to the Commander, Seventh Fleet in Manila. No (—suspicion—) (++impression++) was created in the Headquarters of Commander, Seventh Fleet that this intelligence involved the *Indianapolis*.

The *Indianapolis* was scheduled to have arrived at Leyte at (—0200 Z on 31 July—) (++11:00 A.M., July 31++). (—This was at 1100, 31 July, Leyte time and date.—) It is probable that under normal conditions, no concern as to her nonarrival would have been felt until she was eight or nine hours overdue. Several additional hours would (++have++) elapse(d) incident to the dispatch traffic necessary to check her movements so that, in all probability, search for her would normally not have commenced until she would have been approximately twenty-four hours overdue. That would have been sometime in the forenoon of (—1 August—) (++August 1++). The survivors of the *Indianapolis* were actually sighted at about (—1025—) (++10:25 A.M.,++) Leyte time on (—2 August—) (++August 2++), by a plane on routine patrol.

(++A++) Commander in Chief, Pacific Fleet Advance Headquarters dispatch (—260152—) of July (++26++), in which CTF 95 (Vice Admiral Jesse B. Oldendorf, USN) and CTG 95.7 (Rear Admiral Lynde D. McCormick, USN), were information addressees, contained the sailing orders of the *Indianapolis*. It was ordered that the vessel upon its arrival in Leyte report by dispatch to CTF 95 for duty and directed CTG 95.7 to arrange ten days' training for the vessel in the Leyte area. Neither Commander, Seventh Fleet, Commander, Philippine Sea Frontier nor any shore-based commands in the Philippines were included in the addressees of this dispatch. This dispatch was received and understood by CTF 95 who was, at the time, at Okinawa. It was received in garbled form by CTG 95.7 who was in the Leyte area. CTF 95 noted that the actual dates of departure from Guam and of the arrival of the vessel in Leyte were not given. CTF [sic] 95.7 did not decode this dispatch since the garbled address as received did not include his command. CTG 95.7 was at sea conducting training exercises at the time (—when—) the *Indianapolis* was scheduled to arrive in Leyte.

(++A++) Port Director, Guam dispatch (—280032—) of July (++28++) included as an action addressee CTG 95.7 and as an information addressee CTF 95. In this dispatch the routing of the *Indianapolis* was given, including the date of her departure from Guam and the date of her arrival in Leyte. This dispatch was not received by CTF 95 who was, therefore, still uninformed of the date on which the *Indianapolis* should have been expected to report to him by dispatch. The Port Director, Tacloban, was an action addressee on this dispatch.

The acting Port Director at Tacloban, Leyte, Lieutenant Commander Jules C. Sancho, USNR, was not aware that the *Indianapolis* had not arrived as was scheduled and that she (—could—) (++should++) be considered as being overdue. It, however, was his duty in his capacity as Acting Port Director, to keep himself informed of such matters.

Lieutenant Stuart B. Gibson, USNR, the Operations Officer under the Port Director, Tacloban, was the officer who was immediately concerned with the movements of the *Indianapolis*. The nonarrival of that vessel on schedule was known at once to Lieutenant Gibson who not only failed to investigate the matter but made no immediate report of the fact to his superiors.

While not excusing the failure of Lieutenant Commander Sancho and Lieutenant Gibson to use the initiative and ordinary good judgment in this connection which would have been expected of naval officers, this dereliction may be (—attributed—) (++related++) to the (—weakness—) (++difficulties++) of an organization which had been brought on by the exceedingly rapid expansion of the Navy to meet its wartime requirements.

In view of the volume of shipping which was being handled by the Port of Tacloban, it would have been desirable that the important assignments of Acting Port Director and of Operations Officer of the Port should have been given to more experienced officers.

(—The Commander in Chief, U.S. Pacific Fleet and Pacific Ocean Areas, in a directive dated 26 January 1945 and an identical directive by Commander, Seventh Fleet, under whom the naval activities in the Philippines were operated and administered,—) In order to reduce the volume of radio traffic and increase security, (++the Commander in Chief, U.S. Pacific Fleet and Pacific Ocean Areas, in a directive dated January 26, 1945, and the Commander, Seventh Fleet, under whom the naval activities in the Philippines were operated and administered, in an identical directive,++) made specific provision that the arrival of combatant vessels was not to be reported. In preparing this as well as in the preparation of all directives issued by their headquarters, these two commanders were mindful of the fact that these instructions would be given general dissemination and that officers who were relatively inexperienced in naval matters would be charged with their execution. For this reason, every attempt was made to insure that the wording was clear, concise, and that the meaning could not be misinterpreted. Although these directives were prepared with thought and care, that they were subject to misinterpretation is shown by the inference drawn by Lieutenant Gibson. It was not the intention to prohibit in these directives the reporting of the nonarrival of combatant ships. Nonarrivals were expected to be reported. However, no mention of this was made in the letter and the inference was drawn by this officer that since arrival reports were not to be made for combatant ships, by the same token neither were reports of nonarrivals to be made. This matter has since been clarified in terms which cannot be misinterpreted.

Lieutenant Commander Sancho and Lieutenant Gibson were members of the Philippine Sea Frontier organization. Bearing in mind the lack of experience of these officers in naval matters, it was incumbent upon their superior officers to exercise closer personal supervision over the manner in which their duties were performed than was actually the case. At the time of the loss of the *Indianapolis*, the Commander, Philippine Sea Frontier, Vice Admiral James L. Kauffman, USN, was absent from his command since (—1 July,—) (++July 1,++) 1945 on temporary duty status in the United States; Commodore N. C. Gillette, USN, was in temporary command; and the Operations Officer of the Headquarters Staff, Captain A. M. Granum, USN, was intensively occupied in diversion of shipping in typhoon areas and operations. These facts do not, however, relieve these senior officers of their responsibility connected with the failure of their subordinates to take appropriate action to ascertain the whereabouts of the overdue *Indianapolis* (++.++) (—for—) The junior officers who were directly concerned with this failure were members of the organization which was being administered by these senior officers. For this demonstrated weakness in the organization under their control, brought on largely through their failure to give closer personal attention to the work of these inexperienced juniors, Commodore Gillette and Captain Granum have been held responsible.

CTF 95, at Okinawa, took no action to check on the arrival in Leyte of the *Indianapolis*. It was known to this officer that the *Indianapolis* was directed to report to him by dispatch upon her arrival in Leyte but, for reasons before mentioned, he was not informed of her departure from Guam or of the date of her scheduled arrival in Leyte, (++and++) hence assumed that the ship was still at Guam (++or en route++).

Commander, Philippine Sea Frontier (Commodore N. C. Gillette, USN, Chief of Staff, Acting) was charged with the mission of safeguarding and protecting shipping in the area under his cognizance. He maintained an Operations Board at his Headquarters at Tolosa, Leyte, on which was kept a running record of the scheduled and actual arrival and departure of vessels of all categories in the area under his cognizance. His Headquarters had been given intelligence of all submarine activity in the Philippine Sea and (—was—) (++should have been++) aware that the *Indianapolis* was overdue in Leyte, but no investigation as to her whereabouts was instituted until after her survivors were sighted.

Commander, Marianas, in Guam, felt no particular concern connected with the arrival of the *Indianapolis* in Leyte. He assumed that the *Indianapolis* had reached her destination. No action was taken (++or required to be taken++) by that headquarters until the survivors were sighted.

Aircraft patrols which daily covered a great part of the route followed by the *Indianapolis*, and which were sighted daily by the survivors, failed to sight the oil slick or the survivors for (—several—) (++two++) days after the sinking. Discovery of the survivors by aircraft patrol was largely accidental. Investigation revealed that the planes were flying at altitudes which were considered the optimum for searching the area for enemy craft by search radar and visual lookout. Since, at this time and in this area, enemy craft were almost certain to be submarines, this was, in effect, an anti-submarine patrol. Planes were generally flying too high to see the *Indianapolis* survivors (—whose life rafts did not have radar reflectors—).

At (—1125 local time, 2 August—) (++11:25 A.M., August 2++), while flying in his assigned sector on a routine search mission, (—Lt. (jg)—) (++Lieutenant (junior grade)++) Wilbur C. Gwinn, USNR, flying a twin-engine landplane, sighted an oil slick in position approximately 11-30 north, 133-30 east, approximately 250 miles north of Peleliu. He immediately changed course to investigate and soon sighted a group of about thirty survivors. Dropping a life raft and radio transmitter near the group (—Lt. (jg)—) (++Lieutenant (junior grade)++) Gwinn radioed a report that alerted all commands (—near—) (++in++) the area having search and rescue forces under their control. All air and surface units capable of operations were ordered to the scene. Upon receipt of the report, (—Lt. Comdr.—) (++Lieutenant Commander++) George C. Atteberry, U.S.N.R., took off from his base at Peleliu and arrived on the scene (—1415—) (++2:15 P.M.++). Upon arrival, (—Lt. Comdr.—) (++Lieutenant Commander++) Atteberry, assisted by a Navy patrol seaplane which had been en route to the Philippines and had arrived in the area at (—1345—) (++1:45 P.M.++), conducted a further search, both planes dropping life rafts and rescue equipment near survivors.

The first of the rescue forces hurrying to the scene to arrive was a Navy *Catalina* patrol seaplane. This plane landed in the water about (—1705—) (++5:05 P.M.++) to afford support to those not in life rafts. Coached by (—Lt. Comdr.—) (++Lieutenant Commander++) Atteberry, the *Catalina* seaplane picked up a total of 58 survivors. This plane was so badly damaged on landing and in rescue operations that it could not take off. However, all the rescued were given elementary first aid and a few hours later transferred to a surface vessel.

Later in the afternoon, an Army rescue plane, a flight of seven additional large Navy planes, and two Army bombers arrived in the area, conducted intensive searches and dropped large quantities of life rafts and other rescue gear, to all personnel sighted.

During the night a majority of the available surface craft, consisting of four destroyers, four destroyer escorts, three fast, light transports, plus numerous patrol craft, arrived. Thorough and methodical search and rescue operations were commenced. By night powerful searchlights, flares, and star shells swept the area, and by day, planes coached surface ships to every object sighted.

Before the search was abandoned on August 8th, the area within a 100-mile radius of the center of the survivors group had been so thoroughly searched that there was no possibility that a single individual remaining afloat had been missed.

The following disciplinary action has been taken in connection with the loss of the *Indianapolis*:

Captain Charles B. McVay, III, USN, has been brought to trial by General Court Martial. He was acquitted of failure to give (++timely++) orders to abandon ship. He was found guilty of negligence in not causing a zigzag to be steered. He was sentenced to lose one hundred numbers in his temporary grade of Captain and also in his permanent grade of Commander. The Court and also the Commander in Chief, United States Fleet recommended clemency. The Secretary of the Navy has approved these recommendations, remitted the sentence, and restored Captain McVay to duty.

The Secretary of the Navy has given (—Captain—) (++Commodore++) N. C. Gillette, USN, a Letter of Reprimand, which will become part of his permanent official record.

The Secretary of the Navy has given Captain A. M. Granum, USN, a Letter of Reprimand, which will become part of his permanent official record.

(—The Secretary of the Navy has given Captain Naquin, USN, a Letter of Admonition, which will become part of his permanent official record.—)

The Commander in Chief, Pacific Fleet has given Lieutenant Commander Jules C. Sancho, USNR, a Letter of Admonition, which will become part of his permanent official record.

The Commander in Chief, Pacific Fleet has given Lieutenant Stuart B. Gibson, USNR, a Letter of Reprimand, which will become part of his permanent official record.

Appendix K
Press and Radio Release: Court-Martial of Captain Charles B. McVay, III, U.S.N., Commanding Officer, U.S.S. Indianapolis

(Command File, World War II)

NAVY DEPARTMENT

IMMEDIATE RELEASE
PRESS AND RADIO   February 23, 1946

REPORT ON COURT MARTIAL
OF
CAPTAIN CHARLES B. McVAY, III, USN,
COMMANDING OFFICER, USS *INDIANAPOLIS*

Captain Charles B. McVay, III, U.S. Navy, was tried on December 3-19, 1945, by a Naval Court Martial composed of seven members. His trial followed the sinking of the USS *Indianapolis* by a Japanese submarine and was based upon two charges: First, inefficiency in failing to issue and insure the execution of orders for the abandonment of the USS *Indianapolis*; Second, negligence in "Suffering a Vessel of the Navy to be Hazarded" by neglecting and failing to cause a zigzag course to be steered when visibility conditions and information concerning enemy submarines required him under current United States Fleet Tactical Orders to zigzag in order to minimize the danger from submarine attack. Captain McVay was acquitted of the first charge and therefore was cleared of responsibility for the loss of lives incident to the abandonment of the ship. He was convicted of the second charge. He was neither charged with, nor tried for, losing the *Indianapolis*. The sentence imposed by the court decreed the loss of one hundred numbers in his temporary grade of Captain and one hundred numbers in his permanent grade of Commander. In view of his outstanding previous record, the court unanimously recommended clemency.

The proceedings, findings and sentence were found legal by the

Judge Advocate General and were approved by the Chief of Naval Personnel. This approval, however, was accompanied by the recommendation that, in view of Captain McVay's excellent record and the unanimous recommendation for clemency by the court, the sentence should be remitted and he should be restored to duty. Fleet Admiral King, Commander in Chief and Chief of Naval Operations at the time of the disaster in July, 1945, concurred in the recommendation by the Chief of Naval Personnel. Secretary of the Navy James Forrestal has approved these recommendations and has remitted the sentence of Captain McVay in its entirety, releasing him from arrest and restoring him to duty.

Captain McVay has a record of capable and gallant service to his country. During World War II he had extensive combat duty; he received numerous commendations and the award of the Silver Star Medal for heroism in action and the Purple Heart Medal.

Appendix L
Recommended Awards to Various Members
of the Crew of the U.S.S. Indianapolis

Recommended awards, all posthumous, submitted by Captain Charles B. McVay, III, to James Forrestal, Secretary of the Navy, in memorandums dated September 8, 1945.

It is respectfully requested that the Navy Cross be awarded posthumously to Captain Edward L. PARKE, USMC, for service as set forth in the following citation:

> For extraordinary heroism in rescuing and organizing a large group of men following the sinking of the USS *Indianapolis* on 30 July 1945. Struggling in oil-covered water and without food, drinking water, or life rafts he worked constantly for three days keeping the group together and rounding up stragglers and rescuing men in difficulty. On several occasions he gave away his own life jacket to support exhausted men, finally collapsing himself from exhaustion. His unselfish and heroic

conduct in the face of great personal danger was outstanding and in keeping with the highest traditions of the Naval Service.

It is respectfully requested that the Navy Cross be awarded posthumously to Harold Robert ANTHONY, PhM3/c, for service as set forth in the following *suggested* citation:

For extraordinary heroism while attached to a United States heavy cruiser which was sunk as the result of enemy action three hundred miles north of the Palau Islands on 30 July 1945. ————. The only Pharmacist's Mate in a group of one hundred and fifty survivors, he worked unceasingly to save the lives and bring comfort to many of his shipmates up until the time he gave his life due to complete exhaustion on the morning of 2 August. Although realizing twelve hours before his death that without rest he wouldn't survive, he continued to aid his comrades. His determination and unselfish and heroic conduct throughout were outstanding and in keeping with the highest traditions of the Naval Service.

It is respectfully requested that the Bronze Star Medal be awarded posthumously to Ensign H. C. MOYNELO, Jr., for service as set forth in the following *suggested* citation:

For heroic service in connection with operations against the enemy while attached to a United States heavy cruiser which was sunk——. Immediately following the sinking of his ship he succeeded in rescuing and organizing a large group of men. Despite oil-covered water, and without food, drinking water, or life rafts, he worked constantly for three days keeping the group together by rounding up stragglers and rescuing men in difficulty. On several occasions he gave away his own life jacket to support exhausted men, finally collapsing himself from exhaustion. His unselfish and heroic conduct in the face of great personal danger was outstanding and in keeping with the highest traditions of the Naval Service.

It is respectfully requested that the Bronze Star Medal be

awarded posthumously to Lieutenant Commander Cedric Foster COLEMAN for service as set forth in the following citation:

> For heroic service in connection with operations against the enemy while attached to a United States heavy cruiser which was sunk——. As leader of a group of survivors, he worked unceasingly to keep them together despite the fact that the exertion on his part had such a weakening effect on him that it ultimately caused his death from complete exhaustion. On several occasions, he swam from the group to bring in stragglers, thereby saving their lives. His unselfish and heroic conduct throughout were outstanding and in keeping with the highest traditions of the Naval Service.

It is respectfully requested that the Bronze Star Medal be awarded posthumously to Garland Lloyd RICH, S1c, for service as set forth in the following *suggested* citation:

> For heroic service in connection with operations against the enemy while attached to a United States heavy cruiser which was sunk——. Despite oil-covered water, and without food, drinking water, or life rafts he unceasingly assisted the doctor in caring for the wounded and exhausted men, thereby saving many lives. He supported a badly wounded officer for twenty-four hours and finally, after giving all that was in him, collapsed himself from exhaustion. His heroic and unselfish conduct in the face of great personal danger was outstanding and in keeping with the highest traditions of the Naval Service.

Memorandum from Captain C. B. McVay, III, Commanding Officer, U.S.S. *Indianapolis* (CA 35) to Commander, Cruisers, Pacific Fleet, dated September 5, 1945.

1. On 30 July 1945, the U.S.S. *Indianapolis* (CA 35) was sunk as the result of enemy action about three hundred miles north of the Palau Islands while en route to Leyte, Philippine Islands. As the survivors were not sighted until 2 August, many acts of heroism and courage were performed in the interim, some of which will never be recognized due to the difficult conditions

over which we had no control. However, the following is a list of acts which have been brought to my attention and the recommended awards in the form of suggested citations:

(a)   Commander Lewis L. Haynes (MC), U.S. Navy
        Recommended Award: Bronze Star

For heroic service while attached to a United States heavy cruiser which was sunk——. Although suffering from painful burns, and while the ship was sinking, he administered first aid to the casualties on the quarterdeck until the ship listed to such a degree that all persons were thrown into the water. During the subsequent four days in the water, with no support other than a kapok life preserver, and without benefit of food or water, by his outstanding leadership and spirit he materially aided the more than one hundred officers and men in his group to survive until aid reached them. His determination and heroic conduct throughout were outstanding and in keeping with the highest traditions of the Naval Service.

(b)   John Alton Schmueck, CPhM, U.S. Navy
        Recommended Award: Bronze Star

For heroic service in connection with operations against the enemy while attached to a United States heavy cruiser which was sunk——. Immediately following the explosion he reported to his battle station and began administering first aid and assisting the ship's doctor, remaining there until the ship capsized and sank. During the following four days and five nights, without food, water, or the benefit of life rafts, and even though he was wearing a faulty pneumatic jacket, he continued to administer aid to the wounded and exhausted men. His heroic conduct, performed in the face of great danger to himself, was outstanding and in keeping with the highest traditions of the Naval Service.

(c)   Clarance Upton Benton, CFC, U.S. Navy
        Recommended Award: Bronze Star

For heroic service in connection with operations against the enemy while attached to a United States heavy cruiser which was sunk——. Despite agonizing pain from a bleeding ulcer he aided the senior officer of a group of one hundred fifty survivors who had little food, no good drinking water, and only three rafts by speaking to the half-crazed men in a calm, reassuring voice, thereby reducing the number of men lost by fighting, swimming away, and drowning.* His leadership, courage, and devotion to duty throughout were outstanding and in keeping with the highest traditions of the Naval Service.

(d)   Anthony Francis Maday, AMM1c, U.S. Navy
       Recommended Award: Bronze Star

For heroic service in connection with operations against the enemy while attached to a United States heavy cruiser which was sunk——. In oil-covered water and without food, water, or life rafts he unstintingly gave of his rapidly waning strength to aid the wounded whenever possible. In one instance, he supported a mortally wounded officer for two days until the latter died. His heroic conduct, performed in the face of great danger to himself, was outstanding and in keeping with the highest traditions of the Naval Service.

(e)   Vincent Jerome Allard, QM3c, U.S. Navy
       Recommended Award: Bronze Star

For heroic service in connection with operations against the enemy while attached to a United States heavy cruiser which was sunk——. During the subsequent four and one half days he not only caught fish for the group on the rafts and fashioned hats out of canvas to protect their heads from the sun but also saved the lives of two men shortly after the ship sank by bringing them to the raft. His initiative, heroic conduct in the face of great personal danger, and complete devotion to duty throughout were outstanding and in keeping with the highest traditions of the Naval Service.

---

*The original word typed in this recommendation was suicide. Suicide was subsequently crossed out in pen and the word drowning substituted.

(f)   Eugene Edward Ethier, EM3c, USNR
          Recommended Award: Bronze Star

For heroic service in connection with operations against
the enemy while attached to a United States heavy cruiser
which was sunk——. Although suffering from exhaustion,
exposure, and a fractured foot, he, in company with
another man, supported a survivor who was very ill from
internal bleeding and exposure for two days, thereby saving his life. His unselfishness and heroic conduct throughout were outstanding and in keeping with the highest
traditions of the Naval Service.

(g)   Marvin F. Kirkland, S1c, USNR
          Recommended Award: Bronze Star

For heroic service in connection with operations against
the enemy while attached to a United States heavy cruiser
which was sunk——. Although suffering from exhaustion,
exposure and a fractured jaw, he, in the company of
another man, supported a survivor who was ill from internal bleeding and exposure for two days, thereby saving his
life. His unselfishness and heroic conduct throughout were
outstanding and in keeping with the highest traditions of
the Naval Service.

(h)   James Franklin Newhall, S1c, USNR
          Recommended Award: Bronze Star

For heroic service in connection with operations against
the enemy while attached to a United States heavy cruiser
which was sunk——. With total disregard for his own
safety he voluntarily made three trips into a burning and
smoke-filled compartment, and in so doing, saved the lives
of two men. His heroic conduct, in the face of great danger
to himself, was outstanding and in keeping with the highest traditions of the Naval Service.

(i)   Ensign Harlan Malcolm Twible, U.S. Navy
          Recommended Award: Bronze Star

For heroic service in connection with operations against

the enemy while attached to a United States heavy cruiser which was sunk——. During the period which followed he constantly aided the half-crazed men who were drifting off the raft and swimming away, and, in general, maintained order among the survivors. In addition, he prudently rationed the small supply of food and water which the group had, thereby preventing it from being wasted or destroyed. When a rescue aircraft dropped a boat equipped with flares and signalling equipment, he contributed materially to the success of rescue operations by maintaining contact with the rescue plane which guided surface vessels to the scene. His leadership, courage, and complete devotion to duty throughout were outstanding and in keeping with the highest traditions of the Naval Service.

(j) Lieutenant R. B. Redmayne, U.S. Naval Reserve
Recommended Award: Bronze Star

For heroic service in connection with operations against the enemy while attached to a United States heavy cruiser which was sunk——. Although suffering from severe burns on his fingers and hands, and while the ship was sinking, he made his way to the main engine room where he stayed, securing necessary machinery and spaces until the ship listed to such a degree that the engine room became untenable. During the subsequent three days in the water with no support other than a kapok life preserver, by his outstanding leadership and spirit he materially aided the more than one hundred officers and men in his group to survive until he was completely exhausted and he himself had to be cared for. His determination and heroic conduct throughout were outstanding and in keeping with the highest traditions of the Naval Service.

(k) Loren Charles McHenry, Jr., S1c, USNR
Recommended Award: Bronze Star

For meritorious service in connection with operations against the enemy while attached to a United States heavy cruiser which was sunk——. Although weak from exhaustion and exposure and partially blinded from oil and salt water, he acted as signalman for a group of survivors after a motor whaleboat had been dropped by a transport plane. By his constant devotion to duty the survivors were able to keep in constant contact with the rescue plane which in turn guided the surface vessels to the scene. His courage and untiring devotion to duty throughout were outstanding and in keeping with the highest traditions of the Naval Service.

2. The acts upon which these recommendations are based have not been used as a basis for previous awards.

3. This officer has no knowledge of any previous awards being received by the personnel mentioned herein.

C. B. McVay, III

Bibliography

ALL of the documents shown in the *Primary Source Information* section of this bibliography, will be turned over, by the author, for safekeeping, to:

John D. H. Kane, Jr., Rear Admiral, USN (Ret.)
Director of Naval History
and Curator for The Navy Department
Naval Historical Center, Washington Navy Yard
Washington, D.C. 20374

We believe that this would be the most appropriate depository for them and is well set up to administer this material.

At the author's request, all of this material will be restricted to access only by bona fide scholars and researchers, and this condition will be honored by Admiral Kane and his staff.

General Works

Books

Amrine, Michael. *The Great Decision: The Secret History of the Atomic Bomb.* New York: G. P. Putnam's Sons, 1959.

Buell, Thomas B. *The Quiet Warrior: A Biography of Admiral Raymond A. Spruance.* Boston: Little, Brown & Co., 1974.

Couhat, Jean Lebayle, ed. *Combat Fleets of the World 1976-77: Their Ships, Aircraft, and Armament.* Annapolis: Naval Institute Press, 1976.

Fetridge, William Harrison, ed. *The Navy Reader*. Freeport, New York: Books for Libraries Press, 1943.

Forrestel, E. P. *Admiral Raymond A. Spruance, USN: A Study in Command*. Washington, D.C.: U.S. Government Printing Office, 1966.

Hashimoto, Mochitsura. *Sunk: The Story of the Japanese Submarine Fleet, 1941-1945*. New York: Henry Holt & Co., Inc., 1954.

Helm, Thomas. *Ordeal by Sea: The Tragedy of the U.S.S. Indianapolis*. New York: Dodd, Mead & Co., 1963.

———. *Shark! Unpredictable Killer of the Sea*. New York: Dodd, Mead & Co., 1961.

Hoyt, Edwin P. *How They Won the War in the Pacific: Nimitz and His Admirals*. New York: Weybright and Talley, 1970.

Karig, Walter; Harris, Russel L.; and Manson, Frank A., eds. *Battle Report: Victory in the Pacific*. Vol. 5. New York: Rinehart & Co., Inc., 1949.

Long, Luman H., ed. *The World Almanac and Book of Facts*. 1972 edition. New York: Newspaper Enterprise Association, Inc.

Morison, Samuel Eliot. *History of United States Naval Operations in World War II*. 15 volumes. Esp. vol. 14: *Victory in the Pacific 1945*. Boston: Little, Brown & Co., 1960.

———. *The Two-Ocean War: A Short History of the United States Navy in the Second World War*. Boston: Little, Brown & Co., 1963.

Newcomb, Richard F. *Abandon Ship!: Death of the U.S.S. Indianapolis*. New York: Henry Holt & Co., 1958.

Potter, E. B. *Nimitz*. Annapolis: Naval Institute Press, 1976.

Silverstone, Paul H. *U.S. Warships of World War II*. New York: Doubleday & Co., 1972.

Thomas, Gordon, and Witts, Max Morgan. *Enola Gay*. New York: Stein and Day, 1977.

Wallechinsky, David; Wallace, Irving; and Wallace, Amy. *The Book of Lists*. New York: William Morrow & Co., 1977.

Yokota, Yutaka, and Harrington, Joseph D. *Suicide Submarine* (Formerly *The Kaiten Weapon*). New York: Ballantine Books, Inc., 1962.

Almanac of Naval Facts. Annapolis: United States Naval Institute, 1964.

Dictionary of American Naval Fighting Ships. Esp. vol. 3. Washington, D.C.: U.S. Government Printing Office, 1968.

The Japanese Navy in World War Two. (An anthology by former officers of the Imperial Japanese Navy.) Annapolis: United States Naval Institute, 1969.

Encyclopaedia Britannica. 1972 edition.

Who Was Who in America: A Companion Biographical Reference Work to Who's Who in America. Vol. 2. Chicago: A. N. Marquis Co., 1950.

Periodicals/Magazines

Haynes, Lewis L., and Campbell, George W. "We Prayed While 883 Died." *Saturday Evening Post,* August 6, 1955, p. 28.

Boyd, Carl. "Attacking the *Indianapolis*—A Re-Examination." *Warship International,* Vol. 13, No. 1, pp. 15-25.

Yokota, Yutaka, and Harrington, Joseph D. "Kaiten—Japan's Human Torpedoes." *U.S. Naval Institute Proceedings,* January 1962, pp. 55-68.

"The Captain Stands Accused." *Time,* 10 December, 1945, pp. 23-24.

"Men Against the Sea." *Time,* 27 August, 1945, p. 25.

Newspapers

All of the following are from *The New York Times*.

"Cruiser Sunk, 1,196 Casualties; Took Atom Bomb Cargo to Guam," 15 August, 1945, p. 1.

"The *Indianapolis*" (editorial), 17 August, 1945, p. 16.

"Cruiser's Sinking Laid to Submarine," 18 September, 1945, p. 4.

"Navy Orders Trial for Captain of Sunken Cruiser *Indianapolis*" 28 November, 1945, p. 4.

"Court-Martial of Captain McVay Opens; Lost Cruiser's Skipper Loses Trial Point," 4 December, 1945, p. 3.

"Captain of Cruiser Pleads Not Guilty" (by-line: W. H. Lawrence), 5 December, 1945, p. 5.

"No Alarm Blown on *Indianapolis*," 6 December, 1945, p. 3.

"McVay Gave Order to Leave Cruiser," 7 December, 1945, p. 4.

"McVay Trial Calls Japanese Officer," 9 December, 1945, p. 1.

"Japanese Witness Here," 10 December, 1945, p. 3.

"To Testify at Navy Court-Martial," 11 December, 1945.

"May Bar Hashimoto as M'Vay Witness," 12 December, 1945, p. 15.

"Japanese Tells of Sinking U.S. Cruiser by Torpedoes" (by-line: W. H. Lawrence), 14 December, 1945, p. 1.

"Prosecution Rests in Trial of M'Vay," 15 December, 1945, p. 2.

"Testify for M'Vay at Court Martial," 16 December 1945, p. 2.

"McVay Says Zig-Zag Was Unnecessary" (by-line: W. H. Lawrence), 19 December, 1945, p. 4.

"McVay Acquitted on One Charge; No Report Made on Negligence," 20 December, 1945, p. 1.

"Hashimoto Returning to Japan," 22 December, 1945, p. 8.

"Navy Court Findings on M'Vay Completed," 5 January, 1946, p. 14.

"McVay Guilty in *Indianapolis* Loss; Sentence Is Remitted on His Record" (by-line: W. H. Lawrence), 24 February, 1946, p. 1.

Other Newspapers
"McVay Called 'Negligent,'" *Washington Daily News,* 3 December, 1945, p. 5.
"Why Sharks Make Us Shiver" (by-line: Dick Brass), *New York Daily News,* 2 July, 1978, p. 4.
"Relive True 'Jaws' Story: *Indianapolis* Survivors Meet" (by-line: John D. Burlage), *Navy Times,* 24 September, 1975, p. 43.
"Sharks: What We Don't Know Definitely Can Hurt Us," (Interview of Bernard J. Zahuranec, Marine Biologist, Office of Naval Research, by Gregory Simpkins, Contributing Editor), *Navy Times,* 24 September, 1975, p. 42.
"The *Indianapolis* Sank 15 Minutes After Torpedoing," *New York World-Telegram and Sun,* 16 August, 1945, p. 1.

Miscellaneous
Operation and Engagement Stars. Navy Department: Bureau of Naval Personnel. (NAVPERS 15,632.) August 31, 1945.
Navy Department Communiques 601-624. May 25, 1945, to August 30, 1945, and Pacific Fleet Communiques 373 to 471 with Other Official Statements and Pertinent Press Releases. Washington, D.C.: U.S. Government Printing Office, 1946.
Register of Commissioned and Warrant Officers of the United States Navy and Marine Corps. (NAVPERS 15,018.) Washington, D.C.: U.S. Government Printing Office, 1943.

Smith-Hutton, Henri. *Open Manuscript, Int. 46, at Palo Alto, California, November 14, 1974, by Captain Paul Ryan.* pp. 584-86. Annapolis: United States Naval Institute.

Primary Source Information

All of the following information in this section was obtained from The Department of the Navy, Office of the Judge Advocate General, Washington, D.C.

The two most important sources are:

Record of Proceedings of a General Court-Martial Convened at the Navy Yard, Washington, D.C., by Order of the Secretary of the Navy in the Case of Charles B. McVay, 3rd, Captain, U.S. Navy, December 3, 1945. 3 volumes.

Record of Proceedings of a Court of Inquiry Convened at the Headquarters of the Commander, Marianas, by Order of the Commander in Chief, United States Pacific Fleet and Pacific Ocean Areas for the Purpose of Inquiring into all the Circumstances Connected with the Sinking of the U.S.S. Indianapolis *(CA-35), on or about July 29, 1945, the Rescue Operations, and the Delay in Connection with Reporting the Loss of That Ship. August 13, 1945.*

Additional Material:

Letter from J. Weldon Jones to Rear Admiral John M. Smeallie, Commandant, Sixteenth Naval District. "Letter of Commendation on Lieutenant Commander Charles B. McVay, III, as Naval Aide on the Staff of the Acting United States High Commissioner, Manila." Dated October, 20, 1939.

Report from Raymond A. Spruance, Commander, Fifth

Fleet, to the Chief of Naval Personnel. "Special Report on Performance of Duty—Captain Charles B. McVay, III." Dated May 3, 1945.

Memorandum for the Secretary of the Navy from R. S. Edwards, Vice Chief of Naval Operations. "Mochitsura Hoshimato [sic], General Court Martial Witness—Return to Japan of." Dated January 3, 1946.

Brief in the General Court Martial Case of Captain Charles B. McVay, 3rd, U.S. Navy, Tried on 3 December, 1945.

Memorandum in defense of Hashimoto Testimony to the Judge Advocate General from James Snedeker, Colonel, USMC, Chief Military Law Division. "H. Con. Res. 116 'To Expunge the Testimony of an Alien Enemy Officer from the Naval Court Records.'" Undated.

Memorandum from R. S. Ashby, Lieutenant Commander, USNR, Officer Performance Division, Bureau of Naval Personnel, to the Commandant, Potomac River Naval Command. "Captain Charles B. McVay, III, U.S. Navy—Record of, for Use in Trial by General Court Martial." Dated December 5, 1945.

"Routing Instructions." From Port Director, Guam, to Commanding Officer, USS *Indianapolis* (CA-35) with attachment thereto, "Intelligence Brief for Guam to Philippines." Dated July 27, 1945.

COMINCH F-32 Combatant Damage Card on USS *Indianapolis*.

Memorandum from the Chief of Naval Personnel to the Secretary of the Navy. "The General Court Martial in the Case of Captain Charles B. McVay, 3rd, U.S. Navy." Dated January 22, 1946.

Memorandum from Fleet Admiral E. J. King, U.S. Navy, to the Secretary of the Navy. "Record of Proceedings in General Court-Martial." Dated January 25, 1946.

Memorandum from C. W. Nimitz, Fleet Admiral, U.S. Navy,

Commander in Chief, U.S. Pacific Fleet and Pacific Ocean Areas, to Vice Admiral Charles A. Lockwood, Jr., U.S. Navy. "Directing Establishment of Court of Inquiry." Dated August 9, 1945.

Memorandum from Captain Charles B. McVay, III, U.S.N. (Ex-USS *Indianapolis*) to the Secretary of the Navy. "List I: Roster of Officers Attached to the Ship and One Passenger. List II: Officers and Enlisted Men of Com. 5th Fleet Staff Aboard the USS *Indianapolis* (CA-35). List III: Roster of Two (2) Officers and Thirty-Seven (37) Marine Personnel Attached to the USS *Indianapolis* (CA-35). List IV: Roster of Enlisted Personnel Aboard Ship and Roster of Aviation Detail. List V: Report of Navy Dead and Wounded. List VI: Report of Wounded Marines. List VII: Roster of Dead and Wounded at Base Hospital #20." Dated August 9, 1945.

Statement from Lieutenant (jg) Wilbur C. Gwinn, USNR, U.S. Pacific Fleet Air Force, Patrol Bombing Squadron 152, to Commander Fleet Air Wing Eighteen. "Statement Concerning Sighting of Survivors of CA-35 USS *Indianapolis* on 2 August, 1945." Dated August 3, 1945.

Leyte Gulf Expected Arrivals and Departures Lists of July 31, 1945, August 1, 1945 and August 2, 1945. Compiled by Commandant, Naval Operating Base, Leyte Gulf.

List of Men Buried at Sea (Partially or Entirely Identified by Rescue Ships). Compiled by Headquarters, Commander Marianas, Guam.

Letter from Francis B. Sayre to the Commander in Chief, Asiatic Squadron. "Letter of Commendation on Lieutenant Commander Charles B. McVay, III, as Naval Aide the United States High Commissioner, Manila, from July 28, 1939 to July 30, 1940. Undated.

Temporary Duty Orders. From Commandant, U.S. Naval

Operating Base, Navy 3964, to Lieutenant Commander Jules C. Sancho, USNR. Undated.

Change of Duty. From Commandant, U.S. Naval Operating Base, 3964, to Lieutenant Commander Jules C. Sancho, USNR. Dated July 29, 1945.

Temporary Duty Orders. From Commanding Officer, U.S. Naval Station 3149, to Lieutenant Commander Jules C. Sancho, USNR. Dated July 8, 1945.

Change of Duty. From Commanding Officer, U.S. Naval Station 3149, to Lieutenant Commander Jules C. Sancho. Dated August 2, 1945.

Leyte Gulf Ships Present List for July 31, 1945, August 1, 1945, and August 2, 1945.

Memorandums (5) from Vice Admiral C. H. McMorris, Chief of Staff of Commander in Chief, U.S. Pacific Fleet and Pacific Ocean Areas, to Captain Alfred M. Granum, USN; Lieutenant Commander Jules C. Sancho, USNR; Commodore Norman C. Gillette, USN; Rear Admiral Lynde D. McCormick, USN; and Commodore Jacob H. Jacobson, USN. "Court of Inquiry Regarding Loss of USS *Indianapolis* (CA-35)." All dated August 29, 1945.

Memorandum from Commodore Norman C. Gillette, USN, to Commander in Chief, U.S. Pacific Fleet and Pacific Ocean Areas. "Court of Inquiry Regarding Loss of USS *Indianapolis* (CA-35)." Dated September 1, 1945.

Memorandum from Commodore Jacob H. Jacobson, USN, to Commander in Chief, U.S. Pacific Fleet and Pacific Ocean Areas. "Court of Inquiry Regarding Loss of USS *Indianapolis* (CA-35)—Statement." Dated August 31, 1945.

Personal Narrative of Captain Charles B. McVay, III, USN. (Not to be confused with Narrative dated 9/27/45.) Made Exhibits 1(7), 1(8), and 1(9) of Court of Inquiry. Undated.

Memorandum from Lieutenant Commander Jules C. Sancho, USNR, to Commander in Chief, U.S. Pacific Fleet and Pacific Ocean Areas. "Court of Inquiry Regarding Loss of USS *Indianapolis* (CA-35)." Dated August 31, 1945.

Memorandum from Captain Alfred M. Granum, USN, to Commander in Chief, U.S. Pacific Fleet and Pacific Ocean Areas. "Court of Inquiry Regarding Loss of USS *Indianapolis* (CA-35)." Dated September 1, 1945.

Memorandum from Rear Admiral L. D. McCormick, USN, Commander Battleship Division Three (formerly Commander Task Group 95.7, Philippine Training Group of Task Force 95), to Commander in Chief, U.S. Pacific Fleet and Pacific Ocean Areas. "Court of Inquiry Regarding Loss of USS *Indianapolis* (CA-35)." Dated September 22, 1945.

Memorandum from Fleet Admiral C. W. Nimitz, U.S. Navy, Commander in Chief, U.S. Pacific Fleet and Pacific Ocean Areas, to the Judge Advocate General of the Navy. "Court of Inquiry to Inquire into All the Circumstances Connected with the Sinking of the USS *Indianapolis* (CA-35), and the Delay in Reporting the Loss of That Ship." Dated September 27, 1945.

Memorandum from T. J. O'Brien, Captain, USN, Director of Welfare, to the Secretary of the Navy. "Status of Men Missing/Killed in Action Aboard USS *Indianapolis*." Dated September 27, 1945.

Memorandum from the Chief of Naval Personnel to the Secretary of the Navy. "Court of Inquiry to Inquire into the Sinking of the USS *Indianapolis* (CA-35), and the Delay in Reporting the Loss of That Ship." Dated October 4, 1945.

Memorandum from E. J. King, Commander in Chief, United States Fleet and Chief of Naval Operations, to the Secretary of the Navy. "Court of Inquiry to Inquire into All the

Circumstances Connected with the Sinking of the USS *Indianapolis* (CA-35) and with the Delay in Reporting the Loss of That Ship." Dated September 25, 1945.

Memorandum from E. J. King, Commander in Chief, United States Fleet and Chief of Naval Operations, to the Secretary of the Navy. "Court of Inquiry to Inquire into the Sinking of the USS *Indianapolis* (CA-35), and the Delay in Reporting the Loss of that Ship." Dated October 8, 1945.

Memorandum from E. J. King, Chief of Naval Operations, to the Naval Inspector General. "Further Investigation into the Sinking of the USS *Indianapolis* (CA-35) and the Delay in Reporting the Loss of That Vessel." Dated October 18, 1945.

Memorandum from the Chief of Naval Personnel to the Secretary of the Navy. "Court of Inquiry—Sinking of USS *Indianapolis* (CA-35); CONV by C in C, PAC FLT & PAC Ocean Areas, 9 August 1945." Dated November 8, 1945.

Memorandum from the Chief of Naval Personnel to the Secretary of the Navy. "Court of Inquiry—Sinking of USS *Indianapolis* (CA-35); Deaths of and Injuries to U.S. Naval Personnel; CONV by C in C, PAC FLT & PAC Ocean Areas, 9 August 1945." Dated March 5, 1946.

Memorandum from the Chief of Naval Operations to the Secretary of the Navy. "Court of Inquiry—Sinking of USS *Indianapolis* (CA-35); Convened by C in C PAC, PAC FLT, POA, 9 August 1945." Dated November 10, 1945.

Memorandum from Captain T. J. Ryan, Jr., USN, Judge Advocate, to the Secretary of the Navy. "Declassification of Classified Documents, or Parts Thereof, Necessary to Conduct of the Case—GCM of Captain C. B. McVay, III, USN." Dated November 28, 1945.

Memorandum from Rear Admiral O. S. Colclough, USN,

Judge Advocate General of the Navy, to the Secretary of the Navy. "General Court Martial in the Case of Captain C. B. McVay, 3rd, USN." Dated November 29, 1945.

Memorandum from the Secretary of the Navy to Commandant, Potomac River Naval Command. "McVay, Charles B., 3rd, Captain, U.S. Navy, Trial of by General Court Martial." Dated November 29, 1945.

Memorandum from C. P. Snyder, Naval Inspector General, to Commander Clarke Withers, USNR. "Communication Received by USS *Hyperion.*" Dated December 6, 1945.

Memorandum from the Secretary of the Navy to Captain Alfred M. Granum, USN. "Reprimand." Undated.

Memorandum from the Secretary of the Navy to Commodore Norman C. Gillette. "Reprimand." Undated.

Memorandum from C. W. Nimitz, Commander in Chief, Pacific Fleet and Pacific Ocean Areas, to Lieutenant Stuart B. Gibson. "Letter of Reprimand." Dated September 6, 1945.

Memorandum from C. W. Nimitz, Commander in Chief, U.S. Pacific Fleet and Pacific Ocean Areas, to Lieutenant Commander Jules Sancho. "Letter of Admonition." Dated September 6, 1945.

Memorandum from the Bureau of Ships to the Chief of Naval Operations. "Abandon Ship Equipment—Criticism of in Connection with Loss of USS *Indianapolis.*" Dated March 7, 1946.

Memorandum from the Bureau of Ships to the Secretary of the Navy. "Court of Inquiry—Sinking of USS *Indianapolis* (CA-35); Deaths of and Injuries to U.S. Naval Personnel; Convened by Commander in Chief, U.S. Pacific Fleet and Pacific Ocean Areas." Dated June 19, 1946.

Memorandum from O. S. Colclough, Judge Advocate General of the Navy, to the Secretary of the Navy. "Charles

B. McVay, 3rd, Captain, U.S. Navy, Trial of by General
Court Martial." Undated.

Memorandum from C. W. Nimitz, Chief of Naval Operations,
to the Secretary of the Navy. "Court of Inquiry—Sinking
of USS *Indianapolis* (CA-35); Deaths of and Injuries to
U.S. Naval Personnel; Convened by C in C PAC and
POA, 9 August, 1945." Dated October 9, 1946.

U.S.S. CA 35, Booklet of General Plans. Bu. C&R No. 166011.
Corrected to suit ship as of December 1, 1944, by Mare
Island Navy Yard.

Memorandum from Roy W. M. Graham, Officer in Charge,
Joint Communications Activities, Guam, to Com-
mander, Marianas, (containing 23 dispatches). "Radio
Transmissions 28 and 29 July, 1945 Concerning Enemy
Submarines." Dated November 28, 1945.

Memorandum from Lieutenant J. L. Blackman, USNR, Air
Combat Intelligence Officer to Air Operations Officer,
Sub Area, covering the period from August 2, 1945,
through August 8, 1945. "Operations of VPB-23 to Date
on *Indianapolis* Rescue." Undated.

Progress Report of USS *Indianapolis* Case. Report from the
Office of the Naval Inspector General. Undated.

Memorandum from the Naval Inspector General to the Chief
of Naval Operations. "Report of Progress on Further
Investigation of the Sinking of the USS *Indianapolis*
and the Delay in Reporting the Loss of That Ship."
Dated November 30, 1945.

Memorandum from the Naval Inspector General to the Chief
of Naval Operations. "Investigation of the Sinking of
the USS *Indianapolis* and the Delay in Reporting the
Loss of That Ship." Dated January 7, 1946.

Report by the Naval Inspector General, and made part of the
Naval Inspector General's Memorandum to the Chief of
Naval Operations dated January 7, 1946, under Enclo-

sure "A." "Discussion of Facts in the Further Investigation of the Sinking of the USS *Indianapolis* and the
Delay in Reporting the Loss of This Ship."

Report by the Naval Inspector General, and made part of the
Naval Inspector General's Memorandum to the Chief of
Naval Operations dated November 30, 1945, under
Enclosure "A." "Facts and Discussion of Facts."

Memorandum from C. P. Snyder, Naval Inspector General,
to Fleet Admiral King. Dated November 10, 1945.

Memorandum from the Naval Inspector General to the Chief
of Naval Operations. "—Status of—Supplementary Investigation into the Sinking of the *Indianapolis*." Dated
November 10, 1945.

The following dispatches are also from the office of the
Judge Advocate General of the Navy. These dispatches are
"Date/Time" dispatches. Each dispatch contains six (6) digits. The first two digits give you the day it was sent, and since
we are operating in a limited time frame, i.e., late July and
early August, it is easy enough to ascertain. The last four
digits are the time it was sent but don't get confused since the
dispatches encompass a number of different time zones, and
in the book we have converted many of these to "ship's time."

NUMBER	FROM	TO
260152	CINCPAC ADV HQ	*Indianapolis*
280032	PD Guam	SCOMA/PD Tacloban/ CTG 95.7
290027	CINCPAC AD HQ	COMPHIBSPAC
300230	COMPHIBSPAC	CINCPAC AD HQ
310620	COMPHIBSPAC	CINCPAC ADV HQ
020125	Plane 19/Flight 258	COMMARIANAS, et.al.
020245	Plane 19/Flight 258	COMMARIANAS, et.al.
020155	OINC/Flight 258	Plane 19/Flight 258
020400	COMWESCARSUBAREA	*Cecil J. Doyle* (DE 368)

NUMBER	*FROM*	*TO*
020409	COMMARIANAS	CTG 94.5
020430	K9244	CTG 94.5
020321	Officer Controller	Plane 70
	Flight 258	Flight 258
020445	Plane 19/Flight 258	COMMARIANAS, et.al.
020445	K9244	CTG 94.5
020450	Plane 70/Flight 258	COMMARIANAS, et.al.
020453	COMMARIANAS	LCI(L) 990
020540	(Unknown)	AAGS/Peleliu
020430	(Unknown)	CTG 94.5
020445	(Unknown)	CTG 94.5
020617	CINCPAC ADV HQ	Kwajalein (CVE-98)
020516	COMPHILSEAFRON	CTU 75.2.16, et.al.
020502	COMPHILSEAFRON	CTU 75.2.16
020651	CINCPAC ADV HQ	CTG 94.17
020709	CTG 94.17	COMPHILSEAFRON
020737	COMWESCARSUBAREA	*Madison* (DD-424) and *Ralph Talbot* (DD-390)
020744	CINCPAC ADV HQ	*Ringness* (APD-100) and *Register* (APD-92)
020601	CTU 94.6.2	*Ralph Talbot* and *Madison*
020747	COMPHILSEAFRON	COMWESCARSUBAREA
020822	CTG 94.17	COMPHILSEAFRON, et.al.
020848	CTF 75	PD Guam
020625	RDO Peleliu	Plane 72/Flight 256
020400	COMWESCARSUBAREA	*Cecil J. Doyle*
021105	CTG 94.17	CINCPAC ADV HQ
021303	CINCPAC ADV HQ	CTG 94.17
021435	CTG 94.1 (7?)	CTF 94
020700	CTU 75.2.15	COMPHILSEAFRON
021342	COMPHILSEAFRON	CTU 75.2.15 and CTU 75.2.16
021500	*Cecil J. Doyle*	COMWESCARSUBAREA
021407	USS *Bassett*	COMPHILSEAFRON
021404	COMWESCARSUBAREA	*Ralph Talbot*, et.al.
021645	USS *Bassett*	COMPHILSEAFRON
022115	COMMARIANAS	CINCPAC
022203	CINCPAC ADV HQ	COMINCH

NUMBER	*FROM*	*TO*
030041	PD Guam	CTF 75
030125	COMWESCARSUBAREA	ATCOM Ulithi
030150	CINCPAC ADV HQ	CTG 94.5 and *Tranquillity*
030228	CINCPAC ADV HQ	COMSERVPAC
030231	CINCPAC ADV HQ	COMMARIANAS and COM 7th Fleet
030250	CO *Madison* SOPA	COMPHILSEAFRON, et.al.
030315	COMWESCARSUBAREA	CTU 94.6.11
030634	ATCOM Ulithi	COMWESCARSUBAREA
030705	COMWESCARSUBAREA	*Madison* (DD 425)
030715	CTU 94.6.2	COMMARIANAS and CTU 94.5
030250	*Madison*	COMPHILSEAFRON, et.al.
030855	*Ringness*	CINCPAC AD HQ
030923	COMMARIANAS	ARL 18, LC 369, ARV 1, and AGL 297
031112	CTU 94.6.2	DD 425 *Madison*
031158	PD Ulithi	CTG 94.5
031406	COMPHILSEAFRON	ALL PD'S, PHILSEAFRON
031040	COMWESCARSUBAREA	USS *Madison*
031408	COMPHILSEAFRON	COMWESCARSUBAREA
032341	ISCOM Tinian	COMMARIANAS
030810	CTG 94.5	USS *Madison*
040015	COMWESCARSUBAREA	CTG 94.6
032348	JCC Guam	COMMARIANAS
040052	COMWESCARSUBAREA	*Cecil J. Doyle* and *French*
040125	ISCOM Saipan	COMMARIANAS
040225	COMWESCARSUBAREA	*Register* and *Ringness*
040530	COMWESCARSUBAREA	CTG 94.6
040709	COMMARIANAS	CTU 94.7.1
040349	ISCOM Iwo	COMMARIANAS
040758	CINCPAC ADV HQ	COMWESCARSUBAREA
040806	CTU 94.7.1	USS *Herndon* (DD-638) and USS *George* (DE-697)
040741	COMWESCARSUBAREA	CINCPAC both HQ and COMMARIANAS
040302	COM Allied NAV Forces SW PAC	ALLNAVSHORADSTAB and SOPACAREA

NUMBER	FROM	TO
041441	COMMARIANAS	CTU 94.7.1
040720	COMWESCARSUBAREA	Rescue Ships
040753	CNS Samar	COMMARIANAS, et.al.
041215	USS *Tranquillity*	CTG 94.5
041845	CTU 94.7.1	*Herndon* and *George*
042219	COMPHILSEAFRON	COMMARIANAS
050204	CTU 94.6.2	COMWESCARSUBAREA
050446	COMWESCARSUBAREA	*Madison*
050416	COMWESCARSUBAREA	*Madison*
050550	COMWESCARSUBAREA	USS *Madison* and USS *Ralph Talbot*
050609	COMMARIANAS	CINCPOA ADV HQ
050317	USS *Madison*	COMWESCARSUBAREA
050931	*Alvin C. Cockrell*	COMWESCARSUBAREA
050401	COMWESCARSUBAREA	USS *Tranquillity*
051605	COMWESCARSUBAREA	*Alvin C. Cockrell*
052026	*Ringness*	CTU 95.7.5
052210	COMWESCARSUBAREA	COMMARIANAS
060133	COMMARIANAS	Port DIR Leyte
052247	ISCOM Peleliu	COMMARIANAS
060604	PD Tacloban	COMMARIANAS
060331	PD Peleliu	CINCPAC ADV HQ and PD Guam
060040	COMWESCARSUBAREA	COMPHILSEAFRON
060443	COMWESCARSUBAREA	*Cecil J. Doyle* and *French*
060329	PD Peleliu	CINCPAC ADV HQ
060809	CINCPAC ADV HQ	*Tranquillity* (AH-14)
060317	*Alvin C. Cockrell*	CTG 94.5
060651	*French*	COMWESCARSUBAREA
070021	COMMARIANAS	CINCPOA ADV HQ
070115	*French*	COMWESCARSUBAREA
070825	COMWESCARSUBAREA	*French*
070827	COMPHILSEAFRON	*Alvin C. Cockrell*
080246	*French*	COMWESCARSUBAREA
080604	COMWESCARSUBAREA	*French*
081027	*French*	COMWESCARSUBAREA
160213	COMMARIANAS	CTG 95.7
160740	COMBATDIV 3	COMMARIANAS

All of the following information in this section was obtained from the Department of the Navy, Naval Inspector General, Office of the Chief of Naval Operations, Washington, D.C.

The most important source is:

Investigation of Sinking of the USS Indianapolis, *by Order of the Chief of Naval Operations and Conducted by the Naval Inspector General. 5 volumes.*

Additional Material:

Memorandum from the Deputy Chief of Naval Operations (Administration), to "OP-00." "Report of Progress on Further Investigation of the Sinking of the USS *Indianapolis* and the Delay in Reporting the Loss of That Ship." Dated December 6, 1945.

Memorandum from W. R. Smedberg, III, Office of the Chief of Naval Operations, to Commodore Thomas E. Van Metre. Dated October 31, 1945.

Memorandum from the Commander in Chief, U.S. Pacific Fleet, to the Chief of Naval Personnel. "Letter of Reprimand—Reply to." Dated November 17, 1945.

Memorandum from Commander, Philippine Sea Frontier, to the Chief of Naval Personnel. Dated October 26, 1945.

Memorandum from Lieutenant Stuart B. Gibson to the Chief of Naval Personnel. "Letter of Reprimand—Reply to." Dated September 24, 1945.

Memorandum from Commander Lewis B. Haynes, (MC) USN, to the Naval Inspector General. "An Account of Survivors Following the Sinking of the USS *Indianapolis* with Recommended Changes in Life Saving Equipment." Dated November 26, 1945.

Memorandum from R. M. West, USCGC *Bibb* to the Naval Inspector General. "Distress Message Connection Loss of USS *Indianapolis*—Report on." Dated January 9, 1946.

Memorandum from the Naval Inspector General to the Commanding Officer, USCGC *Bibb*. "Distress Message Connection Loss of USS *Indianapolis*." Dated December 20, 1945.

Memorandum from Commander Clarke Withers, USNR, to the Naval Inspector General. "Distress Message Received by USS *Hyperion* from the USS *Indianapolis*." Dated January 20, 1946.

Memorandums (5) from Captain C. B. McVay, III to the Secretary of the Navy. "Awards—Recommendation For." Dated September 8, 1945.

Memorandum from Captain C. B. McVay, III, U.S. Navy, to Commander Cruisers, Pacific Fleet. "Awards—Recommendation For." Dated September 5, 1945.

Memorandum from the Naval Inspector General to the Chief of the Bureau of Ships; the Chief of the Bureau of Medicine and Surgery; the Chief of the Bureau of Supplies and Accounts. "Abandon Ship Equipment—Criticism of in Connection with the Loss of USS *Indianapolis*." Dated February 1, 1946.

Memorandum from the Naval Inspector General to the Chief of Naval Operations. "Reprimand—Statement in Regard To—Captain Alfred M. Granum, USN." Dated April 22, 1946.

Memorandum from the Naval Inspector General to the Chief of Naval Operations. "Reprimand—Statement in Regard To—Commodore N. C. Gillette, USN." Dated April 10, 1946.

Memorandum from T. E. Van Metre to Admiral Snyder, Naval Inspector General. "Progress Report of *Indianapolis* Case (I-58 Transmission). Dated November 2, 1945.

Memorandum from Vice Admiral Forrest Sherman, USN, to Admiral Ramsey, et.al. "Rough Draft of Narrative of the Circumstances of the Loss of the USS *Indianapolis.*" Dated February 20, 1946.

Letter from Captain Armand Morgan, USN, Planning Officer, U.S. Navy Yard, Portsmouth, New Hampshire, to Captain C. E. Coney, USN, Office of the Naval Inspector General, Washington, D.C. Dated December 10, 1945.

Letter from Donald R. Cowen, FC3c, Ex-USS *Indianapolis* to Charles McVay. Dated November 28, 1945.

Affidavit of Lieutenant Elmer C. Brewton. Dated September 19, 1945.

Supplemental Report to the Naval Inspector General's Investigation of the Sinking of the USS *Indianapolis.* "Facts (Numbered)." Undated.

Supplemental Report to the Naval Inspector General's Investigation of the Sinking of the USS *Indianapolis.* "Details of Whether the Auxiliary Radio Was Ever in Use." Undated.

Supplemental Report to the Naval Inspector General's Investigation of the Sinking of the USS *Indianapolis.* "The Dispatch Received on the *Indianapolis* of Which Captain McVay Had No Knowledge and Its Origin or Source." Undated.

Extracts from CinCPac War Diary for July 28, 1945, and July 29, 1945.

Organization Manual of the Headquarters, Philippine Sea Frontier. August 15, 1945.

Organization Manual of the Headquarters, Philippine Sea Frontier. August 28, 1945.

Wartime Pacific Routing Instructions. (Short Title: WPRI.) Headquarters, U.S. Pacific Fleet and Pacific Ocean Areas, 1945. Serial 18CL-45.

Commander Marianas (and CTF 94) Operation Plan. Commander Marianas No. 3-45, Serial 002298. Guam, July 23, 1945.

Navy Release. "U.S.S. *Indianapolis*." Dated August 11, 1945.

Press and Radio Release. "USS *Indianapolis*." Dated August 14, 1945.

Roster of Officers of the USS *Indianapolis*, NAVPERS—353 (12-43). Dated July 19, 1945.

Navy Department Communique Number 622. Dated August 14, 1945.

Navy Department Press Releases and at CinCPoa Headquarters. "Naval Losses as Announced in Naval Communiques 1-622." Dated August 14, 1945.

Biography. "Captain Charles Butler McVay, III, U.S. Navy." Dated August 10, 1945.

Further Dispatches:

NUMBER	*FROM*	*TO*
250123 (July)	(Unknown)	COMINCH, et.al.
290417 (July)	COM 7th Fleet	7th Fleet
030646 (Aug.)	CINCPAC	All commands
220340 (Aug.)	CINCPAC ADV HQ	All commands
271928 (Nov.)	CINCPAC	CNO
052230 (Dec.)	CNO	SCAP

The following data was obtained from The Department of the Navy, Naval Historical Center, Operational Archives Branch, Washington, D.C. (Reference: NRS 462, July 30, 1976.)

Most of the following reports and memorandums are what are commonly known as "Action" or "After-Action" reports.

Memorandum from Charles Butler McVay to the Secretary of the Navy. "Report of Commanding Officer, U.S.S.

Indianapolis (CA-35)." Routed through Commander Marianas, Serial: 003077. Dated December 8, 1945.

Report from the Commanding Officer, Charles B. McVay, III, USN, to the Commander in Chief, United States Fleet. "Action Report, U.S.S. *Indianapolis*." Dated August 26, 1945.

Narrative of Charles B. McVay, III, USN. "Sinking of USS *Indianapolis*." Dated September 27, 1945.

Report from Commander, Western Carolines Sub Area, to Commander in Chief, I.S. Fleet. "Rescue and Search for Survivors of U.S.S. *Indianapolis* (CA-35) and Recovery, Identification, and Burial of Bodies." Dated August 15, 1945.

Report from Lieutenant Commander W. G. Claydor, Jr., Commanding Officer, U.S.S. *Cecil J. Doyle* (DE-368), to Commander, Western Carolines Sub Area. "Memorandum Report on Rescue of Survivors of U.S.S. *Indianapolis* (CA-35), August 2-4, 1945." Undated.

Report from Lieutenant Commander W. G. Claydor, Jr., Commanding Officer, U.S.S. *Cecil J. Doyle,* to Commander Western Carolines Sub Area. "Report on Search Conducted August 5-9, 1945." Dated August 9, 1945.

Report from M. M. Sanford, Commanding Officer, U.S.S. *Alvin C. Cockrell* (DE-366), to Commander, Western Carolines Sub Area. "Report of Rescue Operations USS *Alvin C. Cockrell* (DE-366), 3 to 6 August, 1945." Dated August 8, 1945.

Report from R. C. Robbins, Jr., Commanding Officer, U.S.S. *French* (DE-367), to Commander, Western Carolines Sub Area. "Search for Bodies, Rafts and Debris from U.S.S. *Indianapolis*." Dated August 9, 1945.

Report from Donald W. Todd, Commanding Officer, U.S.S. *Madison* (DD-425), to Commander, Western Carolines Sub Area. "Narrative of Search Operations 2 to 5

August, 1945, U.S.S. *Madison* (DD-425)." Dated August 6, 1945.

Report from Donald W. Todd, Commanding Officer, U.S.S. *Madison* (DD-425), to the Commanding Officer, U.S.S. *Indianapolis*. "Identification of Bodies Recovered, Report of." Dated August 7, 1945.

Report from K. F. Neupert, Commanding Officer, U.S.S. *Aylwin* (DD-355), to Commander, Western Carolines Sub Area. "Search Operations for 4-5 August, Report of." Dated August 9, 1945.

Report from W. S. Brown, Commanding Officer, U.S.S. *Ralph Talbot* (DD-390), to Commander, Western Carolines Sub Area. "Search and Recovery of Survivors, Report of." Dated August 6, 1945.

Report from J. R. Furman, Commanding Officer, U.S.S. *Register* (APD-92), to Commander, Western Carolines Sub Area. "Search Operations of U.S.S. *Register* (APD-92) for Survivors of U.S.S. *Indianapolis*." Dated August 8, 1945.

Report from A. F. Hollingsworth, Commanding Officer, U.S.S. *Helm* (DD-388), to Commander, Western Carolines Sub Area. "Search for Survivors, Period 4-5 August, 1945, Report of." Dated August 6, 1945.

Report from A. H. Nienau, Commanding Officer, U.S.S. *Dufilho* (DE-423), to Commander, Western Carolines Sub Area. "Rescue—Survivors Search, August 3-6, 1945." Dated August 9, 1945.

Report from G. C. Atteberry, Commanding Officer, Patrol Bombing Squadron 152, United States Pacific Fleet Air Force, to Commander, Western Carolines Sub Area. "Sighting and Air-Sea Rescue of *Indianapolis* Survivors, Report of Participation in." Dated August 9, 1945.

Report from Lieutenant J. L. Blackman, USNR, Air Combat Intelligence Officer, to Operations Officer, Western Carolines Sub Area. "Extracts from VPB-23 Duty Officers Log, Supplemented to Give Fuller Picture of Operations." Dated August 7, 1945.

Report from 1st Lieutenant Richard C. Alcorn, Commanding Officer, Flight D Detachment, 4th Emergency Rescue Squadron, to Sub Area Operations. "Rescue Operations 2 Aug. 45 through 5 Aug." Dated August 6, 1945.

Report from 1st Lieutenant Richard C. Alcorn, Commanding Officer, Flight D Detachment, 4th Emergency Rescue Squadron, to Sub Area Operations. "Search Operations of 7 Aug. 45." Dated August 8, 1945.

Extracts from Commander Western Carolines Sub Area Watch Officers Log Covering Rescue of Survivors from *Indianapolis* (CA-35). Period 1205K August to 0030K August. Enclosure (m) under Report from Commander, Western Carolines Sub Area, to Commander in Chief, U.S. Fleet. Dated August 15, 1945.

Record of Flight Operations in Search for Survivors from U.S.S. *Indianapolis* (CA-35) from 2 August, 1945, through 8 August, 1945. Enclosure (n) under Report from Commander, Western Carolines Sub Area, to Commander in Chief, U.S. Fleet. Dated August 15, 1945.

Identification and Disposal of Bodies and Personal Effects Found on Bodies by U.S. Naval Vessels Engaging in Search for Survivors from U.S.S. *Indianapolis* (CA-35). Enclosure (r) under Report from Commander, Western Carolines Sub Area, to Commander in Chief, U.S. Fleet. (This report was originally directed to the Island Commander, Peleliu.) Dated August 11, 1945.

Questions Asked by Correspondents of Lieut. (jg) W. G. Gwinn, USNR, Lieut. R. A. Marks, USNR, and Lt. Commander G. C. Atteberry. Enclosure (t) under Report from Commander, Western Carolines Sub Area, to Commander in Chief, U.S. Fleet. Dated August 6, 1945.

Memorandum from James Forrestal, Secretary of the Navy, to Captain Thomas J. Ryan, Jr., U.S. Navy, Judge Advocate, General Court Martial, Navy Yard, Washington, D.C. "Charges and Specifications in Case of Captain Charles B. McVay, III, U.S. Navy." Undated.

Press Release. "Memorandum to the Press Dated December 12, 1945, on the Appearance of Commander Ike [sic] Hashimoto at the General Court Martial of Captain Charles B. McVay, III, USN."

Press Release. "Sample Exchange of Correspondence Between Fleet Admiral Chester W. Nimitz, U.S. Navy, Chief of Naval Operations and Next-of-Kin of Personnel Lost Aboard the U.S.S. *Indianapolis*." Dated February 23, 1946.

Press Release. "Report on Court Martial of Captain Charles B. McVay, III, USN, Commanding Officer, USS *Indianapolis*." Dated February 23, 1945.

The following information is also from The Department of the Navy, Naval Historical Center, Operational Archives Branch, Washington, D.C., but without references to NRS 462.

Rear Admiral Charles Butler McVay, III, United States Navy, Retired. Navy Biographies Section, 01-440.

Press Release. "Narrative of the Circumstances of the Loss of the U.S.S. *Indianapolis*." Dated February 23, 1946.

Radio Release: 9 P.M. (E.W.T.), Thursday, October 26, 1944, and Newspaper Release: Friday, October 27, 1944. "The USS *Indianapolis*, Heavy Cruiser."

The following documents can be obtained from General Services Administration, Military Archives Division, Navy and Old Army Branch, Washington, D.C.

Deck Log of the U.S.S. Indianapolis, March 15, 1945, through June 30, 1945.

Deck Log of the U.S.S. Tranquillity (AH-14), August 2, 1945, through August 10, 1945.

Deck Log of the U.S.S. Cecil J. Doyle (*DE-368*), August 1, 1945, through August 9, 1945.

Deck Log of the U.S.S. Aylwin (*DD-355*), August 2, 1945, through August 7, 1945.

The following documents can be obtained from Office of the Chief of Naval Operations, Awards and Special Projects and Deck Logs Branch, Op-09B19, Washington, D.C.

Deck Log of the U.S.S. Alvin C. Cockrell (*DE-366*), August 2, 1945, through August 7, 1945.

Deck Log of the U.S.S. French (*DE-367*), August 3, 1945, through August 9, 1945.

Deck Log of the U.S.S. Madison (*DD-425*), August 1, 1945, through August 6, 1945.

Deck Log of the U.S.S. Ralph Talbot (*DD-390*), August 1, 1945, through August 6, 1945.

Deck Log of the U.S.S. Helm (*DD-388*), August 2, 1945, through August 7, 1945.

Deck Log of the U.S.S. Register (*APD-92*), August 1, 1945, through August 5, 1945.

Deck Log of the U.S.S. Ringness *(APD-100),* August 1, 1945, through August 5, 1945.

Deck Log of the U.S.S. Dufilho (*DE-423*), August 1, 1945, through August 6, 1945.

Deck Log of the U.S.S. Bassett (*APD-73*), August 1, 1945, through August 6, 1945.

Acknowledgments

I want to express my gratitude to John C. Reilly, Jr., at the Naval Historical Center in Washington, who aided my research immensely by directing me to the right people. Dr. Dean C. Allard, head of the Operational Archives Branch at the Naval Historical Center, supplied me with much information in his files. John T. Mason, Jr., former Director of Oral History at the United States Naval Institute, was particularly helpful in the preliminary stages of my research. Harry W. John and Michael L. Miller, both of the Reference Branch, General Archives Division of the General Services Administration, furnished me with information and led me to other valuable sources.

I want to thank Timothy K. Nenninger at the National Archives who enabled me to obtain expeditiously the Deck Logs of the various ships. Perry W. Gilbert, Director Emeritus at the Mote Marine Laboratory in Sarasota, Florida, was kind enough to convey to me the contents of their "International Shark Attack File, Case No. 1755."

I had access to the 385-page transcript of the court martial of Captain McVay along with hundreds of pages of exhibits; since these documents left more questions unanswered than answered, I am especially grateful to Congressman Otis G. Pike, whose assistance was invaluable in obtaining for me a copy of the secret proceedings of the Naval Court of Inquiry into the sinking of the *Indianapolis*.

I want to thank Colonel B. B. Ferrell, USMC, former Assistant Judge Advocate General (Military Law) and Colonel W. Donovan,

USMC, former Deputy Assistant Judge Advocate General (Investigations) whose cooperation was helpful.

In November, 1945, the Naval Inspector General did his own independent investigation into the sinking. In August, 1978, I asked to see the results of this investigation and received voluminous material, including many documents never before seen by the American public. It is within these papers that the secrets of the *Indianapolis* tragedy were contained. I am grateful, as the readers of this book may also be grateful, to Rear Admiral Stanley W. Anderson, the Naval Inspector General who honored my request, and Edward Hidalgo, former Secretary of the Navy, who gave the requisite approval for this information to be released to me.

For material in the Epilogue I am grateful to Henry S. Turner, a friend of Captain McVay's, who enabled me to meet Mr. Albion Dudley, who in turn shared with me his experiences of November 6, 1968. Florence Regosia also kindly provided her recollections.

I am immensely indebted to Richard F. Newcomb, who a quarter of a century ago wrote an admirable book on the sinking of the *Indianapolis* entitled *Abandon Ship!* Though he was unable to obtain from the Navy the previously secret documents that helped me piece together these events, Mr. Newcomb's expertise was invaluable and he was most generous in allowing me access to whatever information he had and to his memory.

None of the people I have mentioned, of course, shares my responsibility for what is contained in this book. Mine is the sole responsibility.

I want to thank also my publisher, Sol Stein, and my editor, Patricia Day, for their enthusiasm, cooperation, and confidence. And I owe a special thanks to my wife and two children, who were considerate throughout the experience of researching and writing this book and who can now have their dining room back.

Raymond B. Lech
Hauppauge, New York
July, 1982

Index

305

DEFEAT INTO VICTORY
Battling Japan in Burma and India, 1942–1945
Field-Marshal Viscount William Slim
New introduction by David W. Hogan Jr.
576 pp., 21 b/w maps
0-8154-1022-0
$22.95

THE MEMOIRS OF FIELD-MARSHAL WILHELM KEITEL
Chief of the German High Command, 1938–1945
Edited by Walter Gorlitz
New introduction by Earl Ziemke
296 pp., 4 b/w maps
0-8154-1072-7
$18.95

CANARIS
Hitler's Master Spy
Heinz Höhne
736 pp., 21 b/w photos, 1 map, 2 diagrams
0-8154-1007-7
$19.95

KASSERINE PASS
Rommel's Bloody, Climactic Battle for Tunisia
Martin Blumenson
358 pp., 18 b/w photos, 5 maps
0-8154-1099-9
$19.95

THE GI's WAR
American Soldiers in Europe During World War II
Edwin P. Hoyt
with a new preface
664 pp., 29 b/w photos, 6 maps
0-8154-1031-X
$19.95

THE MEDICAL CASEBOOK OF ADOLF HITLER
His Illnesses, Doctors, and Drugs
Leonard L. Heston, M. D., Renata Heston, R. N.
Introduction by Albert Speer
192 pp., 3 b/w photos, 4 graphs
0-8154-1066-2
$17.95

OCCUPATION
The Ordeal of France, 1940–1944
Ian Ousby
366 pp., 16 b/w photos
0-8154-1043-3
$18.95

SWING UNDER THE NAZIS
Jazz as a Metaphor for Freedom
Mike Zwerin
with a new preface
232 pp., 45 b/w photos
0-8154-1075-1
$17.95

THE HITLER YOUTH
Origins and Development, 1922–1945
H. W. Koch
382 pp., 40 b/w photos
0-8154-1084-0
$18.95

Available at bookstores; or call 1-800-462-6420

 Cooper Square Press

150 Fifth Avenue
Suite 911
New York, NY 10011